UNDERSTANDING CONSTRUCTION CONTRACTS

UNDERSTANDING CONSTRUCTION CONTRACTS

Alonzo Wass

Reston Publishing Company, Inc.
A Prentice-Hall Company
Reston, Virginia 22090

Library of Congress Cataloging in Publication Data

Wass, Alonzo.
   Understanding construction contracts

   Includes index.
   1. Building - Contracts and specifications - United States. I. Title.
KF902.Z9W37   343.73'07869   81-19168
ISBN 0-8359-8021-9   347.3037869   AACR2

© 1982 by Reston Publishing Company, Inc.
A Prentice-Hall Company
Reston, Virginia 22090

All rights reserved. No part of this book may be reproduced, in any way or by any means, without permission in writing from the publisher.

10   9   8   7   6   5   4   3   2   1

Printed in the United States of America
Interior design and production: Jack Zibulsky

CONTENTS

Preface, xi

1 TYPES OF BUSINESS OWNERSHIP

1.1 Individual Proprietorship (Entrepreneurship), 1
1.2 Operating the Business from Your Own Home, 3
1.3 Key-Man Insurance, 4
1.4 Notes on Preliminary Partnership Agreement, 4
1.5 Suggested Articles of Partnership Agreement, 6
1.6 Limited Partnerships, 8
1.7 Corporations, 8
1.8 Cooperative (Co-Ops), 9
1.9 Class Research, 10
Review Questions, 11

2 LAND

2.1 Tables of Land Measure—Linear and Metric, 13
2.2 Metes and Bounds, 14
2.3 Land Definition—A Glossary of Land Terms, 15
2.4 Surveyor's Batter Boards, 16
2.5 Fee Simple Estate, 16
2.6 Option to Purchase Land, 18
2.7 Zoning, 18
Review Questions, 22

3 TORTS

3.1 Definitions, 23
3.2 Dialogue, 24
Review Questions, 25

4 DIALOGUE BETWEEN BUILDER, REALTOR, AND ATTORNEY

4.1 Definition of Terms, 27
4.2 Tort, 28
4.3 Contract, 29
4.4 Land Title, 30
4.5 Liens, 31
4.6 Arbitration, 34
4.7 Mortgage Definitions, 34
4.8 Judgment, 39
4.9 Caveat Emptor, 39
4.10 Points of Law, 40
Review Questions, 52

5 ZONING LAWS

5.1 Zoning Laws, 53
5.2 Land Use, 54
5.3 Zoning Symbols and Descriptions, 54
Review Questions, 60

6 NOTARIES PUBLIC

6.1 Appointment of Notaries Public, 61
6.2 Historical Notes, 62
6.3 Dialogue Concerning Modern Notaries, 62
Review Questions, 64

7 CONSTRUCTION CONTRACTS

7.1 Contracts, 65
7.2 Dialogue on Contracts, 66
7.3 Dialogue on Building Construction Contracts, 67
7.4 Dialogue on Real Estate Contracts, 68
7.5 Typical Examples of Instructions to Bidders, 71
Review Questions, 74

8 REAL ESTATE APPRAISAL

8.1 The Real Estate Appraiser, 75
8.2 Appraising Property, 76
8.3 Appraising Land for Speculation Building, 76
8.4 Reasons for Land Appraisal, 78
8.5 Methods of Appraising Real Estate, 78
8.6 Appraising the Cost for a New Building, 78
8.7 Appraisers' House Checklist, 81
Review Questions, 84

9 WILLS AND PROBATE

9.1 Glossary of Terms, 85
9.2 Dialogue on the Drawing and Probating of a Will, 87
9.3 Bureau of Vital Statistics, 89
Review Questions, 90

10 RENTING; LEASING; APARTMENTS; CONDOMINIUMS

10.1 Definitions, 91
10.2 Dialogue on Leasing, 94
10.3 Dialogue on Leaseback, 95
10.4 Dialogue on Apartments, 96
10.5 Dialogue on Condominiums, 96
10.6 Dialogue on Timesharing Condominiums, 97
10.7 Dialogue on Cooperatives, 98
Review Questions, 99

11 INSURANCE

11.1 Dialogue on Insurance Terms, 101
11.2 Updating Insurance, 104
11.3 Personal Property Inventory, 105
11.4 Homeowners Warranty, 109
11.5 Limited Warranty: Home Warranty Agreement, 148
11.6 Experience Rating, 152
11.7 Certificates of Insurance . . . No Clerical Detail, 153
11.8 Coverage Checklist, 155
Review Questions, 160

12 ARBITRATION

12.1 Arbitration, 161
12.2 Mediation Clause, 162
12.3 Conciliation, 162
12.4 American Arbitration Association, 162
12.5 The Arbitrators' Institute of Canada, 166
Review Questions, 174

APPENDIX A

Glossary of Legal Terms, 175

APPENDIX B

Glossary of Real Estate Terms, 205

APPENDIX C

Common Terms Used in the Building Industry, 225

INDEX, 235

PREFACE

Included in this book are all the legal aspects that the author has experienced during his building activities; all legal aspects that were brought to his attention by colleagues; and legal aspects about which a builder should be aware.

This book is written in laypersons' language, by a layperson, for the layperson. By studying it, readers may find out *who* to see about *what*.

The author extends thanks to all who have contributed in any way to the presentation of this book and especially to Rosamond Gladwys Cox, for her continued encouragement and enthusiasm, for her reading and adopted suggestions; to Cindi Arden, for her efficient secretarial work; and finally, to my wife Joan Rose Wass, who had the patience to suffer me while I wrote this, my tenth book.

I have been much guided by the following quotation:

> Words are like leaves; and where they most abound,
> Much fruit of sense beneath is rarely found.
> Alexander Pope, 1688–1744

Alonzo Wass

Readers of this book are cautioned that there are differences in law between states of the U.S.A., and also between provinces of Canada. Consequently, local research should be made regarding all subject matter dealt with throughout the book.

This publication is designed to provide accurate and authoritative information in regard to the subject matter concerned.

It is sold with the understanding that neither the publisher nor the author is engaged in rendering legal or other professional service.

If legal advice or other expert assistance is required, the services of a competent professional person should be sought.

UNDERSTANDING CONSTRUCTION CONTRACTS

1 TYPES OF BUSINESS OWNERSHIP

In this chapter we shall discuss four types of business ownership: sole ownerships (entrepreneurships), partnerships, corporations, and cooperatives, with special emphasis on partnerships.

For all those intending going into business it is well to remember that all big businesses were once small ones.

1.1 INDIVIDUAL PROPRIETORSHIP (ENTREPRENEURSHIP)

In an individual proprietorship the total operation of the business is the prerogative of one person, often with the help of the family or a few employees. Legally, only one person is responsible for the indebtedness or profit of the business. Some of the advantages and disadvantages of sole ownership are as follows:

Advantages
a) There is high personal motivation, challenge, low cost of starting up and of terminating the business, no legal expenses.

2 TYPES OF BUSINESS OWNERSHIP

b) The Profits of the business are your own.
c) Speedy decisions can be made.
d) There are no complications with others about responsibilities and rewards.
e) As owner, you may direct your own policy.
f) You may set your own working day, working week, and annual holidays.
g) You can cut overhead expenses by operating your business from your own home (see Article 1.2).

Disadvantages

a) Your liabilities include your business and personal assets, such as your car, savings, and valuables.
b) You are handicapped by having limited talent in areas of buying, selling, manufacturing, financing, accounting, advertising, dealing with the public, and in employee relationships.
c) In case of business failure, your personal and business assets are subject to seizure and sale.
d) The liability of a married man is subject to his own personal property; that listed in his wife's name cannot be touched (unless it was transferred to her name just after the owner had reason to know that he was in difficulty in the financing of the business). Persons entering business in the province of Quebec must go through legal proceedings to determine to what extent the property of the one is separate and distinct from the other.
e) The business is usually small in size and must compete with large organizations that enjoy the services of professionals with expertise in all phases of business management.
f) A small business cannot purchase materials in quantity and at comparable rates of discount as can its larger competitors.
g) Upon the death of the owner, the administrators of the estate may carry on the business under letters of administration until the estate is settled and the business handed over to the heirs and successors; this may cause the business to suffer (see Key-Man Insurance, Article 1.3).

If you wish to add "and Company" to your name, or to use an entirely different name than your own, such a change must be registered in the state or province in which you are doing business. The public must be protected and know with whom they are doing business and to whom they may serve legal papers should they wish to do so. Note carefully that upon the death of a sole owner of a business, it ceases to exist except as in (g).

1.2 OPERATING THE BUSINESS FROM YOUR OWN HOME

To save expenses, many small general contractors use part of their homes as offices. This is acceptable practice for the purpose of federal taxes, under legally established conditions. The cost of the physical maintenance and depreciation of your office and its contents (furnishings and business machines) will appear as claims against the business for taxation purposes. Some of the items that may be claimed are as follows:

a) Rent
b) Light and power
c) Water
d) Heat
e) Sewage
f) Telephone
g) Office maintenance
h) Depreciation of office contents
i) Fire insurance
j) Fire equipment
k) Public liability
l) Stationery and supplies
m) Car parking expenses for any business

The allowable charges on these items is based upon the percentage of floor area that you use as an office. Assume that your home has a floor area of 2,000 sq ft and your office area is 200 sq ft. In that case you are using one-tenth of your home as an office for the purpose of earning your living, and you are entitled to deduct one-tenth of each charge listed. Check with the taxation department or a chartered accountant.

Some of the considerations concerning the suitability of using part of your home as an office are expressed in the following questions:

a) Is it quiet enough?
b) Are you detached sufficiently from other members of your household to give undivided attention to your office work?
c) Is your office subject to noise from television or radio?
d) Are you on a party-line telephone system?

4   TYPES OF BUSINESS OWNERSHIP

e)   Are you disturbed by household chores?
f)   Does your office have a private entrance?
g)   Is your office a suitable place for receiving members of the public?
h)   Are you equipped with regular office furniture?
i)   Is there adequate parking?
j)   Is your home close to banks, the post office, and shopping?
k)   Will you have regular office hours?

It is recommended that as soon as it is financially possible for you to maintain an office away from your home, you should do so. In this way you will have a regular pattern of going out to your business, and your office location will afford a good advertising status for you.

1.3   KEY-MAN INSURANCE

A Key-Man Insurance Plan: This type of plan assures against the loss of profits that might result if your business were deprived of the managerial skill and experience of an important man. The policy is applied for and owned by the business, which pays the premiums and is named the beneficiary. Regardless of whether the man lives, dies, retires, or is disabled, such insurance provides protection for your business.

While Your Key Man Lives: The plan builds up cash value available to your firm for loans or collateral, and represents a growing cash reserve.

If Your Key Man Dies: The income to your business will lighten the financial shock and make it easier to select a qualified successor and thus to minimize any loss of business profits. The money paid to the business is completely free of federal income tax and can be used to purchase any interest the key man may have in the business. It may be used to continue his salary to his dependents for a limited period of time.

If Your Key Man Is Disabled: If the key man becomes totally and permanently disabled, no further premiums would be required if the waiver of premium benefit is included in the policy. Even though no premiums are paid during disability, the policy would be in full force for its face amount, and all guaranteed values and dividends would increase exactly as if the premiums were being paid.

1.4   NOTES ON PRELIMINARY PARTNERSHIP AGREEMENT

Partnership Name: The name selected by a partnership identifies the firm to the business world. Persons transacting business under a

1.4 NOTES ON PRELIMINARY PARTNERSHIP AGREEMENT

partnership should have an attorney draw up the terms of agreement and file a certificate of partnership in the Government Office of Public Records, setting forth the names and addresses of the partners. A statement should also be filed in the same office upon dissolution of the partnership. The public has a right to know with whom it is doing business, or upon whom it may wish to serve legal notices. For this reason anyone, by paying a small fee, has the right to inspect the partnership agreement as registered.

Partners who have entered into partnership with one another are collectively known as a "firm."

Profit: A partner, in the absence of an agreement otherwise, has a right "irrespective of the amount he has invested in the partnership" to share equally in the profits; in like manner, he must share in losses. A partner has no right to salary; each partner is expected to devote his time and skill to the affairs of the partnership without expecting payment for his services. Irrespective of the amount of capital individually invested, every partner may take part in the management of the business.

Some Partners May Only Invest Their "Know-How": Subject to an agreement between partners, every partnership is dissolved upon the death or bankruptcy of a partner. Any difference arising concerning ordinary matters of the partnership may be decided by a majority of partners.

Withdrawal of a Partner: In the absence of an agreement specifying otherwise, a partner may withdraw at any time without incurring liability in the action. When a partner withdraws in violation of the agreement, he is liable for damages or harm he causes to his partner(s). Upon the withdrawal of a partner, the partnership becomes *ultra vires* (a nullity, not legal, beyond his powers).

Partners' Liability: Each partner is liable for the debts of the partnership, even to the limits of his personal assets; a corporation is liable for its debts, but its shareholders are liable only to the amount they have invested in the corporation.

Investment in a Partnership: If a person wishes to invest capital, but not actively participate in the business of the partnership and to receive his share of the profits, such a partner is considered to be a creditor of the partnership rather than a partner.

Creditors: Some states do not permit a partnership creditor to proceed against a partner's individual property until he has exhausted all means to satisfy his judgment from partnership property.

New Partners: Upon the introduction of a new partner, the old partnership becomes null and void and a new partnership agreement must be registered in the government office of Public Records. Some states prohibit

6 TYPES OF BUSINESS OWNERSHIP

married women from forming business partnerships with their husbands, but married women may become business partners with others.

Goodwill: The goodwill of a business is the worth to the business of its good name. For example, the Hoover Company vacuum cleaner became so well known in England that housewives used to refer to "hoovering the room." That was goodwill on the assumption that prospective vacuum-cleaner purchasers may give first consideration to seeing a demonstration of the Hoover vacuum cleaner before others.

1.5 SUGGESTED ARTICLES OF PARTNERSHIP AGREEMENT

Articles of a partnership agreement should be drawn up and registered by an attorney who is familiar with the type of business intended. For example, the brothers Joe and Alec Doe are planning on entering into a building construction partnership agreement with Fred Stark. They meet several times, making handwritten notes. At the third meeting they finalize and type their notes, then meet with an attorney who is familiar with their line of business and who draws up the articles of agreement based on the notes, and files them in the Office of Public Records. Their notes may read as follows:

a) State the name of the business.
b) State the purpose of the agreement.
c) State the starting date of the agreement.
d) Name the starting date of the fiscal (financial) year of the business.
e) State the names and addresses of the following: the partners, the accountant, the bankers, the partner who will keep custody of the company books and records, to which all partners shall have access at any reasonable time.
f) Specify the powers and duties of each partner: Joe Doe to be the building superintendent and to have sole charge of the hiring and firing of construction employees; Alec Doe to be the purchasing agent and to have sole charge of the hiring and firing of office staff; Fred Stark to be in charge of all advertising, business promotion, searching for and purchasing new building land and having it surveyed. Also, the expediting of all ordered building materials, and the expenses of business promotion, lunches, and so on shall be a charge upon the company, but for the first year a sum of $200 shall be provided for this purpose and future year's expenses shall be budgeted annually.
g) All checks shall require the endorsement of any two partners.

1.5 SUGGESTED ARTICLES OF PARTNERSHIP AGREEMENT 7

h) State the manner in which a partner may withdraw from the business and the manner in which the partnership shall be terminated (and such termination filed in the Office of Public Records).

i) A partner has the right to share equally in the management and conduct of the business, even where the sharing of capital contributions are unequal.

j) Where a partner invests equipment or physical stock in the company, such material shall be given an appraised monetary value and such partner shall be paid from the company funds, in cash, for such material. In this manner, all partners shall have only a cash investment in the company.

k) Partners shall devote full normal working business hours to the company; they shall not be allowed to engage themselves in any other business venture in the building industry during the lifetime of this agreement.

l) There shall be an annual meeting that will be attended by an attorney (if so desired by any partner). Amendments, additions, rescindments, or new articles may be dealt with at this time, and any such changes shall be registered with the government Record Office. The goodwill of the business shall be assessed annually (see Article 1.4).

m) The annual meeting shall present a budget for the ensuing year.

n) No retiring member shall be permitted to operate in the building construction industry within 50 miles of the operation of this company and neither will such retiring member be permitted to join any other building construction company during the life of this company, within the same radius.

o) Key-man insurance shall be taken out by the company in the name of all partners [see Article 1.3].

p) If a partner withdraws from the partnership, accounting procedures shall prevail so that such a withdrawing partner may receive equitable compensation dating from the starting date of the first fiscal business year including: accounts receivable, uncollected debts, stock on hand, plant and machinery owned by the partnership, unfinished building projects, and considering such items as bad debts and liens by subcontractors on completed properties.

q) No new partner shall be admitted into the partnership without the unanimous agreement of all partners.

r) The registered name of the company shall be "The Elmton Building Construction Company."

s) Joe Doe shall be the Chairman and Alec Doe shall be Secretary/Treasurer, and all resolutions shall require at least a two to one majority vote (see Key-Man Insurance, Article 1.3).

8   TYPES OF BUSINESS OWNERSHIP

t) No other person shall be accepted into partnership without the agreement of all other partners. If they so agree, the original partnership is by law terminated and a new partnership agreement shall be entered into. Partners may agree on any kind of profit or loss arrangement, but if their agreement is silent on the division, then the profits and losses are shared equally, regardless of each partner's contribution to the partnership. Each partner shall be entitled to receive profit and shall bear any loss according to his percentage of invested capital.

Note: Each partner is required to make a full disclosure of all material facts within his knowledge relating to the partnership's affairs. Each partner is personally liable to creditors for all partnership debts. If the partnership assets are insufficient to satisfy the claims of creditors, the creditors may resort to personal assets of any one or more partners. In effect, a partnership agreement is a written constitution between legally consenting individuals and one article or more should be a written remedy for differences arising between partners.

Insurance on Partner's Life: Life insurance is extensively used by partnerships to offset losses of a partner during the period of adjustment following his death. Partners are well advised to consult an attorney as well as a life insurance agent or broker before procuring this insurance. There are many legal and tax problems to be considered (see Key-Man Insurance, Article 1.3).

1.6   LIMITED PARTNERSHIPS

In a limited partnership, one or more partners operate the business and one or more invest cash only. The former are general partners and are liable to creditors for both their business and private assets. The latter are *limited* to creditor's claims only to the amount of cash they have invested in the business. No claim may be made against their personal assets.

Individuals considering entering into partnerships should meet informally several times, itemize the articles they would like included in the articles of agreement, and *have it drawn up by an attorney with knowledge of their field of business.*

1.7   CORPORATIONS

A corporation is an association of one or more persons legally capable of acting as one entity under a common name. A corporation continues to exist even though its members may change. It may engage in business, or it may be a charitable, social, or religious association. It can own property, may sue, and can be sued. A charter issued by a government is a document granting certain rights to a person or group of persons or a corporation. A corporation has been defined by the United States Supreme Court as "an artificial being, invisible, intangible, and existing only in contemplation of law."

A corporation can come into existence only in accordance with statutory provisions in the state of incorporation. It is managed by a board of directors elected by the shareholders; it may have to be registered in other states if it wishes to do business there.

The business corporation is the main instrument of big business and is a legal entity. The most distinct attribute of a large corporation is the separation of management and ownership.

The formation of a corporation is accomplished by registration of a document with the appropriate government department. This document sets forth a memorandum of the company (called a "memorandum of association") and the corporation becomes legal as soon as it has been legally registered. In some areas this document may be called Letters Patent; this is an offspring of the Royal Charter, and the Charter. Almost all commercial corporations are incorporated either by memorandum of association or by Letters Patent. Such documents set out the bare essentials of the company's constitution, its name, its objects, and its authorized capital. If the company is a private one, this must be stated in its charter.

1.8 COOPERATIVES (CO-OPS)

A cooperative is an incorporated organization of five or more persons who subscribe their skills, talents, and efforts to produce services and/or goods for themselves at cost price.

The first recorded cooperative was formed by 28 weavers in Rochdale, England, in 1884. In 1916 the Co-operative League of the U.S.A. was formed in New York.

In the early twentieth century, "housing" cooperatives were financed through credit unions. Membership in cooperatives is open to all over the age of 16 and irrespective of race, color, creed, religion, sex, or political affiliation. Each member is entitled to only one vote irrespective of the number of shares held. Every member has at least one share and not more than twenty-five. The chairperson has an extra casting vote in case a vote is tied.

To become incorporated, an association must submit a memorandum of agreement or have an attorney draw one up and submit it to the state government, where it will be filed in the public record office and to which the public must have access. It is important in a democracy that the public may know with whom it is doing business or upon whom it may serve legal papers, if necessary.

The memorandum of agreement shall clearly set forth:

a) The services which it is intended to render to its members
b) The names, addresses, and occupations of the first directors and the number of shares that each member will hold and the length of the term of office of such directors
c) The address of the co-op. upon being granted a charter
d) The effective date of incorporation, as shown on the charter;

The memorandum of agreement shall be submitted together with the prescribed fee to the superintendent of co-ops:

a) The first copy is for the Superintendent of Co-ops.
b) The second copy is to be filed in the Office of Public Records
c) The third copy is returned to the co-op. for its files.

Co-op. records are subject to internal and to government audit.

1.9 CLASS RESEARCH

For those offering courses using this book, it is suggested that consideration be given to apportioning chapters among the students for research, and having them make an oral report to the class, and then giving a typescript and any other gathered material of their findings to each student and the instructor.

REVIEW QUESTIONS

1. List ten advantages of operating a builder's business from one's own home.
2. Define key-man insurance.
3. List eight articles that you would insist on being written into a partnership agreement for a residential construction business.
4. In not more than 150 words, describe a limited partnership.
5. What are the main differences between a cooperative and a corporation?

It is important to remember that the law differs in many states, and also in the provinces of Canada. Research locally.

2 LAND

In this chapter we shall discuss tables of land measure, and explain how to identify the owners of land and how to find out how much tax they pay on it. We also discuss land registration, building and zoning laws, and how to conduct market research on the salability of a speculatively built house on a parcel of land in a given district.

2.1 TABLES OF LAND MEASURE—LINEAR AND METRIC

Linear Measure:

12 ins = 1 ft	= 3048 mm
3 ft = 1 yd	= 9144 mm
5½ yds = 1 rd (rod)	= 5.029 m
4 rds = 1 ch (chain)	= 20.1168 m
22 yds = 1 ch	= 20.1168 m
10 chs = 1 fur (furlong)	= 201.168 m
8 furs = 1 mi	= 1.609 km

Square Measure:

144 sq in = 1 sq ft	= .0929 m²
9 sq ft = 1 sq yd	= .8361 m²
4840 sq yds = 1 acre	= 4046.86 m²
640 acres = 1 sq mi / 1 section	= 259.008 m²
36 sections = 1 standard township	
1 standard township = 36 sq mi (6 mi each way)	

14 LAND

A *range* is a single row of townships lying between meridian lines.

Longitude is the geographical distance east and west on the earth's surface measured by the angle contained between a known meridian such as the Prime Meridian, which passes north-south (through Greenwich, England) and a particular place. Such angles are expressed in degrees, minutes, and seconds: thus

1 degree = 60 minutes . . . 1 minute = 60 seconds

2.2 METES AND BOUNDS

The oldest method of describing land is by metes and bounds.

Metes are linear measurements; *bounds* define and encompass an area of land enclosed within natural or man-made observable objects (see Figure

Because of the technical competency required to derive directional bearings north, south, east, and west with accuracy to minutes and seconds of degrees, metes and bounds descriptions should be prepared only by registered land surveyors. In metes and bounds descriptions as shown in the following circular diagram, the bearings or course of a line of direction is the angle that line makes from the central point of a departure parallel with a meridian.

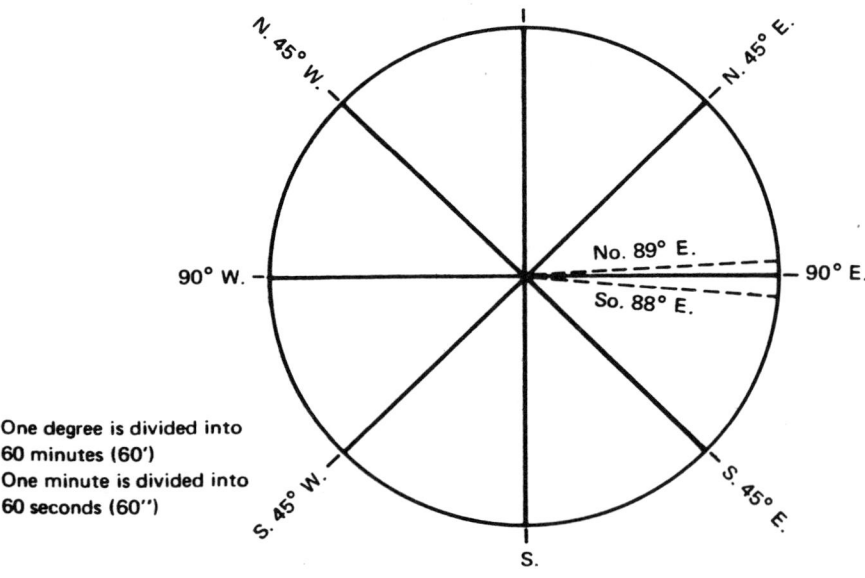

FIGURE 2.1   Directional bearings.

2.1*). Natural objects include such things as a river bank, a tree, or an outcrop of rock. A man-made object may be a cairn (pile of rocks) concealing and protecting a surveyor's metal peg. In open, flat country the survey crew may protect a surveyor's metal peg by mounding or piling earth over it. In both cases the pegs are protected and such man-made observable objects become known as monuments and are readily identifiable.

Latitude is the angular distance north and south of the equator of the earth's surface. *Land* is a geographic location on the earth's surface delineated by survey.

2.3 LAND DEFINITION–A GLOSSARY OF LAND TERMS

Throughout this book a *parcel of land* means a piece, lot, or block of land registered in the relevant Land Title Office as one unit. A *plot* is a small piece of land; or a *plot* is the plan of a city block; *tract* is an extent of land or water as shown on a map; *estate* refers to acreage or a large parcel of land.

Every parcel of land must be uniquely and legally described. For the purpose of registration, a postal address is not acceptable.

There are two kinds of property: *real* (nonconsumable and immobile)—land—and *personal* (consumable and mobile)—such as jewelry, clothing, and such things as a thief could be punished for stealing.

Real property (land) is registered by legal description in the government county office of the area in which it is located.

No two parcels may bear the same legal description. A legal description is effected either in words, or by determining the parcel's geographical location by surveyed bearings in degrees, minutes, and seconds from known internationally accepted bearings. Bearings may be described by magnetic north–south lines by astronomical bearings, in which case they are known as *true bearings*.

The immobility and indestructibility of land indicates that it cannot be lost, stolen, destroyed by fire, or in any other way consumed, as opposed to personal property, which may be moved with or without the consent of the owner.

Real property consists of land including soil, gravel, rock, minerals, both solid and liquid, including the depth below the surface and the space above it.

---

*Figure 2.1 has been excerpted from *Real Estate Principles and Practices*, 7th ed., published by Prentice-Hall, Inc., 1972, by Alfred E. Ring, and is reproduced here with the permission of the copyright holder.

16   LAND

Although the ravages of war may completely destroy whole cities, and land remains, and may be resurveyed into small parcels with each one being uniquely and legally described by compass bearings, or in words, or by both means.

When closing land deals, the realtor should carefully list the things that go with the sale and those that are personal property of the vendor and which he will take away. For example, a clock on the shelf of a house is personal property, but a concrete sundial in the garden is real property because it is attached to the earth and is real estate.

2.4   SURVEYOR'S BATTER BOARDS

Once a determination has been made to purchase a parcel of building land, a registered surveyor should be engaged to establish its boundary pegs. The surveyor may also get from the municipality a profile of the sewer lines, which shows the depth of the lines below the existing and future grades of the center of the road and of the elevation of the finished sidewalk (see Figure 2.2).

The surveyor will also, if requested, set up the batter boards (see Figure 2.3). Batter boards are frames placed adjacent to (but on the outside corners of) proposed excavations, over which a taut mason's line (or wire, for large jobs) is strung to delineate building lines when excavations are completed. It is as imperative that a building be lawfully placed at its correct elevation in space as that it is correctly placed on its building lot.

2.5   FEE SIMPLE ESTATE

A *fee simple estate* title may also be known as a "certificate of indefeasible title" or, in the case of an owner holding property without any registered encumbrances on it, it may be known as "fee simple absolute." The certificate is issued from the county land titles office and is the most definite type of evidence stating that the registered holder owns the rights to

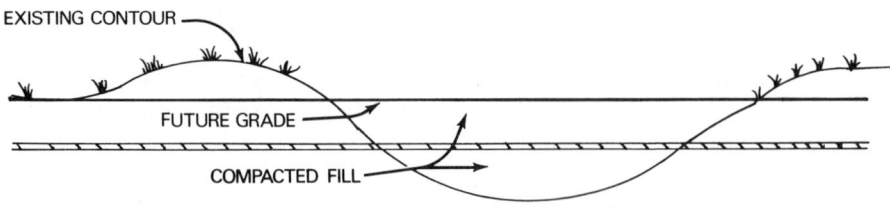

FIGURE 2.2   Elevation of proposed sewer line.

2.5 FEE SIMPLE ESTATE

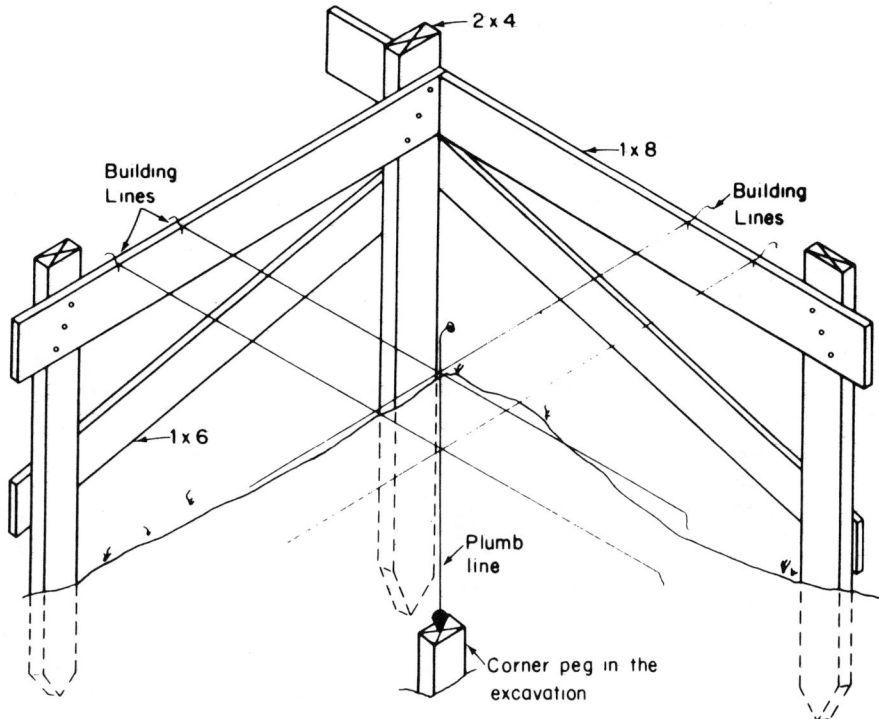

FIGURE 2.3   Batter boards.

the property, which is free from all encumbrances such as mechanic's liens, tax indebtedness to the municipality, mortgagers' claims, court judgments, or anything else that may hinder the new owner from selling the property. In effect, the registered owner has the right to possess the property for as long as he lives. It cannot be taken away, defeated, or voided by any claims whatsoever, except by *eminent domain*, which means that the public interest is supreme and maintains the right of government to take private property for public use, provided it serves a necessary public use and that fair compensation is paid to the owner.

An *encumbrance* is a debt on a property. Anything that burdens (encumbers) a property is known as causing a *cloud on the title* of the land (being opposite to a *clear title*, which has no cloud on it).

Before land can be purchased, an attorney must search the title to find out if any of the above-mentioned or other encumbrances have been registered against the property; this includes court judgments against the vendor. A *judgment* is a court's final decree, and before a "fee simple absolute" is issued, the issuing officer checks the record to be sure there is no outstanding and unsatisfied judgment against the would-be vendor.

2.6 OPTION TO PURCHASE LAND

It is imperative for a speculative builder to arrange for an option to purchase building land for his future needs.

An *option* is a written instrument which, for a consideration (payment), gives a person the right to buy or lease property within a stated time on the terms set forth in the agreement. Such an agreement should be drawn up by a lawyer.

For example: a builder may buy a parcel of land from an owner who has subdivided it from his estate (acreage); he then may erect a house on it and sell it. The builder may then be given the option to purchase further parcels subdivided from the original estates of the owner as and when he sells other completed houses. He may pay, say, 10 percent down on other parcels in the subdivision and pay the remaining 90 percent upon the sale of newly constructed houses. In this manner the builder has most of his working capital free for his building activities, and the vendor has an excellent prospective sale for his lots. It is seldom that a person becomes rich by using his own money—many builders become rich in land and poor in working capital.

Option: In contracts, an option is the privilege existing in one person, for which he has paid money, which gives him the right to buy certain merchandise or certain specific securities from another person, if he chooses, at a time within the agreed period, at a fixed price; or to sell such property to such other person at an agreed price and time. If the option gives the choice of buying or not, it is denominated a "call." If it gives the choice of selling or not, it is called a "put." If it is a combination of both these, and gives privilege to either buying or selling, it is called a "straddle" or "spread eagle." These terms are used in stock exchanges.

A *continuing offer* is a contract by which one person stipulates with another that the latter shall have the right to buy property at a fixed price within a certain time; and an *agreement* is only an option, with no obligation resting on the party to make any payment except such as agreed on between parties as consideration to support the option until he has made up his mind within the time specified to complete the purchase.

2.7 ZONING

Historically, zoning bylaws have been developed to assure orderly planning of cities, with the prime object of protecting residential areas from industrial districts.

Zoning bylaws differ from region to region and are designed for the of more than five acres within the city, and to encourage creativity and innovation in development. The district provides a wider range of options for land use mixes through the offer of design flexibility in return for a higher degree of review and regulatory authority over development by the city council in the insurance of essential standards of public health, safety, morals, and general welfare. The over-all objective is to encourage land uses within the city which are more beneficial to the city and to the developer than are permitted under other existing zoning districts; to encourage development which improves public health, convenience or welfare and to foster future development of the city to the end that transportation systems be carefully planned; that new community centers be developed with adequate highway, utility, health, educational, and recreational activities; that the needs of industry and business be recognized in future growth; that residential areas be provided with healthy surroundings for family life; and that the growth of the community be consonant with the efficient and economical use of public funds.

The more specific objectives include:

Beneficial use of land. The failure to develop land in a manner compatible with and beneficial to the community of which it is a part is both widespread and widely lamented. Contributing factors have included:

The exclusive zoning of large areas for one specific purpose or another, but prohibiting the possibility of mutually beneficial mixtures, thus forcing unnecessary demands for transportation between areas and the consequent costs on both the city and the developer.

Zoning and development practices which have divided rather than united the city and the developer in a common cause which is the betterment of the community at large.

This district has been designed to bring the city and the developer together to promote the planning and development of land uses in a manner which best serves the interests of both parties.

Coordinated provision for services. Unless the demand for services generated by a development can be met by existing facilities, considering all other sources of demand which can be foreseen, new facilities must be planned for, budgeted and constructed to meet the demand as it develops. Failure to do so creates serious and inexcusable problems for both the new users and the prior users of those services.

This district has been designed to make the development of land and the provision of services a coordinated venture on the part of both the city and the developer.

This district has been designed to encourage mixed developments which are self-supporting with regard to tax-supported services; to reduce the necessity for automobile traffic by encouraging people to live and work in the same area; to encourage innovative mixes of both residential and commercial development which invite both day and evening as well as work day and weekend usage by area residents and businessmen; and to insure that usable play areas and other open relief are provided within a development.

(8) CPD The commercial planned development district has been designed to promote a mixture of commercial and residential uses, with commercial predominating, on appropriate tracts of one acre or more within the city. The district provides a wider range of options for developers through the offer of mixed land use in return for greater review and regulatory authority by the city council to insure essential standards of public health, safety, morals, and general welfare. The overall objective is to recognize the need for offices and shops in future growth; to provide residential areas with compatible sur-

particular city or borough in which they are to operate. Cities may be, for example, educational, retirement, or industrially based centers, and the nature of each city would affect its zoning and building standards and planning.

The following is an example of zoning restrictions for a small market town:

Fairfax City Code

Article II. <u>District Development Standards
and Regulations Generally</u>.

Division 1. Generally.

Sec. 26-8. <u>Conformity with chapter; enumeration and purpose of districts</u>.

(a) No structure shall hereafter be erected, no existing structure shall be moved, altered, added to, or enlarged, nor shall any land or structure be used for any purpose not specifically permitted by this chapter in the district in which the structure or land is located.

(b) There are hereby established the following districts in the city for the general purposes indicated below:

(1) R-1 This district is established to provide areas for single family residences with a minimum lot size of twenty thousand square feet.

(2) R-2 This district is established to provide areas for single family residences with a minimum lot size of twelve thousand five hundred square feet.

(3) R-3 This district is established to provide areas for single family residences with a minimum lot size of nine thousand five hundred square feet.

(4) R-T This district is established to provide for single family development and, under certain conditions, the development of town houses. Town house development should occur where development will be consistent with the master plan, and involves the reuse of land where older structures are removed or as a transitional use of vacant land where a substantial portion of the property has common boundary with an I, C or M district. It is intended that any town house development permitted should result in high quality living units to promote the purposes set forth in section 15.1-489, Code of Virginia, as amended, offering optimum preservation of natural land form and foliage and the clustering of usable open space by the clustering of dwelling units. Clusters of dwelling units should be so arranged to achieve an intimate, internal relationship. Site plans shall be prepared in sufficient detail to permit judgment of compliance with the purpose of this chapter.

(5) RT-6 This district is intended to maintain the character of low-density residential areas by providing for the development of townhouses with adequate open space to serve the needs of its residents.

(6) M-1 This district is established to provide areas for multifamily residences of the garden or low rise type or for retirement homes.

(7) PD The planned development district has been designed to promote a mixture of commercial and residential uses on appropriate tracts

2.7 ZONING

roundings; and to guide community growth consonant with the efficient and economical use of private land and with careful attention to the impact of such growth on adjacent developments, both existing and planned, and on the city's existing and proposed public facilities.

The more specific objectives include:

Beneficial use of land. The failure to develop land in a manner compatible with and beneficial to the community of which it is a part is both widespread and widely lamented. Contributing factors have included:

The exclusive zoning of large areas for one specific purpose or another, but prohibiting the possibility of mutually beneficial mixtures, thus forcing unnecessary demands for transportation between areas and the consequent costs on both the city and the developer.

Zoning and development practices which have divided rather than united the city and the developer in a common cause which is the betterment of the community at large.

This district has been designed to bring the city and the developer together to promote the planning and development of land uses in a manner which best serves the interests of both parties.

Coordinated provision for services. Unless the demand for services generated by a development can be met by existing facilities, considering all other sources of demand which can be foreseen, new facilities must be planned for, budgeted and constructed to meet the demand as it develops. Failure to do so creates serious and inexcusable problems for both the new users and the prior users of those services.

This district has been designed to make the development of land and the provision of services a coordinated venture on the part of both the city and the developer.

This district has been designed to encourage mixed developments which are self-supporting with regard to tax-supported services; to reduce the necessity for automobile traffic by encouraging people to live and work in the same area; to encourage innovative mixes of both residential and commercial development which invite both day and evening as well as work day and weekend usage by area residents and businessmen; and to insure that usable play areas and other open relief are provided within a development.

(9) C1-L This district fills the need for a zoning classification which will allow limited office development. The intent is to permit, in transitional districts between residential and commercial areas, office buildings which in height and appearance resemble residential development and which will not adversely affect the character of any nearby residential community.

(10) C-1 This district is established to provide areas for offices for business, governmental and professional uses.

(11) C-2 This district is established to provide areas for general business establishments and related activity.

(12) C-3 This district is established to provide areas for business establishments of curb service or drive-in nature and related activity.

(13) I-1 This district is established to provide areas for light industrial uses.

(14) I-2 This district is established to provide areas for general industrial uses. (12-7-60, § 3; 4-17-63; 4-6-65; Ord. No. 1979-1, § 2.)

REVIEW QUESTIONS

1. Define longitude.
2. Define metes and bounds.
3. What is a parcel of land?
4. List six points that a speculator builder of homes should check before buying a parcel of land.
5. Define and make a freehand sketch of a batter board, as used in light construction work.
6. How could you obtain a drawing of the profile of the municipal sewage line to a property?

3 TORTS

In this chapter we shall discuss *torts*—past, present, and future. The law of torts exists for the purpose of preventing persons from hurting one another, whether in respect to their property, their persons, their reputations, or anything that they own.

3.1 DEFINITIONS

a) A person of legal age and competence is responsible for his/her own torts (wrongs).
b) Torts are civil wrongs against persons, their reputations, or their property.
c) The law of torts encourages people to accept civilized standards of behavior, and to enforce penalties against wrongdoers.
d) Tort in law is a wrong, other than a breach of contract, for which the law prescribes compensation.
e) As a general statement, tort law requires payment for damages.

Criminal law entails possible imprisonment for tort as a warning to others.

24 TORTS

3.2 DIALOGUE

Q *Define the tort of defamation.*
A A spoken false statement about a person or persons.

Q *Define the tort of slander.*
A A written false statement about a person or persons.

Q *Define* respondant superior.
A "Let the master respond."

    This is from the old English Master and Servant Act. In tort cases, the servant was in the employment and under the control of the master. While this was the case, any tort of the servant was deemed to be the liability of the master. It is still thought by some that "he who makes the most profit out of a venture should bear the cost and award of the lawsuit in tort." It was also considered that the employer was better able to bear the cost of the court award.

    As language changes, law adapts. An example is in the word "gay." Fifty years ago the word simply meant "happy." At this time of writing, the use of the word "gay" about a person could be defamatory and hence a *tort*.

    At the beginning of the twentieth century, it was not a tort to drive an automobile at 150 miles per hour. It was not possible to do so. Now the tort of automobile accidents is so common that insurance companies offer comprehensive insurance policies to compensate the driver not in the wrong.

    We are liable in tort for our animals. Some years ago a dog jumped onto a butcher's open stall in a country market and absconded with a leg of lamb. The stall owner said to his neighbor, "Did you see that ?" "Yes," replied the other, "that is the attorney's dog; you should go and see him." The butcher did. He explained himself to the attorney, who replied, "You should sue the owner of the dog for the price of the meat." "It was your dog and the price of the leg of lamb was $2.50." "Good," said the attorney. "My fee for consultation in the matter is $2.50." We can only speculate about future torts that may be committed due to computerization. So it is that law, language, and inventiveness evolve.

REVIEW QUESTIONS

1. What persons are liable for torts?
2. In general terms, define the difference between tort and criminal law.
3. Do you believe that in the future people will be prosecuted for torts that they could not commit at the present time?
4. If your answer to Question 3 is yes, give two examples.

4 DIALOGUE BETWEEN BUILDER, REALTOR, AND ATTORNEY

In this chapter we discuss torts, contracts, liens, and other matters of importance in developing an understanding of construction law, within the framework of a dialogue of questions and answers that might take place between a builder, a realtor, and an attorney. (For reference to specific questions, see the index.)

4.1 DEFINITION OF TERMS

Words ending in two *e*'s indicate the receiver of something, thus:

Address: To direct in speech or in writing

Addressee: One to whom speech or a written message is directed

Assign: To endorse over to another

Assignee: One to whom property is transferred, as in a deed or mortgage

Assignor: One who assigns

Mortgage: An instrument (document) used to convey (transfer) property from one party to another

Mortgagee: One who lends money on the security of a deed or mortgage

Grantor: One who conveys (transfers) title of property to another by deed or mortgage

Grantee: One who acquires title to property by deed (legal transfer)

Addresser: One who addressess, such as the addresser of a letter

Addressee: Person to whom a letter is sent; the receiver

Assigner: One who assigns a right to property

Assignee: A person to whom an assignment is made

Endorser: One who endorses (to acknowledge receipt) by writing his or her signature on a document

Endorsee: One to whom a note (say, mortgage) or bill is assigned

Vendor: One who sells

Vendee: One to whom a thing is sold

Option: The action of choosing yes or no in consideration of something

Optionor: One who gives an option (such as option to purchase)

Optionee: One who enjoys an option to do something

Covenant: Formal agreement of legal validity

Covenanter: One who makes a promise (covenant)

Covenantee: One to whom a promise (covenant) is made

4.2　TORT

Q *What is a tort?*

A A tort consists of some act done by the defendant whereby without just cause or excuse some form of harm is suffered by the plaintiff. The law of tort exists for the purpose of preventing persons from hurting one another whether in respect of their property, their persons, their reputations, or anything that is theirs. A classic case of a tort is an automobile accident in which neither driver intended to harm the other, but someone has to indemnify the one that was not in the wrong. Automobile insurance exists so that such torts are covered by comprehensive insurance policies.

Q *Define defendant.*

A The party in a legal action or proceeding, against whom a charge or claim is made.

Q *Define plaintiff.*

A One who brings an action at law.

4.3 CONTRACT

Q *Define contract.*

A In a contract there must be three factors present:
  a) There must be acceptance
  b) There must be agreement
  c) There must be consideration unless under seal

    A seal originally was melted wax upon which was imprinted the seal of the ring worn by the maker. It was extensively used when few people could read or write their names.

    An offer not accepted within a reasonable or stated time lapses. Whenever an offer has lapsed or has been rejected, it is gone and cannot be revived except by the original offeror making it again. Once an offer has been accepted, it makes little difference who was the offeror and who the offeree. The offeror is one who makes the offer, the offeree is the one who accepts the offer.

    Regarding the phrase "terms to be agreed" or its equivalent: The courts consistently point out that an agreement to agree is nothing, and the courts will not make the agreement for the parties. *It is important to see an attorney* **before,** *not after signing any legal document.*

    Consideration means that each party involved in a contract must give someting as an act of good faith. It may be money, or it may be a promise to do or not to do some legal thing. It is a basic principle of law that an offer can be withdrawn at any time before it is accepted, but notice of withdrawal must reach the offeree (the one to whom it is offered) before that person has accepted it. An irrevocable offer or tender is in fact a contradiction in terms. What is meant by those words is an agreement not to withdraw an offer for a stated period—*this, then, is an option.* (See Chapter 6 for an in-depth discussion on contracts.)

Q *In the event of the death of a partner in any business, what action should be taken by the survivors?*

A Upon the death of a partner in any business, the partnership ceases to exist. In such a case, the surviving partner(s) should enlist the services of a public accountant and have him or her draw up a balance sheet showing the state of the business at the time of the death of the partner. Then it is necessary to consult with the attorney who drew up the original articles of partnership; he or she will transmit this information to the clerk of the court, who will register it on the original registered partnership file. Then, the surviving partner(s) should have the attorney draw up a new set of articles of agreement and register the new partnership in the county court house. The public must always be able to find out with whom it is doing business.

4.4 LAND TITLE

Q *What is a lien claim on land?*
A This is a legal claim of debt against a property that is officially registered in a county land titles office against a parcel of land. A successful claim may result in foreclosure (forced sale) of the land to redeem the indebtedness from the proceeds of sale.

Q *What is title to land?*
A It is a lawfully recorded instrument (document) on which is enfaced the name of the legally and uniquely described parcel (piece) or land. This document is filed in a secure, fireproof land titles office. No two parcels of land may bear the same description. The original document is filed in the government office and the owner of the land is issued a certified true copy of the original document. For a nominal charge, any citizen may obtain a certified true copy of a title to any land.

Q *What is searching a title?*
A This is a reading of all enfacements (written records) appearing on the document. The reading is usually done by an attorney or by one of his experienced clerks. To *search* means, in this case, to read, to find out whether or not there are any encumbrances registered on the title. If there are any registered encumbrances, the title is known as having a cloud on it. A title without registered encumbrances is known as a clear title.

> In a legal transaction involving transfer of property in New Orleans, a firm of New York lawyers retained a New Orleans attorney to search the title and perform other related duties. The New Orleans attorney sent his findings, back to the year 1803. The New York lawyers examined his opinion and wrote again to the New Orleans lawyer, saying in effect that the opinion rendered by him was all very well, as far as it went, but that title to property prior to 1803 and not been satisfactorily answered.
>
> The New Orleans attorney replied to the New York firm as follows:
>
> I acknowledge your letter inquiring as to the state of the title of the Canal Street property prior to the year 1803.
>
> Please be advised that in the year 1803 the United States of America acquired the territory of Louisiana from the Republic of France by purchase. The Republic of France acquired title from the Spanish Crown by conquest. The Spanish Crown had originally acquired title by virtue of the discoveries of one Christopher

Columbus, sailor, who had been duly authorized to embark upon the voyage of discovery by Isabella, Queen of Spain. Isabella, before granting such authority, had obtained the sanction of His Holiness, the Pope; the Pope is the Vicar on Earth of Jesus Christ; Jesus Christ is the Son and Heir Apparent of God. God made Louisiana.

4.5 LIENS

Q *Define a lien.*

A A lien is the right given to a creditor to have a debt or charge satisfied out of property belonging to the debtor. Liens may entitle the holder to have the realty sold whether or not the owner wishes it. Such a forced sale is known as foreclosure. There are several types of liens such as:

a) A mortgage lien voluntarily entered into by the owner in which he mortgages (pledges) his interest in the land as security against a mortgage loan.

b) A mechanic's lien, which may be registered for unpaid work done to the property by a mechanic (tradesman).

c) A material supplier's lien, which may be registered for material delivered to the land for which payment has not been paid.

d) A lien registered by the municipality for unpaid taxes.

e) A lien registered by the municipality for unpaid special taxes for local improvements made to the property (for example, for a new road, sidewalk and curb, police protection, fire protection, etc.). If such special levies are not paid, the property may be foreclosed and the taxes and court expenses recovered from the proceeds of the sale.

The following Mechanics Lien article and claim of lien form have been excerpted from *Real Estate Principles and Practices* by Alfred A. Ring, and published by Prentice-Hall Inc., and is here reproduced with the permission of the copyright holder.

MECHANIC'S LIENS

The mechanic's lien is purely statutory, having no origin in common law or equity. It may be defined as a security claim given by statute to those who perform labor or furnish material in the improvement of real property. Predicted on the principle of unjust enrichment, laws have been enacted by the various state legislatures recognizing the claims of materialmen and laborers against the property to which they have added value. This right to a mechanic's lien is in addition to the right or action against the person who made the contract of employment or purchase. The lien is specific, as it affects only the property benefited and is governed by the provisions of the statute under which the right is obtained. The entire subject of mechanic's liens is highly technical; the laws vary materially in the different states; and everyone dealing with alterations or improvements to real estate should secure from an attorney in his own community legal advice as to his rights and obligations. A mechanic's lien is usually asserted through the filing of a notice of the claim with the county clerk. This notice must be under oath of the lienor or his agent and must set forth the claim in detail and substantially in form as follows:

Claim of Lien

STATE OF ....
COUNTY OF ....
    Before me, the undersigned authority, personally appeared ......, who being duly sworn, says that he is the lienor herein [or (agent) (attorney) of the lienor herein] .... whose address is .... and that in pursuance of the contract with ...., lienor furnished labor, services, or materials consisting of .... on the following described real property in ....County, of .... State, owned by .... of a total value of $.............. of which there remains unpaid $.............. and furnished the first of the same on .... 19....., and the last of the same on .... 19....., and (if the lien is claimed by one not in privity—direct contact—with the owner) that the lienor served his notice of claim to owner on .... 19....., by ....
    Sworn to the subscribed before me this ...... day of ...., 19...... .
....
Notary Public
My Commission expires:

    In many states, in order to perfect the right to a mechanic's lien claim, the statutory regulations provide for the recording of a notice of commencement of contract work with the clerk of records and for the posting of a certified copy thereof on the premises. Such notice identifies the parties involved, the property affected, and the work to be performed. Where such constructive notice is mandatory, work, that is, the improvements described, must be commenced within a stipulated time (generally thirty days), otherwise such notice is void and of no legal consequence.

MECHANIC'S LIENS

Q *What are the actual steps required in the registration and discharge of a lien?*

A The form of claim for a lien is prescribed by a government "act" (statute). Blank forms may be purchased from any legal stationer. The form must be correctly filled in (preferably by an attorney) and signed by the claimant, who swears an affidavit that the statements are true. The claim is then filed in the county courthouse and it is written onto the title deed (registered). A discharge of lien is described in the "act" as a receipt in writing acknowledging that the claim has been paid. The discharge is also signed by the claimant and is registered on the title in the county courthouse or county clerk's office. In this manner that particular cloud on the title has been lifted. In short, when the registration of the lien and its discharge are both registered in the same county office and both are registered on the correct title document, the latter nullifies the former.

Q *What is escheat?*

A Escheat is lapse of ownership of land, whereupon it returns to government.

Q *What is the difference between a mortgage and a deed of trust?*

A A mortgage is a sum of money (or other consideration) given and recorded with the land, and used as collateral or pledged security for the loan.

A deed trust (trust deed) is the temporary conveyance of title to land to a third party until all the terms of the loan have been complied with. The land is then reconveyed to the owner.

Q *What is a certificate of estoppel?*

A This is a certificate showing the amount of mortgage outstanding at the time of issue. It shows the original amount of mortgage, the amount paid as of date of issue, the amount still outstanding, and the terms under which the unpaid balance is to be paid.

Q *What is severalty ownership?*

A This is sole ownership of property (such as a house or an apartment block) as opposed to ownership by partners.

Q *With regard to real estate, what is a writ or judgment?*

A This is a record of a court's judgment which is filed in the county courthouse. Before a title to land is conveyed, a search is made of the file, and if there is a recorded judgment against the vendor of land, it is recorded on the land title. In this manner, a prospective purchaser of that land will know what indebtedness is attached to it. *Caveat emptor* ("Let the buyer beware"): before transfer of the title may be made to another party, the indebtedness attached to the land must be paid. In effect, this means that the land may be foreclosed and the debtor satisfied before transfer may be made. Otherwise the buyer would himself be indebted to the amount stated in the judgment. Debt that is attached to land is in effect owed by the owner of such land.

4.6 ARBITRATION

Q *What is arbitration?*

A Some contracts include a clause outlining the procedure to be adopted in case of dispute between parties. This states that any dispute between parties shall be resolved through arbitration. When this is necessary, an arbitration board may be established by each contesting party, each appointing one or more arbitrators of their own choosing; the appointed arbitrators then appoint a further arbitrator agreeable to themselves to act as chairman. The general procedure for arbitration may be stated in the contract, and may refer to the rules of procedure of an applicable arbitration association such as the AMERICAN ARBITRATION ASSOCIATION®.

Disputing parties pay the fees of their own appointees and half the fee of the chairman and all other expenses.

Elected arbitrators are persons of sound judgment who are experienced in the industry in which they are to deliberate. The award or determination of the arbitration board shall be binding on all parties, but in some jurisdictions the recommendation of the board shall not preclude any party the right of access to a court of law for a final judicial ruling.

The AMERICAN ARBITRATION ASSOCIATION® is a public service not-for-profit, nongovernmental organization dedicated to the resolution of disputes of all kinds through the use of arbitration, mediation, democratic elections, and other voluntary methods. Membership in the Association is open to all individuals and organizations interested in voluntary arbitration. The association is located at

> 140 West 51st Street,
> New York, New York 10020
> Phone: (212) 484-4000.

4.7 MORTGAGE DEFINITIONS

Q *Please define mortgage.*

A A mortgage is a conditional transfer of property to a creditor as security for repayment of money.

4.7 MORTGAGE DEFINITIONS

To mortgage land is to pledge the land as security for something else, usually money. A mortgagor (borrower) is the person who mortgages property. A mortgagee (lender) is the person to whom property is mortgaged.

Q *Assume that a foreclosure (forced sale) of land yields $40,000 and the indebtedness is $30,000: Who gets the excess of realized funds?*

A The mortgagor.

Q *When a property is mortgaged, who pays the fire insurance premium?*

A The mortgagor pays the premium but the mortgagee should have possession of the document.

Q *What is discharge of mortgage?*

A This is a recorded admission, recorded on the respective land title in a county clerk's office, affirming that the indebtedness attached (claimed against) the land has been extinguished.

Q *What is a chain of title?*

A This is the recorded history of the owners of land.

Q *What determines the priority of a mortgage?*

A The date and time of day that a mortgage is registered.

Q *Who pays the recording fee for a mortgage?*

A The mortgagor.

Q *Is a mortgage a lien?*

A Yes, and the first mortgage registered takes priority over a second and succeeding registered mortgages.

Q *What procedures must be taken before a parcel of land may be subdivided?*

A The reasons for subdividing must be given; these reasons will be thoroughly studied by the local authority for such things as compliance with local zoning laws, pollution laws, bylaws, restricting heights and sizes and types of buildings for allowable industries in the given area. The object is to ensure orderly development of districts.

Q *What is the difference between solicitors, barristers, and lawyers?*

A In England and Quebec, solicitors are office lawyers; barristers receive briefs from lawyers for arguing cases in court. In the United States, the distinction is broken down to one title—"attorney." The legal profession in Canada is organized in provincial areas (by state in the the United States) each with its own "bar" (barristers' society). A lawyer's membership in one provincial or state bar association does not constitute permission to practice in another.

Q *What is a bill of sale?*

A Usually in the transfer of real estate, a bill of sale is unnecessary, but if the vendor is leaving personal and portable things in the house and the purchaser of the land wishes to buy them, all such items should be listed separately in a bill of sale and dealt with entirely separately from the sale of the real estate.

Q *What is a riparian owner?*

A This is an owner whose property is in contact with water such as a lake or river.

Q *What is a subpoena?*

A A subpoena is a judicial writ or process commanding, under threat of penalty, the attendance in court of the witness upon whom it is served; or the presenting to court of enumerated stated documents as exhibits.

Q *What is a municipal ordinance?*

A It is an authoritative direction or decree, such as a municipal building bylaw, which is enforceable by law.

Q *What is the difference between tort and contract?*

A In a contract, terms are set between contracting partners who voluntarily assume obligations to obey certain standards. The courts may interfere to forbid the obligations of parties when these obligations are contrary to the public interest.

Q *How soon after purchase should a person occupy land?*

A Not until the attorney is satisfied that all the terms of purchase have been met. After a purchaser occupies a property, the courts may interpret this as being acceptance of terms of contract.

Q *What is the maximum number of persons who may own equal rights to a land title?*

A Any number.

Q *What is a life estate?*

A This is a type of property title specifying that a stated person has the use of a property for life.

Q *Should a life estate be registered?*

A Everything affecting the status of land should be officially registered.

Q *What is an option?*

A It is an agreement in writing whereby the owner (optionor) gives to another (optionee) the exclusive right for a limited period of time to purchase (or lease) real estate upon certain terms or conditions.

4.7 MORTGAGE DEFINITIONS 37

Q *Define dedication of land.*

A It is the public acceptance of a parcel of land from a person or persons (party) who has dedicated (given) the land for public use.

Q *What is an encroachment on land?*

A Any overhang, such as a porch, beyond the permissible municipality building line is an encroachment.

Q *What should a prospective purchaser of a parcel of land do to ensure that there is no encroachment upon it?*

A It must be officially surveyed by a registered surveyor.

Q *Define severally.*

A As an example, if a partnership fails, a creditor may sue the partnership as a unit or he may seek complete satisfaction from any individual partner.

Q *In case of default of a mortgagor, what are the options open to the morgagee?*

A The mortgagor may be sued according to the mortgage. For example,
   a) A writ may be issued for possession of the premises.
   b) Action may be taken to foreclose (seize the property). Note that after foreclosure the mortgagee can still take legal action against the mortgagor for outstanding debt under the original agreement.

Q *What is an easement by prescription?*

A When someone has openly and without interruption or dispute used property without the owner's express or implied permission for a statutory (prescribed by law) number of years; it is deemed an easement and the use of the property may be continued in the same manner.

Q *What is the difference between "joint tenants" and "tenants-in-common"?*

A If two or more persons buy an interest in land and wish to be joint tenants, this fact must be stated on the deed of grant (mortgage). When one party dies, the property automatically goes to the survivors. This form is common between married couples.

"Tenants-in-common" each own an interest in the whole property and are entitled to sell this interest. On the death of a tenant-in-common, the interest of the deceased passes to the beneficiary referred to in that person's will. On selling the property all tenants-in-common must join in the sale.

Q *What are the implications of default concerning mortgage payments?*

A Most mortgages carry strict terms designed to protect the land. If a payment is missed, the default may allow the mortgagee to demand immediate payment of the entire mortgage because the contract has been breached. A default may occur for allowing a fire insurance policy to lapse. If the mortgagee believes the owner has allowed the property to become run-down, he may claim that this is a default and seek remedial action through the courts.

Q *What is an assignment of property?*

A This is the legal transfer of rights and obligations of property from one person or persons (party) to another. An assignor is the one who assigns, or transfers, a negotiable instrument (such as salable stocks or bonds) or right to another. An assignee is one who receives an assignment.

Q *What is a power of attorney?*

A It is the written authority (instrument) that a responsible adult may grant to another to speak or act in his or her behalf in matters of legal consequence.

Q *What is collateral security?*

A There are many types of security that a lender may require as collateral security for a loan, such as:
   a) A pledge of stocks or bonds together with the power of attorney signed by the borrower authorizing the lender to sell these items as his (the borrower's) agent, if need be.
   b) Chattel mortgage.
   c) A real estate mortgage.
   d) A guarantee by a third party (co-signor).

Q *Is there any other way in which a mortgage may be terminated (taken back) other than by full payment of the amount borrowed?*

A A forced sale (foreclosure) will extinguish a mortgage.

Q *By whom is a mortgage executed (performed/carried out)?*

A By the mortgagor (person who pledges property against a loan).

Q *If an injury is sustained by a person on an icy sidewalk adjoining a mortgaged property, who is liable for damages?*

A The mortgagee (the borrower) or tenant or lessor, providing he is living on the property.

Q *How should a mortgagee protect himself against such an eventuality?*

A By covering himself with public liability insurance. He is insuring himself against a possible tort.

4.8   JUDGMENT

Q *What is a judgment?*
A It is a court ruling in the determination of the right of contesting parties through a court trial.

Q *What is a writ of judgment?*
A A court recorded statement. When recorded on a title deed, it shows that at a certain time and place a judgment was handed down by a court of law stating that the party in whose name the title stands was indebted to another party for some service or goods for which payment was not made. These services or goods could be indebtedness to multiple stores, garages, and so on. This instrument is a *caveat emptor* (notice to beware) that the party who has filed the caveat has an interest in the property that must be taken into account before any change of ownership is made.

4.9   CAVEAT EMPTOR

Q *What does* caveat emptor *mean?*
A This is Latin, meaning "Let the buyer beware." If the vendor of land makes no representation about the title of the land regarding registered encumbrances on the property, then it is in the interest of the prospective purchaser to "beware." For this reason he usually employs the services of an attorney to "search the title" (read) so that the prospective purchaser may be made aware of anything (such as debts) attached to the property for which he may become liable by purchase.

Q *May a mortgagor sell or in any other way dispose of his property?*
A Yes, subject to the rights of the mortgagee.

Q *What is a discharge of mortgage?*
A It is an attested certificate confirming that indebtedness on a mortgage has been redeemed (paid out). It is then registered on the original, applicable title deed. (For a typical list of forms that can be purchased from a legal stationers, see sample of a legal stationer's price list at the end of this chapter).

Q *What is the difference between a mortgage and a trust deed?*
A When a mortgage is concluded there are two parties—i.e., the mortgagor (the borrower) and the mortgagee (the lender). With a trust deed there are three parties—i.e., the mortgagor (the borrower), the mortgagee (the lender), and a trustee.

The title to the property is conveyed to the trustee (usually a trust company) to be held by that entity until the mortgage (amount borrowed) has been paid out in full. The title is then conveyed to the mortgagor.

Q *Who is liable for personal injury incurred on mortgaged land?*

A When the mortgagor takes control over the mortgaged property, he is responsible.

Q *Relating to the last question, what remedy has a mortgagor against incurring heavy penalty?*

A He should cover himself by taking out public liability insurance.

Q *What is an amortized mortgage payment?*

A It is a stipulated sum paid to the mortgagee at stated times throughout the lifetime of the mortgage. Payments include the total interest charge on the outstanding balance from the time of the previous payment.

Q *If a mortgagor enlarges a house after the mortgage has been placed, and the house is then foreclosed, can the mortgagor make claim for the value of improvement he made?*

A No.

Q *What is a satisfaction piece?*

A That part of a mortgage that has been retired (paid off) and recorded on the title.

4.10   POINTS OF LAW

Q *What is an affidavit?*

A It is a sworn statement made in writing before an officer authorized to administer oaths, such as a lawyer or notary public.

Q *What is a notary public?*

A A notary public is a person authorized by law to administer oaths (see chapter 6).

Q *What is an abstract of title?*

A This is an up-to-date digest of relevant and present records affecting title to property. An abstract of title may be used in a court of law and is an acceptable exhibit up to the date and time of day that it was issued.

Q *What is a garnishee?*

A This is a person served with a summons (a garnishment). It is a summons to appear in litigation already pending between others. It is a warning served on a person to hold (subject to the court's direction) money or salary or wages belonging to the defendant. Thus a person's wages may be subject to garnishment, and the employer may be obliged to pay into court a certain percentage of an employee's earnings. It is a court process, generally used by creditors to attach goods or debts due them. A court may direct that earnings be paid into court, but the court in most jurisdictions will not go out to collect such withheld earnings from the employer holding them.

Q *What is a foreclosure by suit in equity?*

A This is a bill for foreclosure filed in a court of equity. This bill sets out the mortgagee's rights as provided for in the mortgage and shows breaches of the covenant (agreement) justifying foreclosure. The court issues a certificate of sale. The proceeds are used to pay

a) The court costs
b) The mortgage indebtedness
c) Inferior liens in order of priority

The remainder of the proceeds is paid to the former owner.

In some states it is provided that within a stated period of time the mortgagor or other persons having interest in the property may redeem it. After the redemption period has elapsed, the mortgagor's claim to the property is extinguished (terminated).

Q *What are dower rights?*

A These refer to interest of a wife in her husband's estate after his death.

Q *Define co-signatory.*

A This is one who signs a note certifying that if the borrower does not pay, he will. *See an attorney* **before, not after,** *signing any legal document.*

Q *What is meant by the statute of limitations?*

A A statute imposing limits on the period during which certain rights, such as the collection of debts, may be legally enforced.

Q *What is a setback ordinance?*

A It is a local building bylaw requiring owners to keep building lines at a legal distance from the lot boundaries.

Q *What is the statute of frauds?*

A Some state laws require that certain agreements be in writing to be enforceable.

SAMPLE PRICE LIST OF LEGAL FORMS

Bankruptcy Forms

		25	50	100
360	Proof of Claim	2.50	4.25	7.00

Chattel Mortgage Act

		25	50	100
13-15	Bill of Sale - Absolute (3 pages)	7.00	11.50	19.00
203	Discharge of Chattel Mortgage	3.00	5.00	8.50
21-23	Chattel Mortgage (to secure sum of) (3 pages)	7.00	11.50	19.00
214	Conditional Sales Contract (2 pages)	4.50	7.75	13.00
69-72	Chattel Mortgage (to secure promissary note) (4 pages)	9.00	15.00	25.00
77-79	Assignment of Chattel Mortgage (3 pages)	7.00	11.50	19.00

Company Act

NEW NUMBER IN BRACKETS

		25	50	100
10	Notice of New Directors	2.25	3.50	6.00
	10 & 10A (11) Combined Form	2.25	3.50	6.00
10A (11)	Notice of Directors Ceasing to Act	2.25	3.50	6.00
14 (15)	Statement on Registration of Extra Provincial Company	5.25	8.75	14.50
15 (16)	Notice of Change of Attorney	2.25	3.50	6.00
17 (18)	Annual Report	2.25	3.50	6.00
18 (19)	Annual Report - (Extra Provincial Company)	2.25	3.50	6.00
185	Statutory Declaration (Re: Form 18 (19))	2.25	3.50	6.00
19 (20)	Ordinary Resolution	2.25	3.50	6.00
20 (21)	Special Resolution	2.25	3.50	6.00
3	Notice of Offices	2.25	3.50	6.00
361-362	Annual Shareholders Minutes (2 pages)	4.50	7.75	13.00
371-372	Annual Directors Minutes (2 pages)	4.50	7.75	13.00
375	Articles (42 pages)			5.00 per set
	(in Quantity) 25			3.50 per set
	50			3.00 per set
375A	Table A — Articles (9 pages)			1.50 per set
	(in Quantity) 25			.90 per set
	50			.80 per set
378	Transfer of Shares (padded in 100's)			5.00
4	Notice to Change Offices	2.25	3.50	6.00
4(a)	Directors Resolution	2.25	3.50	6.00
5	Particulars of a Mortgage of Motor-Vehicle	2.25	3.50	6.00
6	Notice of Satisfaction of Mortgage of Motor-Vehicle	2.25	3.50	6.00

Conveyancing

		25	50	100
1-3	Mortgage (Short) (3 pages)	7.00	11.50	19.00
100	Guarantor's Clause	3.00	5.00	8.50
10A	Sub. Pg. 10 (Mortgage) Canada Interest Act Clause	3.00	5.00	8.50
201	Bulk Sales Declaration	3.00	5.00	8.50
202	Discharge of Mortgage (Long) (2 pages)	4.50	7.75	13.00
204	Statutory Declaration	3.00	5.00	8.50
205	Option to Purchase Land (3 pages)	7.00	11.50	19.00
209	Affidavit for Attorney (padded in 100's)			5.00
210	Transfer and Consent (padded in 100's)			5.00

SAMPLE PRICE LIST OF LEGAL FORMS

		25	50	100
211	Discharge of Mortgage (Short)	3.00	5.00	8.50
221	Partial Discharge of Mortgage	3.00	5.00	8.50
223	Builders Lien Act	3.00	5.00	8.50
224-225	Builders Lien - Discharge (2 pages)	4.50	7.75	13.00
25-27	Assignment of Agreement - Purchaser (3 pages)	7.00	11.50	19.00
29-31	Assignment of Mortgage (3 pages)	7.00	11.50	19.00
37-38	Quit Claim Deed (2 pages)	4.50	7.75	13.00
49-50	Assignment of Lease (2 pages)	4.50	7.75	13.00
561-564	Agreement for Sale of Land (4 pages)	9.00	15.00	25.00
9-12	Mortgage (Long) (4 pages)	9.00	15.00	25.00

County Court

		25	50	100
401	Writ of Summons	2.50	4.25	7.00
402	Praecipe	2.50	4.25	7.00
425	Affidavit of Personal Service of Summons	2.50	4.25	7.00
503	Praecipe (old - 8½" x 7") (padded in 100's)			5.00

Court of Appeal

501	Praecipe in the Court of Appeal (padded in 100's)			5.00
607	Appeal (Factum) Paper - 1000			42.00
	500			24.00
	100			5.50
FB-BE	Factum Backs — Blue			12.00
FB-BF	Factum Backs — Buff			12.00
FB-GN	Factum Backs — Green			12.00

Default Judgment

		25	50	100
383 (A)	Debt or Liquidated Demand Action - No Costs/No Interest	2.50	4.25	7.00
383 (B)	Debt or Liquidated Demand Action Interest Pursuant to Contract Occuring after Date of Writ to Date of Order, and Costs	2.50	4.25	7.00
383 (C)	Debt or Liquidated Demand Action, Interest Pursuant to Prejudgment Interest Act from Date Cause of Action Arose to Date of Order, and Costs	2.50	4.25	7.00
383 (D)	Unliquidated Damages to be Assessed, and Costs	2.50	4.25	7.00
383 (E)	Judgment for Delivery of Goods Detained by the Defendant or their Value to be Assessed, and Costs	2.50	4.25	7.00
383 (F)	Judgment for the Value of Goods Detained by Defendant, and Costs	2.50	4.25	7.00
383 (G)	Judgment for Debt or Liquidated Demand and Costs/No Interest	2.50	4.25	7.00
383 (H)	Judgment for Debt or Liquidated Demand, Interest Pursuant to Contract Occuring after Date of Order, and Costs	2.50	4.25	7.00
383 (I)	Judgment for Debt or Liquidated Demand, Interest Pursuant to Prejudgment Interest Act from Date Cause of Action Arose to Date of Order, and Costs	2.50	4.25	7.00

SAMPLE PRICE LIST OF LEGAL FORMS

		25	50	100
383 (J)	Judgment for Unliquidated Damages to be Assessed, and Costs	2.50	4.25	7.00
383 (K)	Judgment for Delivery of Goods Detained by the Defendant or their Value to be Assessed, and Costs	2.50	4.25	7.00
383 (L)	Judgment for the Value of Goods Detained by the Defendant and Costs	2.50	4.25	7.00

Land (Wife Protection) Act

WPA-A	Forms A Affidavit	2.50	4.25	7.00
WPA-B	Certificate of Acknowledgement by Wife	2.50	4.25	7.00
WPA-C	Application for Entry	2.50	4.25	7.00
WPA-D	Forms D Affidavit (Homestead Rights)	2.50	4.25	7.00
WPA-E	Application for Cancellation of an Entry	2.50	4.25	7.00

Land Title Act

LTA 2	Affidavit of Witness, Sections 43(a) and 44(a) (padded 100's)			5.00
LTA 7	Affidavit of Witness (Ignorance of English Language) (padded 25's)	1.75		
LTA 7(a)	Affidavit of Witness (Physical Disability or Illiteracy) (padded 25's)	1.75		
LTA 14	Application for Cancellation of Interior Lot Lines	2.50	4.25	7.00
LTA 11	Application for Deposit of Reference or Explanatory Plan (Fee-Simple) on the Consolidation of Surveyed Parcels	2.50	4.25	7.00
LTA 11(a)	Application for Deposit of Reference or Explanatory Plan (Charge)	2.50	4.25	7.00
LTA 10	Application to Deposit a Subdivision Plan	2.50	4.25	7.00
LTA 22	Application for Duplicate Certificate of Title	2.50	4.25	7.00
LTA 20	Application by Owner of Absolute Fee for Certificate of Indefeasible Title	2.50	4.25	7.00
LTA 28	Assignment of Judgment	3.00	5.00	8.50
LTA 41	Assignment of Purchaser's Interest in Right to Purchase with Mortgage Back to Assignor (2 pages)	4.50	7.75	13.00
151	Application Stamp (Section 151)			27.50 each
152	Application Stamp (Section 152(1))			27.50 each
220	Application Stamp (Section 220)			27.50 each
LTA 38	Caveat	2.50	4.25	7.00
LTA 39	Caveat — Withdrawal of	3.00	5.00	8.50
LTA 40	Caveator — Notice To	2.50	4.25	7.00
LTA 12	Certificate as to Highway in Statutory Right-of-Way Plan	2.50	4.25	7.00
LTA 3	Certificate of Acknowledgement of Transferor (padded 100's)			5.00
LTA 31	Certificate of Lis Pendens (Section 213(1))	3.00	5.00	8.50
LTA 32	Certificate of Lis Pendens (Section 213(5))	3.00	5.00	8.50
LTA 33	Certificate of Lis Pendens (Section 213(6))	3.00	5.00	8.50
LTA 34	Certificate of Lis Pendens (Section 213(7))	3.00	5.00	8.50
LTA 35	Declaration of Building Scheme	2.50	4.25	7.00
LTA 37	Mortgage — Discharge of	3.00	5.00	8.50
LTA 27	Mortgage — Transfer of	3.00	5.00	8.50
LTA 13	Notice of Amendment of Land Records to Show Receipt of Notice of Establishment			

SAMPLE PRICE LIST OF LEGAL FORMS

		25	50	100
	of Land in Statutory Right-of-Way Plan as Highway and of Vesting in the Crown	2.50	4.25	7.00
LTA 15	Notice of Change of Address	2.50	4.25	7.00
LTA 19	Notice of Intention to Register on Non-Production of Instrument	2.50	4.25	7.00
LTA 36	Notice of Objection to Registration Free from Mortgage	2.50	4.25	7.00
LTA 8	Notice of Revocation of Power of Attorney	2.50	4.25	7.00
LTA 29	Notice to Judgment Creditor of Intention to Register Free of Judgment	2.50	4.25	7.00
LTA 24	Postponement Agreement (2 pages)	4.50	7.75	13.00
LTA 6	Proof of Execution by Corporation (padded 100's)			5.00
LTA 42	Real Property Transfer Record	2.50	4.25	7.00
600	Receipt of Document - Vancouver (padded 100's)			5.00
601	Receipt of Document - New Westminster (padded 100's)			5.00
506	Required a Certificate of Charge (padded 100's)			5.00
LTA 30	Release of Judgment	3.00	5.00	8.50
RC 14	Required a State of Title Certificate as to the Following Lands	2.50	4.25	7.00
604	Search Sheets (padded 100's)			8.00
LTA 16(A)	Statement as to Citizenship	2.50	4.25	7.00
LTA 16(B)	Statement as to Citizenship of Directors of a Corporation (Personal Knowledge)	2.50	4.25	7.00
LTA 16(C)	Statement as to Citizenship of Directors of a Corporation (Information and Belief)	2.50	4.25	7.00
LTA 16(D)	Notice of Change of Citizenship Particulars	2.50	4.25	7.00
LTA 5	Statutory Declaration where Attorney is a Corporation	2.50	4.25	7.00
LTA 4	Statutory Declaration where Attorney is not a Corporation	2.50	4.25	7.00
LTA 18	Summons to Produce Documents	2.50	4.25	7.00
LTA 23	Transfer of an Estate in Fee-Simple	3.00	5.00	8.50

Leases

		25	50	100
39-41	Lease — Statutory (3 pages)	7.00	11.50	19.00
45-47	Lease — House (3 pages)	7.00	11.50	19.00
53-56	Lease — Commercial (4 pages)	9.00	15.00	25.00

Miscellaneous

BDB-1S-12	Blue Backs - 1 Score 9x12		10.00 per C
BDB-3S-12	Blue Backs - 3 Scores 9x12		10.00 per C
BDB-1S-15	Blue Backs - 1 Score 9x15		12.00 per C
BDB-4S-15	Blue Backs - 4 Scores 9x15		12.00 per C
BDB-PL-12	Blue Document Backs, Plain, 12"		10.00 per C
BDB-PL-15	Blue Document Backs, Plain, 15"		12.00 per C
DC-1	Blue Document Corners	3.35 per C	31.85 per M
	White Document Corners	3.75 per C	36.10 per M
L15-A	Client's Ledger Sheets (per 100)		11.00 per C
CM-1	Client's Memo Forms (pad 50)		2.75 per pad
CD-1	Client's Diary Cards		3.00 per C
53085	Legal Seals "E" (pkg. 60)		.75 pkg.
			7.80 doz.

SAMPLE PRICE LIST OF LEGAL FORMS

R707	Legal Seals, Self Adhesive (roll 500)	3.70 roll
LIS-1	Lawyer's Instruction Sheets (pad 100)	8.00 per C
8551	Lawyer's Ledger Sheets (per 100)	11.00 per C
LTS-1	Lawyer's Time Sheets (pad 100)	8.00 per C
LBC	Legal Brief Covers (Manilla).......... each	.80 each
	(9 x 12 or 9 x 15)............................(10s)	.70 each
	....(20s)	.60 each

Mortgage Brokers Act

		25	50	100
MBA6	Disclosure Statement	2.50	4.25	7.00

Notarial

212	Notarial Certificate of True Copy (padded 100's)	5.00

Power of Attorney

73-74	Power of Attorney - General (2 pages)......	4.50	7.75	13.00
75	Power of Attorney - Short	3.00	5.00	8.50
222	Irrevocable Stock Power - (padded in 100's)...............................			5.00
379	Irrevocable Power of Attorney (Stocks/Bonds 100's)			5.00

Real Estate Forms

6M69	Sales Record Pads	Each	2.25
		10 Pads	20.00
1900	Sales Record Sheets 8½ x 14	100	3.50
		1000	31.50
1890	Sales Record Sheets 8½ x 14	100	3.50
		1000	31.50
11	Exclusive Listing Pads 8½ x 11 - Padded 50	Each	1.85
		10 Pads	17.00
A1	Appointment of Exclusive Agent 8½ x 11 - Padded 50..	Each	1.75
		10 Pads	15.75
60	Application for Rent of Suite 6¼ x 10 - Padded 25 sets in Dup	Each	3.25
		10 Pads	29.25
REL/100	Interim Agreement - 6 Part Carbon Snapset - 8½ x 11 - 10		3.00
	25..		6.30
	50..		13.50
	100		25.00
REL/200	Listing Contract - 3 Part Carbon Snapset - 8½ x 11 - 10		2.00
	25..		4.50
	50..		8.50
	100		15.00

SAMPLE PRICE LIST OF LEGAL FORMS 47

Real Estate Publications

		Each
41	Blended Payments for Loans - 10% to 25%	3.95
424	Monthly Amortized Mortgage Payments - 8% to 9% by 1/4% — 9% to 12% by 1/8%. Also 12 1/2%	3.95
69	Monthly Payments for Mortgage Amortization — 5% to 10% by 1/8%	3.95
351	Monthly Mortgage Tables	6.95
450	Monthly Payments for Mortgages (Interest Semi-Annually)	6.95
100	Mortgage Value Tables (for Loans with equal Monthly Payments)	5.00
200	Loan Value Tables (for quarterly Payment Loans)	5.00
400	Loan Payments Handbook	7.00
500	Financial Loan Tables	7.00
RDR	Real Estate Dictionary and Reference Guide	6.95
MLT	Monthly Lease Tables	12.00
595	Real Estate Buying/Selling Guide	5.95

Record Book SHARE CERTIFICATES

		100
2104	No. C1 Blue - 1 Restriction Clause 8 1/2 x 14	15.00
	No. C10 Orange - 2 Restriction Clauses 8 1/2 x 14	15.00
D1 or D1 1/2	No. C2 Blue - 1 Restriction Clause 8 1/2 x 14	15.00
	C11 Orange - 2 Restriction Clauses 14 x 8 1/2	15.00
306, 316, 326	No. C3 Blue - 1 Restriction Clause 11 x 8 1/2	15.00
	C12 Orange - 2 Restriction Clauses 11 x 8 1/2	15.00

Record Books Complete

2104	4 Ring (Hard Cover)	Each	16.50
		10	15.40
		20	14.30
2104-2	4 Ring (Hard Cover)	Each	29.00
		10	25.00
D1	"D" Ring 14 x 8 1/2 - 1	Each	16.50
		10	15.40
		20	14.30
D1 1/2	"D" Ring 14 x 8 1/2 - 1 1/2	Each	17.00
		10	15.95
		20	14.85
P306	3 Ring 11 x 8 1/2 - 1	Each	13.20
		10	12.10
		20	11.00
P316	3 Ring 11 x 8 1/2 - 1 1/2	Each	13.75
		10	12.65
		20	11.50
P326	3 Ring 11 x 8 1/2 - 2	Each	14.30
		10	13.20
		20	12.10

SAMPLE PRICE LIST OF LEGAL FORMS

Indexes and Registers Only
for All Above .... Each   10.00
                                                                        10   8.80
                                                                        20   7.70
Registers Only 100   6.00

Small Claim Act

		25	50	100
SCA 1	Summons	2.50	4.25	7.00
SCA 10	Notice to be Sent With All Warrants of Execution Against the Goods	2.50	4.25	7.00
SCA 11	Affidavit in Support of Garnishing Order Before Judgment	2.50	4.25	7.00
SCA 12	Affidavit in Support of Garnishing Order After Judgment	2.50	4.25	7.00
SCA 13	Garnishing Order Before Judgment (Attachment of Debts)	2.50	4.25	7.00
SCA 14	Garnishing Order After Judgment (Attachment of Debts)	2.50	4.25	7.00
SCA 15	Affidavit in Support of Garnishing Order Before Action	2.50	4.25	7.00
SCA 19	Application	2.50	4.25	7.00
SCA 2	Notice of Payment Out of Money Paid Into Court by Garnishee (padded in 100's)			5.00
SCA 3	Summons to Witness	2.50	4.25	7.00
SCA 31	Interlocutory Judgment	2.50	4.25	7.00
SCA 32	Notice of Discontinuance	2.50	4.25	7.00
SCA 33	Notice of Hearing	2.50	4.25	7.00
SCA 34	Notice of Intention to Dispute	2.50	4.25	7.00
SCA 35	Notice of Intention to Proceed	2.50	4.25	7.00
SCA 36	Counter Claim	2.50	4.25	7.00
SCA 6	Default Judgment for Plaintiff	2.50	4.25	7.00
SCA 64	Judgment for Plaintiff	2.50	4.25	7.00
SCA 7	Judgment Summons	2.50	4.25	7.00
SCA 8	Warrant of Commitment	2.50	4.25	7.00
SCA 9	Warrant of Execution Against the Goods of Defendant	2.50	4.25	7.00
SCA A	Certificate of Judgment	3.00	5.00	8.50

Society Act

704	List of First Directors	2.50	4.25	7.00
705	Notice of Address of Society	2.50	4.25	7.00
706	Letter Requesting Incorporation	2.50	4.25	7.00
710	Copy of Resolution	2.50	4.25	7.00
711	Annual Report	2.50	4.25	7.00
7B	Bylaws of Society	Per Set		1.10

Strata Titles Act

Form A	Certificate of Full Payment	2.25	3.50	6.00

Supreme Court

301	Writ of Summons	2.50	4.25	7.00
302	Praecipe	2.50	4.25	7.00
418	Affidavit of Service of Summons (Pers)			7.00

SAMPLE PRICE LIST OF LEGAL FORMS 49

		25	50	100
423	Affidavit of Service of Writ of Summons..	2.50	4.25	7.00
504	Praecipe (8½" x 7") (padded in 100's)			5.00
370	(V.S. 112) In the Matter of the Name Act	2.50	4.25	7.00

Supreme Court — Divorce

79	Answer.................	2.50	4.25	7.00
80	Certificate of Means	2.50	4.25	7.00
81-86	Petition for Divorce (6 Pages)	13.00	22.00	37.00
87	Affidavit of Service	2.50	4.25	7.00
88	Notice of Trial........................	2.50	4.25	7.00
89	Divorce Information Sheets (padded 100's)			8.00
90	Judgment by Way of Decree Absolute	2.50	4.25	7.00
90A	Judgment by Way of Decree Absolute (Respondent Petitioner by Way of Counter Petition).........................	2.50	4.25	7.00
91	Decree Absolute at Hearing	2.50	4.25	7.00
92	Affidavit in Support of Decree Absolute — By Solicitor..........................	2.50	4.25	7.00
92A	Affidavit in Support of Decree Absolute — In Person...........................	2.50	4.25	7.00
93	Application for Decree Absolute	2.50	4.25	7.00
94A	Praecipe — Re Application for Decree Absolute.............................	2.50	4.25	7.00
95	Registrar's Certificate of Pleadings...........	2.50	4.25	7.00
96	Praecipe Divorce	2.50	4.25	7.00
97A	Judgment by way of Decree Nisi (2 pages)	4.50	7.75	13.00
98	Divorce Registration (3 part snapset)	5.25	9.25	14.00
99A	Praecipe — Re Restoration of Maiden Name	2.50	4.25	7.00
99B	Order — Re Restoration of Maiden Name	2.50	4.25	7.00
99C	Affidavit — Re Restoration of Maiden Name	4.50	7.75	13.00
99-3	Set of Above (99A, 99B and 99C) (4 pages)	9.00	15.00	25.00

Supreme Court — In Probate

396	Affidavit of Value & Relationship (2 pages)	4.50	7.75	13.00
398	Wills Notice	2.25	3.50	6.00
399	Declaration of Transmission (2 pages)	4.50	7.75	13.00
400	Application for Search of Wills Notices (2 part)...........................	5.00	9.00	15.00
502	In Probate — Supreme Court Praecipe	2.50	4.25	7.00
Form 1	Affidavit of Executor..................	2.50	4.25	7.00
Form 2	Affidavit of Administrator	2.50	4.25	7.00
Form 3	Affidavit of Administrator (With Will Annexed)............................	2.50	4.25	7.00
Form 4	Notice.............................	4.50	7.75	13.00
466	Affidavit of Executor (2 pages)	4.50	7.75	13.00
467	Affidavit of Administrator (2 pages)........	4.50	7.75	13.00
468	Affidavit of Administrator Applying for Administration With Will Annexed (2 pages)...........................	4.50	7.75	13.00
469	Notice to Next of Kin..................	2.50	4.25	7.00
470	Administration Bond...................	2.50	4.25	7.00
471	Administration Bond on Resealing	2.50	4.25	7.00
472	Caveat	2.50	4.25	7.00
473	Notice to Caveator....................	2.50	4.25	7.00
474	Citation to Accept Probate as Executor ..	2.50	4.25	7.00
475	Answer (Re: Form 474).................	2.50	4.25	7.00
476	Citation to Propound an Alleged Will........	2.50	4.25	7.00
477	Answer (Re: Form 476).................	2.50	4.25	7.00

SAMPLE PRICE LIST OF LEGAL FORMS

		25	50	100
478	Citation to Bring In a Will	2.50	4.25	7.00
479	Subpoena to Bring in Testamentary Documents	2.50	4.25	7.00
480	Affidavit to Lead to Resealing of Grant	2.50	4.25	7.00
481	Affidavit in Supp. of App. to Pass Accounts (2 pages)	4.50	7.75	13.00
482	Citation to Bring in Grant	2.50	4.25	7.00

Supreme & County Courts

304	Notice of Hearing of Petition	2.50	4.25	7.00
307	Appearance	2.50	4.25	7.00
308	Notice of Appointment or Change of Solicitor	2.50	4.25	7.00
310	Notice of Change of Address for Delivery	2.50	4.25	7.00
314	Notice to Defendant by Counterclaim	2.30	4.25	7.00
318	Appointment to Examine for Discovery	2.50	4.25	7.00
319	Subpoena	2.50	4.25	7.00
322	Appointment	2.50	4.25	7.00
323	Notice of Order	2.50	4.25	7.00
324	Notice of Discontinuance	2.50	4.25	7.00
325	Notice of Withdrawal	2.50	4.25	7.00
326	Notice of Payment In	2.50	4.25	7.00
327	Notice of Acceptance of Money Paid In	2.50	4.25	7.00
328	Declaration	2.50	4.25	7.00
329	Particulars of Application for Payment Out Other Than Judges Order	2.50	4.25	7.00
333	Notice of Trial	2.50	4.25	7.00
334	Certificate of Readiness	2.50	4.25	7.00
336	Notice to Produce Documents, etc., at Trial	2.50	4.25	7.00
341	Appointment to Settle	2.50	4.25	7.00
342	Writ of Seizure and Sale	2.50	4.25	7.00
343	Writ of Sequestration	2.50	4.25	7.00
344	Writ of Possession	2.50	4.25	7.00
345	Writ of Delivery	2.50	4.25	7.00
346	Writ of Delivery or Assessed Value	2.50	4.25	7.00
348	Subpoena to Debtor	2.50	4.25	7.00
349	Notice of Motion for Committal	2.50	4.25	7.00
351	Certificate of Result of Sale	2.50	4.25	7.00
352	Notice of Motion	2.50	4.25	7.00
356	Notice of Appeal (2 pages)	4.50	7.75	13.00
359	Order Giving Leave to Register Foreign Judgment	2.50	4.25	7.00
361	Offer to Settle	2.50	4.25	7.00
362	Revocation	2.50	4.25	7.00
363	Consent to Judgment	2.50	4.25	7.00
384	Judgment Upon a Consent to Judgment Given After An Offer To Settle	2.50	4.25	7.00
385	Examiner's Report	2.50	4.25	7.00
403	Petition (3 pages)	4.90	9.90	18.00
414	Garnishing Order After Judgment	2.50	4.25	7.00
415	Affidavit in Support of Garnishing Order Before Judgment	2.50	4.25	7.00
416	Affidavit in Support of Garnishing Order After Judgment	2.50	4.25	7.00
417	Affidavit in Support of Garnishing Order Before Action	2.50	4.25	7.00
419	Garnishing Order Before Judgment	2.50	4.25	7.00
421	Certificate of Judgment	2.50	4.25	7.00
DD	Demand for Discovery of Documents	2.50	4.25	7.00

Will Forms & Will Paper

44	Will Forms		25.00 per C	
			1M	**500**
120-2	Ezerase Bond — 2 Margin		56.00	33.60
320-1	Gilbert Bond — 1 Margin		55.00	30.60
320-2	Gilbert Bond — 2 Margin		55.00	30.60
420-1	Colonial Bond — 1 Margin		51.00	29.35
420-2	Colonial Bond — 2 Margin		51.00	29.35
420-3	Colonial Bond — 3 Margin		51.00	29.35
WB-1	Will Backs		24.00 per 100	
WE-1	Will Envelopes		42.00 per 100	

REVIEW QUESTIONS

1. Define endorsee, grantee, and vendee.
2. What three factors must be present for the making of a lawful contract?
3. Define three different lien claims that may be registered on a land title.
4. Define indefeasible title to land.
5. How may a person obtain the legal description to a parcel of land?
6. How would you register a mechanic's lein on a parcel of land?
7. Review the subject matter of chapter 4 and research for any differences in law in your own district.

5 ZONING LAWS

In this chapter we shall discuss legally enforceable municipal (local government) zoning laws and building codes.

The first zoning laws in America were enacted in New York City in 1916, and in 1926 the Supreme Court of the United States ruled that zoning laws were constitutional.

5.1 ZONING LAWS

Without zoning laws there could be no town planning. Originally, landowners believed that zoning laws were an infringement on their personal land rights. Now it is agreed that legally enforceable zoning laws allow for an orderly development of cities and counties. There are two schools of thought about land ownership. One believes that the title owner to land should have an absolute right to do anything that he likes with it, such as to denude it entirely of trees, or to change the contours of it without any public consent. The other side contends that title owners of land are in reality only the custodians of the land during their lifetime or ownership time, and that the land itself is time enduring, while the title owner is merely transient and should enjoy the land during his tenure of it but not change it if it offends the public interest. As a result of this latter view, zoning and pollution laws are becoming more stringent in our democratic societies.

54 ZONING LAWS

Before purchasing land, any citizen or his agent may see a map of the area in which any land (in which he is interested) is located and ask at the municipal office (city hall) to see the ordinance so that he may know how he may (or may not) use it. He may then purchase a copy of the local building code, which decrees the minimum building standards for any particular area.

Zoning laws are not immutable; their intention is to assure that the public good shall prevail. A zoning law may be changed by application to the local zoning board, but before any changes are allowed, the matter must be presented for public debate. The law may be waived by "variance"; for example, if a building has been in use many years before the zoning law was applied to that particular building, provided that this use has been without detriment in any way to the public, such a building may be excluded from the zoning law during its lifetime. Thus a zoning law may be repealed, or mitigated by "variance."

5.2 LAND USE

Restrictions may be placed on land in many ways; for example, the floor areas and heights of buildings may be restricted. The allowable heights of buildings are important because, as in the case of an apartment building, the higher the building, the more suites available for rent or sale and the denser the traffic flow in the vicinity. Also, the higher the building the longer the shadow cast on other property. This is a particular consideration in business areas where people may wish to seek either the sunny side or shady side of the street. Thus one side of the street may have a poorer pedestrian flow than the other, with a poorer business cash turnover.

5.3 ZONING SYMBOLS AND DESCRIPTIONS

The following material has been used with the permission of the California Department of Real Estate, publisher of *Reference Book*, a real estate study manual and guide for Californians. This information may be found on pages 412 through 417 of said book.

That there is little consistency in zoning symbols and descriptions in the political subdivisions of California government has long been well known to real estate brokers and others with real estate interests. This lack of uniformity was graphically portrayed in a study of variations in zoning symbols and descriptions and the possibilities for more uniformity, completed by the Real Estate Research Bureau, Division of Business Administration, California State University, Sacramento in 1965. Incidentally, the

5.3 ZONING SYMBOLS AND DESCRIPTIONS

study was financed by a modest appropriation from the Real Estate Education, Research and Recovery Fund administered by the Real Estate Commissioner. Following are extracts quoted from the study:

"It is obvious that there is a wide variety of zoning symbols used in California. Some jurisdictions apparently need few symbols, others many. A given letter of the alphabet, when used in a zoning symbol often permits quite different land uses, that is, the same letter sometimes means different things, even in the same jurisdiction. There is a distinct lack of uniformity among jurisdictions in the use of symbols and their descriptions. Among the jurisdictions collectively there is inconsistency in the symbols and descriptions used.

"It is assumed, however, although this *was not* part of our investigation, that there are good and sufficient reasons for the differences found. These reasons have their roots in such factors as the date and circumstances under which the jurisdiction was created, the person or persons who drafted the zoning ordinances, the economic and social functions of the city or county, the topography and other natural features of the area, the desires of the residents, the character and rate of change in the economy and population, and so forth.

"Granted that there are reasons for legitimate differences among the ordinances, it is also true that there has not been heretofore a great amount of interest in uniformity. One reason is that many of these ordinances were adopted when there did not appear to be any need for regional, or statewide uniformity. Another reason is that there have not been, in the state, the standards, guides or models available statewide to suggest the desirability or the nature of uniform symbols and descriptions. No group or governmental agency in California, so far as we know, has heretofore developed and made available a uniform set of zoning symbols and descriptions."

Examples of Zoning Symbols and Their Meanings:

The California State University, Sacramento study team referred to above tabulated zoning symbols and their descriptions (or definitions) used by 70 local governments in California: 20 counties and 59 cities, all in Standard Metropolitan Statistical Areas. The tabulation follows:

Zone symbol	Number of jurisdictions using symbol	Description
A	12	Agriculture
A1	23	Agriculture; residential-agriculture; single family
A2	19	Agriculture; poultry and rabbit raising
A3	4	Heavy agriculture; floriculture
A4	1	Agriculture
A5	1	Agriculture
AC	1	Arts and crafts
AE	4	Agriculture; agriculture-exclusive
AG	2	Agriculture; agriculture-exclusive
AL	1	Limited agriculture
AP	6	Airport; administrative-professional
AR	5	Agriculture-residential; administrative-research

56 ZONING LAWS

AV 2 Airport

Summary: Generally "A" indicates agriculture; however, in one case it stands for art; in a few instances it stands for administrative; and in about five cities it stands for airport.

B	1	Buffer
C	5	Business; commercial
C1	64	Limited commercial; retail
C1A	1	Community shopping center
C1S	1	Shopping Center
C½	1	General commercial
C2	63	General commercial; limited commercial; neighborhood shopping
C2GM	1	Central business-general merchandise
C3	33	General commercial; regional shopping; community shopping
C4	12	Unlimited commercial; service stations
C5	2	Commercial
C6	1	General commercial
C10	1	Local retail
C20	1	Shopping center
C25	1	Office-commercial
C30	1	District thoroughfare
C35	1	District commercial
C40	1	Community thoroughfare
C50	1	Central business
C60	1	City service commercial
CA	1	Commercial-agriculture
CB	2	Central business
CC	5	Central commercial; community commercial
CD	1	Civic development
CG	4	General commecial
CH	6	Highway commercial
CL	4	Limited commercial
CM	23	Commercial-manufacturing
CN	6	Commercial-neighborhood
CO	9	Commercial-office; professional office
CP	4	Restricted commercial; administrative-professional
CR	8	Restricted commercial; recreation-commercial; community reserve
CS	4	Commercial shopping
CT	2	Thoroughfare commercial
CX	1	Administrative-research

Summary: Generally "C" indicates commercial; however, in one case it stands for civic; in another, community. In both of these instances a noncommercial land use pattern was noted.

D2	1	Desert-mountain
E1	8	One family residence; estate; executive
E2	7	One family residence; estate; executive; small farms
E3	5	One family residence; estate; mountain estate
E4	3	Small estates
EA	1	Exclusive agriculture

Summary: "E" seems to indicate estates, although it is frequently used to mean executive offices.

F	5	Farm; flood plain; forestry
FP	1	Flood plain
FR	1	Forestry-recreation

Summary: There is no pattern in the use of "F".

5.3 ZONING SYMBOLS AND DESCRIPTIONS

GA	1	General agriculture
GI	1	General industrial
GR	1	Guest ranch
H1	4	Highway
HD	1	High density residential
HI	1	Heavy industrial
HS	2	Highway service
I	1	Industrial
IA	1	Intermediate agriculture
IM	1	Intermediate manufacturing
IP	1	Industrial park
IR	3	Industrial-recreational; industrial-administrative research
LI	1	Light industrial
LM	2	Limited manufacturing

Summary: There is no consistent pattern for zone symbols "G," "H," "I," and "L," although "I" most frequently is used in connection with industrial land use.

M	11	Industrial; manufacturing
M1	60	Light manufacturing; residential-manufacturing
M1A	3	Manufacturing; limited light industrial
M1B	1	Restricted light industrial
M1C	1	Distributive industries
M1S	1	Industrial park
M1X	3	Exclusive light manufacture
M2	57	Light industrial; medium industrial; heavy industrial
M2A	1	Manufacturing
M3	14	Heavy industrial
M4	3	Limited industrial; heavy industrial
M10	1	Special industrial
M20	1	Light industrial
M30	1	General industrial
M40	1	Heavy industrial
MF	1	Industrial frontage
MG	1	General manufacturing
ML	6	Limited manufacturing
MP	4	Industrial park; industrial parking
MR	3	Manufacturing-restricted; multiple residential
MS	1	Special industrial

Summary: Generally an "M" zone indicates an industrial land use; in one case, however, MR is used to indicate a residential use. In the "M" zones there seems to be no pattern for symbols used for restricted, heavy, or general industrial zones.

O	7	Open space; official
OB	1	Office building
OP	1	Office-professional
P	24	Parking; parks
P1	8	Parking
PA	1	Professional and administrative
PB	1	Parking building
PC	2	Planned community
PD	2	Planned development
PF	1	Public facilities
PL	2	Parking-landscaping
PM	1	Planned industrial
PO	1	Professional office
PR	1	Park and recreation
PW	1	Planned working area

ZONING LAWS

Summary: The use of the letter "P" as a zone symbol is the most inconsistent of all the zone symbols. It is truly a trap for the unwary.

Q	3	Quarries
R1	64	Single family residential
R1A	10	Single family residential
R1B	8	Single family residential
R1C	4	Single family residential
R1D	4	Single family residential
R1E	2	Residential estate
R1H	1	Residential hillside
R1S	1	Special single family residential
R2	75	Duplex; multiple family
R3	69	Multiple family; garden apartments; apartment hotels
R3A	3	Multiple family; mountain resort
R3G	1	Garden apartment
R3H	1	High density multiple family
R3P	1	Residential-professional
R3R	1	Restricted multiple family
R4	42	High density multiple family; suburban residential
R4C	1	High-rise apartments
R5	9	High density multiple family; tourist accommodations
R6	2	Single family; hotel apartments
R7	1	Single family
R10	2	Estate residential; single family
R12	2	High density residential; single family
R15	1	Single family-low density
R20	2	Single family-low density
R24	1	Medium density residential
R30	1	Single family
R40	2	Townhouse; single family
R50	1	Garden apartment
R60	1	Medium density residential
R65	1	Single family
R70	1	High density residential
R80	1	High-rise apartments
R90	1	Downtown apartments
RA	17	Residential-agriculture
RB	1	Retail business
RC	2	Residential commercial; professional office
RD	5	Residential duplex
RE	17	Residential estate
RF	2	Recreation-forestry
RG	1	Garden apartment
RHE	1	Residential hillside estate
RM	2	Multiple residential
RO	3	Single family suburban; restricted office
RP	7	Residential professional; unrestricted residential
RR	7	Rural residential; resort-recreation; residential-resort
RRB	1	Restricted roadside business
RS	7	Residential-single family; residential suburban
RT	2	Recreational-tourist; residential transitional
RWY	1	Railway

Summary: "R" generally denotes residential; "R" is also used to denote retail, recreation, resort and railway.

S	2	Scenic highway; motion picture studio

SC	2	Residential-commercial; shopping center
SL	1	Ocean-submerged land
SP	2	Special land use; parking and buffer zone
SR	2	Recreation; scientific research

Summary: The use of the letter "S" as a zone symbol follows no consistent pattern.

T	6	Trailer park
TM	1	Trailer park-motel
TP	2	Trailer park-residential
U	2	Unclassified, hog ranch
W	1	Watercourse area
WA	1	Watercourse area
WR	1	Watershed-recreational

Range in number of symbols used: 40 by one jurisdiction to low of 5 by one jurisdiction.

REVIEW QUESTIONS

1. Define zoning laws.
2. How could you find out what the zoning laws are regarding a parcel of land in your area?
3. May a zoning law be changed? If your answer is yes, how may it be done?
4. List six restrictions that may be placed on a parcel of land.
5. Are you in favor of zoning laws? If your answer is yes, support your argument in not more than 150 words.

6 NOTARIES PUBLIC

In this chapter we shall present a dialogue on notaries public, their qualifications and appointment to office.

6.1   APPOINTMENT OF NOTARIES PUBLIC

Q *How are notaries public appointed?*

A There are different methods of appointing notaries public between states of the U.S.A. and also between provinces of Canada. As examples: in the State of Washington a person desirous of becoming a notary public must make an application on an official form obtainable from the Notary Public Commission, Division of Professional Licensing, P.O. Box 9649, Olympia, Washington, 98504. To become a notary public in B.C. persons must apply to the Society of Notaries Public, answer a questionnaire, pay a fee and take an educational course. Only then may he or she be accepted if there is a vacancy or need for a new appointee. In some states of the United States appointments are made by the governor of the state and in some cases by a senator. Still other states require the recommendation of several free holders residing wherein the applicant resides. It is important for would-be notaries public to check the method of appointing in the desired area of operation.

6.2 HISTORICAL NOTES

Notaries have been in existence since early Roman times. They were called *scibae*, scribes. Coming from varied occupations, they were originally mere copiers of documents.

Some were permanent officials at law courts, where they recorded public proceedings, transcribed state papers, supplied magistrates with legal forms, and registered judgments and decrees. They dealt with matters of private concern such as drafting wills, deeds, and conveyances. Cicero invented a new shorthand for secretaries called *notae* and people who used it were called notaries.

Roman notaries were officially connected with voluntary or non-contentious jurisdiction of the court, and their duties were regulated by law.

6.3 DIALOGUE CONCERNING MODERN NOTARIES

Q *Define a notary public.*

A This is a person authorized by law to attest (bear witness) to documents, administer oaths, authenticate deeds of contract, attest to affidavits (sworn statements made under oath) and to draft and witness the signing of last wills and testaments, etc.

Q *Define a deed.*

A A deed is a legal document by which lands, tenements, and hereditaments (any property that may be inherited) are conveyed (transferred) from one owner to another. This document is signed and sealed before a notary, and delivered to the parties.

Q *Define a notarial instrument.*

A This is a document containing some contract or agreement—for example, one which conveys real estate from a vendor to a purchaser or donee. It is a legal instrument recording the due execution (signing) of the deed, contract, or other writing, verifying some fact or thing done.

Q *Define the necessary contents of a notarial instrument.*

A a) The title
   b) The date
   c) The place of execution
   d) The parties and witnesses
   e) The document or transaction that is the subject of the act

f) The statement to the effect that the document was read to the parties and approved by them
g) The date, which should be written in full
h) The place where the instrument is executed
i) The words "before me" should never be left out.

Q *Define a notarial act.*

A This is the act of a notary public, authenticated by his (or her) signature and official seal, certifying the due execution (signing and sealing) in his or her presence of a deed, contract, or other writing, verifying some fact or thing done in his or her presence. In many countries in which notaries are recognized, whatever is certified by the notary as having been done or said in his or her presence is taken to be beyond dispute, and proved.

Q *What is an authentic act?*

A It is an act executed (signed) on a legal document and certified by an official such as a notary public.

Q *List some types of documents that a notary public may attest.*

A a) A partnership agreement
b) Conveyance documents to buy and sell property
c) An attestation of affidavits (witnessing). An affidavit is a sworn statement written under oath (a solemn appeal before God for verification of the terms of the promise)

Q *How does a person grant a power of attorney?*

A One grants a power of attorney by appointing legally by documentation a party (agent) to act in the place of another (principal) to transact any stated business for the other such as conveyance of property, stocks and shares, a car or anything and everything stated in the document. The power of attorney shall be in the form of a notarized letter (on legal stationery), authorizing one party (agent) to act in behalf of another (principal).

Q *Who is entitled to act as principal?*

A Every person capable of contracting on his or her own account and not personally disqualified (such as a criminal in jail) is competent to appoint an attorney to do for him whatever he or she is legally entitled to do for himself. The interpretation of attorney in this question does not mean that the agent must be a lawyer or attorney at law; it means anyone of legal age and competent in health and record.

REVIEW QUESTIONS

1. How are notaries public appointed to office in your area?
2. Inquire at a bonding agency or insurance company as to the fee for a notary bond. It is $_____.
3. What are the age limits for becoming a notary public in your area?
4. What is the fee for becoming a notary public in your area?
5. Define the contents of a notarial instrument.
6. What advantage may there be to employ the services of a notary public to convey property instead of using the services of an attorney?

7 CONSTRUCTION CONTRACTS

A contract may be described as private law between two subscribing parties. Most contracts are accepted and consummated without recourse to law. Thus, A agrees to purchase land from B. This is a contract. If both parties adhere to the terms, there is no need for a court opinion.

7.1 CONTRACTS

The essentials of a legal contract are:

a) Competent parties
b) An offer and an acceptance
c) Consideration
d) A legal object
e) The contract must be written without mistakes or ambiguities

Competent Parties: These are parties that are legally privileged to enter into a contract. They must be of sound mind, of legal age, and not deprived of civil rights as are these persons in prison. A person while drunk cannot enter into a contract agreement. No contract is lawful unless there has been an offer and an acceptance.

66 CONSTRUCTION CONTRACTS

Consideration: This means that each party must give something. It may be money or it could be love, affection, devotion as from one person to another. It is a basic principle of law that an offer can be withdrawn at any time before it is accepted, but the notice of withdrawal must reach the offeree (the one to whom it is offered) before that person has accepted the offer. An irrevocable offer or tender is a contradiction in terms; what is meant is an agreement not to withdraw an offer for a stated period. This then is an option.

7.2 DIALOGUE ON CONTRACTS

Q *Define rescission.*

A To abrogate, repeal, cancel, terminate something such as a lawful contract which returns both parties to their original positions before the contract was signed.

Q *What methods are there for resolving a breach of contract?*

A The best method is by negotiation between parties. Another method is to arbitrate the differences. A third way is by recourse to a court of law, which may make a monetary award for damages; however, time is important and court proceedings may be long delayed. A breach of contract should be resolved quickly.

Q *What is specific performance?*

A This is a court remedy that requires the party in the wrong to do all those things agreed upon in the contract.

Q *Define liquidated damages.*

A It is a provision in a contract document providing for certain damages in the event of a breach. Many construction contracts call for liquidated damages in favor of the owner for late delivery of the building. Damages are assessed at a specific amount per day.

Q *What are punitive damages?*

A These are damages beyond normally appropriate compensation awarded a plaintiff as a punishment to the defendant. Such punishments are imposed to protect society from obnoxious conduct.

Q *What is an architect's certificate?*

A It is a certificate issued by the architect to the owner, certifying that certain work has been completed and all bills for material and wages have been paid and that the contractor merits being paid the sum stated including 10 percent for his overhead expenses; but a contracted sum, called a holdback (usually 10 to 15 percent), is retained in case there are any liens being registered against the owner's property. In all events, the integrity of the owner's property is paramount.

Q *Can the architect order changes to be made to the building during operations?*

A Only with the consent of the owner. Significant changes must be noted in writing and the contractor's compensation is negotiable.

7.3 DIALOGUE ON BUILDING CONSTRUCTION CONTRACTS

Q *Define a contract between a client and an architect.*

A A contract between a client and a professional person is often referred to as a retainer. It is a contract. Architects often use a standard form of agreement between client and architect, obtainable from the American Institute of Architects (AIA), in which the language used has been polished over the years and the articles have been court-tested.

Q *Who is the owner of the drawings and specifications for a building?*

A The architect. He is considered to have exercised his genius and expertise in making them and his ownership does not require copyrighting.

Q *Who is responsible for ordering changes to be made to the building after start of operations?*

A The owner (usually upon the advice of the architect). Most buildings have changes made during building construction. The architect may order the changes, but he is acting as the agent of the owner.

Q *What are liquidated damages?*

A In the construction industry, these are monetary rewards made to either the owner or the contractor for early or late delivery of the building to the owner. Assume that the owner was to make a projected $1,000 profit per day from a new factory that was late in being delivered. Liquidated damages may be fixed at $500 per day. On the other hand, the builder may be awarded $500 per day for early delivery.

Q *Explain why there are retainage funds withheld from the contractor.*

A As the construction progresses, many workers and material suppliers are engaged by the builder. If they are not paid, they may file liens against the owner's land. The retained funds may then be used to effect release of the liens and restore to the owner the original registered state of the land.

68   CONSTRUCTION CONTRACTS

Q *What are general conditions?*

A These are definitions of rights, responsibilities, and relationships of all parties to the contract.

Q *What are supplementary conditions?*

A They are special conditions imposed by local authorities for construction work in their area of jurisdiction, such as special ground conditions, earthquake-proof construction, and so on, peculiar to the area.

Q *Define specifications.*

A Specifications are written instructions on types of building materials and of how they are to be fitted together. When they are read with the architectural drawings a contractor may arrive at an acceptable and profitable estimate of the cost of the building to the owner.

Q *Where do the legal clauses of the contract appear in the documents?*

A The first few pages are known in trade parlance as being "front-end papers," or "boilerplate." The AIA consistently updates its documents. The language has been polished over the years and many of the clauses have been court-tested.

Q *What is an invitation to tender (bid)?*

A An architect, as agent of the owner, invites a few known contractors to bid on a certain project. The bid itself constitutes an offer only to build the project at the quoted price. It is not a contract to build until it has been accepted by the offeree (the owner).

7.4   DIALOGUE ON REAL ESTATE CONTRACTS

Q *Is an oral agreement to sell or exchange real estate valid?*

A No. There must be a written contract to sell or exchange land. (Note that land covers also any building on it.) Such transactions must be filed in the public land titles office of the city or county in which the land is located.

Q *What are the main provisions in a typical real estate contract of sale?*

A The contract sets forth a legal description of the property, the price, the date of possession, the provisions for prorating the local taxes, the insurance, and the amount of heating oil still left in the furnace tank at the time of settlement of the contract. The contingencies in case of default are outlined, as is the resolution in case of total destruction of the property.

7.4 DIALOGUE ON REAL ESTATE CONTRACTS

Q *Define a contract for a deed by installment payments for a land contract.*

A The purchaser's right to the deed to the property is determined upon contracted payment and any other provisions having been met. The deed is then (sometimes) deposited with an escrow agent (such as a trust company), which holds the deed until all conditions of the contract have been met. The escrow agent administers the accounting for the installment payments and for the insurance coverage, and makes payments to the vendor.

Q *Define an escrow agent.*

A An escrow agent is a neutral party who holds the deed until all conditions of the contract have been met. If they are not met he may (upon legal advice) initiate foreclosure proceedings (making a forced sale of the property), and with the proceeds make payment to the vendor of the outstanding balance owing plus interest up to date, pay for foreclosure proceedings, and deduct his own fee. In short, the escrow agent holds the deed in trust for both parties; thus the purchaser enjoys the use of the property but does not get possession of the actual title until the final payment has been made. (This may be some years after the closing date of the deal. At that time the vendor will grant discharge of mortgage to the purchaser and the purchaser's attorney will file it in the land titles office.)

Q *What is a "subject to" clause in a listing?*

A It means that there cannot be a firm offer to purchase unless the "subject to" clause has been met or removed from the offer to purchase. A typical "subject to" clause may read as follows:

> This offer is subject to the purchaser arranging a first mortgage on his property located at _____ within fourteen (14) business days of the date this offer is made in the amount of $_____ on terms satisfactory to himself.

With this type of interim agreement the prospective purchaser is free to withdraw from the deal unless the "subject to" clause has been consummated or withdrawn.

Another frequently used "subject to" clause may read:

> This offer is subject to the purchaser selling his land located at _____ (legal description) for a minimum of $_____ cash, with completion date prior to the completion date set herein.

The vendor too may include a "subject to" clause, such as:

The vendor reserves the right to accept further offers for the above described property in the event another acceptable offer is received, in which case the offeror shall be given twenty-four (24) hours' written notice in which to remove his "subject to" clause, failing which the vendor shall be free to accept the new offer.

Q *What is a discharge of mortgage or satisfaction piece?*

A It is a written certificate stating that all terms of the mortgage have been met. It is filed in the land titles office and endorsed on the original title certificate as notice to all the world that the mortgage has been redeemed.

Q *What is a second mortgage?*

A This is a mortgage that can only be satisfied after the first mortgage has been satisfied. For example, in case of default of payment to the first mortgagee, such payment must be first applied to the first mortgage and second to the second mortgagee. Second mortgages carry a bigger risk than first mortgages; that is why they earn a bigger interest rate.

Q *Define different types of real estate listings.*

A There are several types of listings:

Net Listing: This is a contract to sell, lease, or rent, and to obtain a minimum set price for the owner. Using this type of listing, the agent should carefully determine his or her compensation for efforts in realizing the contract.

Open Listing: These are simple listings. The owner retains the right to list the property with other agents, or to sell the property himself. The agent who sells the property receives compensation. If the owner sells the property himself, he does not have to pay any commission, unless the agent can prove that it was through his or her agency that the owner met the prospect. This may require a court ruling.

Exclusive Agency Listing: These allow for compensation to the agent named in the listing, regardless of who sells the property. In some states this could include the owner himself.

Exclusive Right-to-sell Listing: This type of listing allows for compensation to the agent named in the listing, regardless of who sells the property, including the owner himself.

Certified Listing: A certified listing grants exclusive right to sell to the listing agent. The client is called upon for a small sum of money to cover the agent making a brief of the property, and also for an accredited appraiser's report. This sum is placed in the trust fund of the broker and is deducted from the broker's commission when he sells the property. The advantage of an appraisal report is that all parties are aware of the true market value of the property. A new zoning law could change the value of property overnight.

Note: It is very important that local research be made to compare or contrast local conditions of this material.

7.5 TYPICAL EXAMPLES OF INSTRUCTIONS TO BIDDERS

Tenders shall be made on the blanks provided, enclosed in an envelope, endorsed _____.
(Here state the name of the work)

_____, sealed and addressed to the Architect. All blanks shall be completely filled in giving all proposals asked and all figures shall be stated in writing. Failure to observe this ruling shall cause rejection of the proposal.

Each tender shall be accompanied by a certified check equal in amount to ten per cent (10%) of the contract price as evidence of good faith and to the effect that should the proposal be accepted, the tenderer shall enter into a contract and furnish satisfactory deposit or bond. The said deposit or certified check to be forfeited if the tenderer whose proposal is accepted shall fail to give satisfactory guarantee deposit or bond or to execute a contract, or shall be returned after guarantee deposit or bond is given and contract executed. Tendered deposits or checks of unsuccessful bidders shall be returned after the award has been given and contract executed.

Persons or firms submitting tenders or proposals shall be actively engaged in the line of work required by the specification and shall be able to refer to work of a similar character performed by them.

They shall be fully conversant with the general technical phraseology in the English language, of the lines of work covered by the drawings and specifications.

Before submitting a tender, bidders shall carefully examine the drawings and specifications, visit the building site or premises, and fully inform themselves as to all existing conditions and limitations.

Tenderers finding discrepancies in or omissions from the drawings, specifications, or other documents, or having any doubt as to the meaning or intent of any part thereof, should at once inform the Architect, who will send written instructions or explanations to all tenderers. Neither Owner nor Architect shall be held responsible for oral instructions.

The Contractor shall bring to the attention of the Architect any obvious omission and/or discrepancies failing which he shall become responsible for completing such work without added compensation.

Failure of the tenderer (should he become the successful bidder) to inform or bring to the attention of the Architect at the time of tendering, any such items as appear obvious, shall be assumed as indicating his willingness to accept the original intent and meaning as may be interpreted by the Architect, within the reason of standard practice, or requirements necessary to obtain a complete work, or any other such work, supply or installation, failing which would jeopardize the structure or leave an unfinished or incomplete work in part or in whole.

Addenda or corrections issued during the time of tendering are to be covered in the proposal and shall become part of the contract documents.

The Architect reserves the right to reject any or all proposals. Contracts when awarded shall be for each branch or division of the work, or for the whole work as deemed for the best interests by the Architect.

The tenderer whose proposal is accepted will be required to furnish a marked check or bond or bonds or Guarantee Bond for supply of proper materials, faithful performance and maintenance of the work as provided for under article "Guarantee Deposit or Bond".

A written request for approval of equivalents for products and materials and/or associated alternative subcontractors shall be submitted in order to reach this office not later than ten days prior to closing date of tender. All subcontractors must be noted in the list submitted by the General Contractor with his tender.

All Contractors are to itemize, with their bids, all contingency and P.C. Sums.

If necessary, one (1) Addendum to the Specifications and Drawings will be issued by the Architect, one (1) week before closing date of tender.

This Addendum will contain all changes and clarifications to the drawings and specifications, as well as a list of equivalent materials and products, as determined by the Architect, or his representative.

No further addenda will be issued after one week prior to tendering and all bidders shall refer to "Interpretations of Specifications and Drawings" as covered in the preface to Instructions to Bidders.

Tenderers shall make allowance for delay in mailing or transportation, or preferably see his tender delivered personally, that they reach the Architect within the stated time, as no allowance can be made for extenuating circumstances.

The mechanical and electrical subcontractors *shall* on acceptance of tender (whether called for by the Owner or by the General Contractor) and when completing agreement, render to the General Contractor a surety bond for 50% of their contract to cover materials and performance for the faithful completion of their contract. They shall therefore allow in their tender figure for the cost of such bond. The General Contractor in his turn shall not conclude any agreement with the mechanical and electrical subcontractors until he has received the covering surety bond.

REVIEW QUESTIONS

1. Describe (in general outlines) a construction contract.
2. The essentials of a legal contract are:
    a)
    b)
    c)
    d)
    e)
3. What methods are there for resolving a breach of contract?
4. Define liquidated damages.
5. Define punitive damages.
6. Define an escrow agent.
7. Under what circumstances may an architect order changes to be made during building operations?
8. In the construction industry, does the architect have a contract with the builder?

8 REAL ESTATE APPRAISAL

8.1 THE REAL ESTATE APPRAISER

The American Institute of Real Estate Appraisers was founded in 1932. It was organized under, and requires the applicant to be a member of, the National Association of Realtors. The Institute issues two certificates: for Residential Members (RM) and for the Member Appraisal Institute (MAI). The MAI designation is considered by many to be the best in its field.

The Society of Real Estate Appraiser, developed primarily from the savings and loan group of staff appraisers, grants three designations: Senior Residential Appraisers (SRA); Senior Real Property Appraisers (SRPA) for commercial properties; and its highest designation, Senior Real Estate Analyst (SREA). Those bearing the last title are qualified to appraise any type of property.

There are a number of real estate appraiser chapters in Canada such as these of the Accredited Appraiser Canadian Institute (AACI) and the Canadian Residential Appraiser (CRA). They may be contacted through the Appraisal Institute of Canada.

An appraiser should be a very experienced realtor who knows intimately the district in which he or she operates.

8.2 APPRAISING PROPERTY

Let us consider the appraisal of a property made for a financial organization that lends money on mortgages. If the appraiser's report gives the value of the property as $100,000, the company would probably make a loan of 60 percent of the appraised value, $60,000. This is done in case the mortgagor does not honor his commitment to make regular agreed repayments on the loan, plus interest. In case of default, the mortgagee has the right to initiate foreclosure proceedings—i.e., a legal forced sale of the pledged property—to cover the defaulted debt. In this manner the loan company feels secure in its investment (of other people's money) by anticipating that the forced sale would yield sufficient money to repay the balance of the outstanding loan plus interest, plus legal expenses.

A forced sale is usually conducted by the sheriff (the chief law enforcement officer). (The word *sheriff* derives from shire reeve, meaning shire bailiff.)

8.3 APPRAISING LAND FOR SPECULATION BUILDING

A speculation builder should have an appraisal and district market survey made of the parcel of land upon which he would like to build a house.

The object of speculation building is to erect the right type of house in the right place and time, on the correct lot at its correct elevation, to suit the purse and aesthetic taste of particular individuals. *It should be remembered that it costs just as much to build an expensive house on a poor lot as it does to build a similar house on an appropriate and sales-appealing lot.*

Here are some points that should be carefully considered before speculatively building houses:

a) Price range of the units to be built.
b) Where the houses should be built.
c) Cost of the land.
d) Probable municipal taxes on the completed units (an assessment may be obtained from the local municipal office).
e) Topographical features of the land: Will it have to be cut and graded, or is it filled with land? The municipality may have a history that will provide this information.
f) Surface water drainage: Is it by gravity or storm sewer drains already in place on the adjoining public road?

8.3 APPRAISING LAND FOR SPECULATION BUILDING

g) Trees or existing buildings or fences: Will they have to be removed?
h) The kind of water supply available.
i) Existence (or nonexistence) of natural gas, power, sewer, telephone, and power lines.
j) Possible existence of any old sewer and service lines still underground on the property: Will they have to be removed back as far as the municipal mains?
k) Existence of projected schools, shopping facilities, libraries, postal facilities, parks, hospitals, churches, and freeways.
l) Other residential construction being built in the area.
m) Location of places in which people will be employed, and access to these places.
n) Local zoning laws. These may be seen at the municipal office where taxes for the property will have to be paid.
o) Suitability of district for small families or retirees.

Before speculatively building a house, a realtor should be engaged to make a research of the district and of the type of house that would be appealing to prospective purchasers. Some of the points for research are as follows:

a) The price range of existing nearby houses
b) The age and salary range of prospective purchasers
c) The floor area, architectural merit, design, and price of the proposed project
d) The probable municipal taxes (an estimate may be obtained at the local municipality)
e) The availability and type of public transportation, accessibility to freeways, distance from the city center
f) The proximity of churches, schools, recreation centers, libraries, hospitals, hairdressers and so on
g) The places at which people will work
h) New developments planned by the local authority
i) The age group to which the new house would be appealing
j) Freedom from pollution
k) The type of driveway
l) The grounds (including such considerations as maintenance, beauty, topography, etc.)
m) The local building and zoning laws.

8.4 REASONS FOR LAND APPRAISAL

The appraisal date and reason for the appraisal are most important and should be written on the statement. A building could be utterly destroyed by fire or earthquake in minutes; conversely, oil or gold could be discovered between dawn and dusk on the property.

There are a number of reasons for making a property appraisal, such as: assessment of city taxes; insurance; sale or exchange of the property; distribution of shares between beneficiaries under the terms of a will; possible need to demolish a house; possible need for the total removal of a house from one lot to another; possibility of takeover of the property by government by right of eminent domain.

An appraisal must take into account the present and probable economic conditions of the state or province; the county within the state; and the district within the county. An appraisal must be made as to whether or not the area is a growing and forward-looking place with a firm industrial base, or a deteriorating district that may be slowly becoming a ghost town. An indication of trends may be made from a comparison table of children of school age over the past few years. Also, research should be made of the number of bankruptcies in the area over recent years.

Sometimes legal necessity requires that an appraisal be made for a previous date, but it is impossible for anyone to make a valid appraisal of property for a future date.

8.5 METHODS OF APPRAISING REAL ESTATE

There are several methods of appraising real estate, among them:

a) By comparative values of recent sales of similar property in the same district
b) By adjusted values against trends of the environment
c) By projected future development in the district by industry or by municipality
d) By the sound, experienced judgment of an appraiser from a study of the existing features and from a study of a historical review of the property retrieved from files on the subject property and its environs.

8.6 APPRAISING THE COST FOR A NEW BUILDING

An approximate estimate of cost for a new building (within, say, 5 to 10 percent either way) is used by architects in their first consultations with

8.6 APPRAISING THE COST FOR A NEW BUILDING

clients. A similar estimate is used by contractors to guide their thinking in the first approach to the probable cost of a new building. There are several ways of determining within reason the cost of a proposed building:

The Square-Foot Method: This method may be used where a comparable building has recently been built in similar ground conditions. First, the square-foot area of a completed building is taken, and the cost per square foot is reckoned by dividing the total cost by the number of square feet. Second, the square-foot cost of the newly completed building is multiplied by the square-foot area of the proposed building. This gives a quick approximate cost. Assume that a recently built warehouse cost $12/sq ft and a proposed 3200-sq-ft warehouse is to be built in the same general area and of similar construction. The preliminary estimate of cost would be $12 × 3200, which is $38,400. This method is used by both the architect and the contractor as a guide.

The Cubic-Foot Method: This method is used by the architect and the contractor in much the same manner as the square-foot method. For some types of structures it might be more valid. As an example, assume that a school building with air conditioning is to be built in a tropical climate. Once the cubic-foot cost of the school built to similar drawings and specifications has been established, it is reasonable to suggest that the new proposed school will cost very nearly the same amount per cubic foot.

The Comparative-Appraisal Method: This method is used by both architects and contractors to get a near-cost price for a proposed new building by comparing its size, design, specifications, and soil conditions with a similar new building.

Assume that the following information is known about the existing building:

a) It is a recently completed single-story elementary school with library, gymnasium, auditorium, storage, and administrative space. It comprises 31,310 square feet. (*Note:* This is an elementary school and could only be compared with such. A high school, college, technical school, or university would cost more.)
b) It has fourteen classrooms, and is designed for 420 student stations, with an average of 30 students per classroom.
c) The total cost was $431,207.

From this information we can derive the following:

a) The cost per sq ft is total cost divided by the number of square feet: this is 431,207 ÷ 31,310 = $13.53/sq ft.

b) The cost per classroom is total cost divided by the number of classrooms: this is 431,207 ÷ 14 = $30,800/classroom.

c) The cost per student station is total cost divided by the number of student stations. This is 431,207 ÷ 420 = $1,026/student station.

Let us make an appraisal of cost for a proposed new single-story elementary school comprising 27,500 square feet, with twelve classrooms designed for 360 student stations, to be built to similar design, specifications, and ground conditions as the fourteen-room school. We may proceed as follows:

a) Assume the cost is $13.53/sq ft, as for the fourteen-room school.

b) The total cost will be the square-foot area times the cost per square foot: 27,500 × $13.53 = $372,075.00 total cost.

c) The cost per classroom will be nearly the same as for the other school, which was $30,800 per classroom. Then 12 × 30,800 = $369,600 total cost.

d) The cost per student station will be near (maybe more) to that of the fourteen-room school—say, 1026 × 360 = $369,360 total cost.

e) Another very quick guide would be to say that if a fourteen-room school cost $431,207, then a twelve-room school with everything else being equal would cost $\frac{12}{14}$ of 431,207, or $369,606.

It can be seen that the guide cost in paragraphs (b), (c), (d), and (e) are very close to each other. But other considerations would have to be taken into account, such as: Would total expenses be more or less for a smaller school? Would the use of heavy equipment be more economical on a bigger job? Would temporary buildings and even the cost of estimating the job be more or less on a smaller job? There are other considerations too, but all these appraisal methods are educated guesses and have value as guides.

In the case of a motel village, the near cost may be appraised by the type and size of each proposed unit against the actual cost of similar compound types and sizes built under similar conditions.

All these methods should be used simply as a guide in the initial thinking. The architect can advise his or her client of the type and size of the building to expect for a given outlay. The estimator can advise his or her manager of the approximate cost. The manager, in consultation with the chief executive officers of the company, would be able to assess their financial obligations if they made a successful bid. There is a limit as to how far each company may become financially involved, as well as to whether or not materials, equipment, and labor will, indeed, be available at the correct time.

Every contracting company only wants to obtain contracts at its own price and build in its own available time. Usually, it is considered that a general contractor for an average new city building is financially involved for about 15 to 20 percent of the total cost. The rest is taken up by subcontractors. It does not require many contracts, even at this rate, for the general contractor to become deeply involved financially.

There are no data for you comparable to that of your own company. It is imperative that a cost analysis of every completed job be made and the records brought up to date. Toward the top left-hand corner of the general estimate stationery sheet is a place for the "subject" to be written. The subject would range from residences, schools, hotels, motels, garages, warehouses, and so on. The completed estimates would then be filed under the appropriate subject heading; the analysis of each job would also be filed under the correct subject heading. An estimator cannot have too many guides to regulate his thinking.

When an analysis of the cost of each job is taken by the square-foot method, the cubic-foot method, and the comparative-appraisal method, any one or, better still, a combination and average of all these methods may be taken to arrive at a reasonable educated guess of the cost of a new proposed building. However, the estimator's detail estimate is the document against which the final bid will be made.

8.7 APPRAISER'S HOUSE CHECKLIST

The minimum checklist for anyone appraising the present value of a house and land would include:

a) Date of the appraisal
b) Name of the applicant for it
c) Civic address of the property
d) Legal description of the property
e) Age of the building
f) Date of any enlargement or renovations to the structure

Lot Information
a) Dimensions
b) Shape
c) Grade, steps leading to outside doors
d) Landscaping
e) Ease with which lawn can be cared for (topography of yard)

f) Type of driveway onto the property, and ease of care (shoveling snow)
g) Utilities available: gas, power, water, sewer mains, and telephone cables in place?
h) Municipal storm water drains, or gravity surface water drainage availability
i) City tax assessments, fuel bills for the previous year

Neighborhood Information
a) Types of nearby property
b) Income range of people living in the district (low, middle, professional, retirees)
c) Nearby properties (predominantly detached, single-family, high-rise apartments, condominiums, townhouses, rowhouses)
d) Distance (in blocks or miles) to nearest freeway, airport, bank, post office, libraries, schools, hospitals, and churches
e) Service by fire protection and postal delivery

Description of Property
a) Full or partial basement, crawlspace, free from termites, foundation walls dampproof, brick foundation walls (concrete block, stone, other), legally finished habitable rooms in the basement, or area suited for office for a small business

Information about Market Appeal of the District
a) Is it improving? deteriorating? well-cared-for homes nearby, or rundown homes in the vicinity?
b) Existence of pollution (noise, air, etc.).

Description of Outside Walls of the House
a) Stucco on wood frame, brick veneer, half stucco and half brick or other, veneer, stone, concrete block, cedar plank, log, clapboard
b) Maintenance required; seasonal or negligible

Description of Interior Walls
a) Lath and plaster, drywall, wallboard, papered, walls and ceilings free of damp stains

Description of Roofing
a) Asphalt, roll roofing, split wood shakes, sawn shingle, clay tile, concrete tile, cold built-up roofing, hot built-up roofing
b) Existence of troughs and downpipes to storm sewer or other

Garage and Parking Information
a) Attached to the house; under the house

b) Location and description of detached garage: served by back lane?
   c) Parking facilities for guests

Kitchen Description
   a) Modern?
   b) All units to be listed on a bill of sale and to become a sale between vendor and purchaser separate from the sale of the real estate.

Lighting Fixtures Information
   a) Ceiling shades, swag lamps, chandeliers to be on a separate bill of sale between vendor and purchaser.

Prorating on Closing Date
   a) Including city taxes, oil left in the tank.

Estimate of Value

I certify that I have personally inspected the property and analyzed sales considered comparable. The statements contained in this report are to the best of my knowledge correct. I have no financial interest in the property and in my opion the fair market values as of (DATE) _____ is $_____ based on normal or typical cash to mortgage financing.
(DATE) _____ (SIGNED) _____
                                        Appraiser

Appraiser's Fee

An appraiser's fee at the time of writing this book was about $100 for a city suburban lot. It is usual for the appraiser's fee to be borne by the party seeking it. It may be paid out of mortgage funds advanced on the property.

REVIEW QUESTIONS

1. Name two certificates that are issued by the American Institute of Real Estate Appraisers.
2. Define foreclosure on land.
3. List four important points that should be considered carefully before speculatively building houses.
4. List four reasons for appraising real estate:
    a)
    b)
    c)
    d)
5. Describe briefly the square-foot method of appraising the cost of a new house.

9 WILLS AND PROBATE

In this chapter we shall present first a glossary of terms, then a dialogue on the drawing (making) of a last will and testament, and of the probating (proving) of such a will. Where the masculine gender is used it shall be understood that we refer to both sexes.

9.1 GLOSSARY OF TERMS

Will: A signed and witnessed document detailing the distribution of a person's estate after his death.

Testator: The maker of a will.

Intestate: Describes a person who dies without leaving a will.

Holographic Will: One that is totally handwritten and executed (signed) by the maker (testator). A standard will form, as purchased from a stationer, could not become a holographic will because of the printed matter on it. Such wills are not valid in some jurisdictions.

Noncupative Will: Made in contemplation of death as in war. In the paybook of some servicemen there are pages set aside for the making of a noncupative will. Should such a will be found on the body of the maker, in some countries such a will is valid.

Beneficiary: A named entity who is bequeathed something in a will.

Bequeath: To name some entity in a will to whom a share of the deceased's estate it to be left.

Executor: The named person in a will who, after probate, executes (carries out) the wishes of the deceased.

Co-Executor: A person acting as an executor with someone else. Any act of any executor or co-executor is binding on the estate.

Probate: The proving of a will by a judge of the probate court.

Probate Court: A court in which wills are proved and where the worth of the deceased's estate is accounted for and verified.

Letters Patent: Documents denoting authority granted by a judge of the probate court confirming the name(s) of the executor(s). In effect these grant them the lawful right to gather together all the property of the deceased, including papers such as stock and bond certificates, government bonds, access to the safety deposit box, insurance certificates, bank accounts, and everything that was in the possession of the deceased at his death. It also includes debts owing to or owed by him. Before a grant of letters patent is given, a fee must be paid to the clerk of the court.

Letters of Administration: Documents denoting authority granted by the judge of a probate court to an executor (named by it), to carry out the duties of an executor and to disburse the proceeds of the estate between named beneficiaries. If the deceased died intestate, the estate is divided among his heirs-at-law.

Devise: A gift of real estate under the terms of a will.

Devisee: The recipient of real estate under the terms of a will.

Legacy: A gift left to some entity under the terms of a will.

Legatee: Recipient of a legacy under the terms of a will.

Testator: The person who makes and executes (signs) the dated will in the presence of witnesses. The following wording concludes the will of the author:

IN WITNESS WHEREOF I have hereunto set my hand this _____ day of _____, 19_____.
SIGNED, Published and declared
by the said Testator (rix) _____, as and for his (her) last Will and Testament in the presence of us both present at the same time who, at his (her) request in his (her) presence and in the presence of each other have hereunto subscribed our names as witnesses.
WITNESS _____   TESTATOR _____

WITNESS _____

9.2 DIALOGUE ON THE DRAWING AND PROBATING OF A WILL

Q *If a person is nominated in a will to be an executor, is he obligated to do so?*

A No. Providing he has not meddled in the affairs of the estate, he may renounce his position by signing (and have notarized) an affidavit of renunciation and presenting it to the probate court.

Q *May a beneficiary under a will also be a witness to it?*

A No.

Q *Define a codicil to a will.*

A This is an updated will which adds or detracts from the original will. A codicil is really a new will and must be treated in every respect like an original will. A will should be read at the latest every five years and annually for aged people.

Q *Is it costly to have an attorney draw up a will for a client?*

A No, the fee is nominal.

Q *Is it costly to have an attorney act as executor to a will?*

A Yes, this can be very costly. Some attorneys have a standard fee for simple estates, but where stock and bond certificates, and land to be transmitted to others are concerned, especially if such real estate is out of state or province, it could take up to a year to probate an estate. In these cases, attorneys often charge a percentage fee of the estate. Assuming that an estate is worth $200,000 with a 2 percent fee, this would amount to $4,000. Makers of wills may inquire for the cheapest attorney in the district.

Q *May a layperson execute the terms of a will?*

A Yes, a simple family will may be executed by following steps set forth in a do-it-yourself guide for probating of wills.

Q *What are the qualifications for being an executor of a will?*

A The person must be of legal age and physically and mentally competent.

Q *Is a last will and testament a legal document?*

A Not until the moment of death of the testator.

Q *Define dissolution of partnership, as related to wills.*

A There is a difference between dissolution and termination. Upon the death of a partner, the partnership is automatically terminated; no further business can be done in that name. At dissolution, there may be charges or profits to be accounted for to the estate of a deceased partner;

88   WILLS AND PROBATE

no disbursements of the proceeds from the estate may be made until the probate court is satisfied that the affairs of the partnership have been legally completed.

Q *Define* per stirps (per stirpes *plural*).

A Next of kin as heirs-at-law.

Q *Define heirs-at-law.*

A The claimants of a will are first the spouse of the deceased, then the nearest blood relations, such as children and parents. Children of the children of the deceased would be *per stirpes*. This situation occurs when a beneficiary under a will dies before he has received his bequest; in that case his share goes to his children.

Q *What is the difference between the transfer and the transmittal of land titles?*

A A transfer of land title is made between living persons. A transmittal of title to land is made between the executor of a will and another living person. The land title's office will require several documents to make the transfer, including a true legal description of the property as it appears on the municipal tax notice, a certified copy of the death certificate and an attached will, a certified copy of letters probate or administration, and a duplicate copy of the certificate of title. In some jurisdictions in Canada a certificate of citizenship of the executor is required. The land registry office charges a fee commensurate with the value of the property to be transmitted.

Q *May a probate court change the wording of a will?*

A No. The court only interprets the intention of the testator.

Q *Define co-executor.*

A This is a person acting as an executor with someone else; both are appointed by the testator. In such a case the act of any executor is binding on the estate.

Q *May a will be revoked?*

A Yes, by making another will or adding a codicil to an existing one. The codicil has the effect of a new will and must be attested and witnessed as if it were a totally new will. An existing will may be revoked by being burned or by being rendered utterly indecipherable.

Q *Define attestation.*

A This is participation in the witnessing of a solemn verbal or written declaration supporting a fact.

Q *What is the role of an attorney in drawing up a will for a client?*

A He puts into words the express wishes of the testator, who signs the will in the presence of witnesses.

Q *Is it obligatory to have an attorney draw up a will?*

A In some jurisdictions, yes.

Q *Define litigation.*

A Proceedings in a court lawsuit. The court finds a remedy for the disputing parties; it may be very costly.

Q *Define surrogate.*

A A person who acts in the place of another or others.

9.3 BUREAU OF VITAL STATISTICS

Government offices of vital statistics record births, marriages, divorces, and deaths of persons.

Upon the death of a person, an undertaker (funeral director, mortician, or funeral home) will be engaged by the family, or the executor of the will, to attend to the funeral rites. This person must call on the doctor of the deceased to get a death certificate, which must be registered at the bureau of vital statistics. There he gets as many typewritten copies of the death certificate as will be necessary to present to organizations with which the deceased did business. The will must be presented with a death certificate to the following institutions:

a) Bank or financial institutions for closing the account and for opening the safety deposit box
b) Insurance companies
c) Stock brokers
d) Directors of corporations
e) Royalty departments of authors and artists
f) Patent office
g) Business partners
h) Land registry office

The law is exacting concerning presentation of death certificates, and must be followed to the minutest detail. These proceedings are necessary to have the name of the deceased removed from records. Finally, the Probate Court must be satisfied that the law has been applied correctly.

If the funeral director fails to obtain sufficient copies of the death certificate at one time, it may delay the distribution of the estate among the beneficiaries and cause hardship. Some probate proceedings take up to a full year.

REVIEW QUESTIONS

1. What is a holographic will?
2. Define a noncupative will.
3. Define the duties of an executor of a will.
4. What is meant by probating a will?
5. Define "the deceased died interstate."
6. If a person is nominated in a will to be an executor, is he obligated to be so?
7. May a beneficiary under a will also be a witness to it?
8. Define "codicil" to a will.
9. What is the difference between transfer and transmittal of land titles?
10. *Research* the subject matter of this chapter for the area in which you live, and note any differences.

10 RENTING; LEASING; APARTMENTS; CONDOMINIUMS

In this chapter we shall present a list of leasing and renting definitions; then follows a dialogue on leasing and the chapter concludes with definitions of apartments, condominiums, and cooperatives.

10.1 DEFINITIONS*

Lease: A contract transferring the right to the possession and enjoyment of real estate for a definite period of time.

Lessor: the owner—one who lets the property.

Lessee: the tenant.

Rent—Rental: the consideration paid by the lessee for the possession and use of the property.

Covenants: clauses in the lease which define the rights and obligations of lessor and lessee.

Term—Lease Term: the specified duration of the lease, i.e., "the lease has a term of 10 years." When used in the plural, this word

---

*From the book *Leases: Percentages, Short and Long Term*, 6th ed., by McMichael & O'Keefe, published by Prentice-Hall Inc., Englewood Cliffs, N.J. 07632, pp. 6-9.

has a different meaning; it is then usually synonymous with "covenants," i.e., "the terms of the lease provide that the tenant must maintain the property in good condition and make all interior repairs."

Leasehold—Leasehold estate: the lessee's interest in the property created by the lease. The full designation for this interest is "leasehold estate" but it is commonly referred to as a leasehold.

Sublessor—Sublessee—Sublease: sometimes a tenant is permitted to lease his interest to a third party. The original lessee thereby becomes a *sublessor*. The new tenant is the *sublessee*. The new agreement between sublessor and sublessee is a *sublease*.

Prime Tenant: when one or more subleases have been made on a property, the original lessee is sometimes referred to as the prime tenant.

Sandwich Lease: intermediary instrument in three or more leases on the same property; i.e., A leases to B, B subleases to C, C subleases to D; the agreement between B and C would be called a "sandwich lease."

Tenancy at Will—Month-to-Month Tenancy: lease agreement cancellable by either party on short notice—usually 30, 60 or 90 days.

Long-Term Lease—Short-Term Lease: there is no clear understanding as to what is a short-term lease and what is a long-term lease. By common usage, people in the real estate business have come to regard a long-term lease as one for a period of 21 years or more.

"Short-term lease," on the other hand, has various relative connotations. Leases on one family dwellings and apartment houses are made customarily for a one-, two- or three-year term. It would be misleading to refer to a ten-year lease on such a property as a "short-term lease."

On the other hand, the purchase lease transaction entered into by insurance companies and business or industrial concerns usually involve a lease term of at least 21 years. A ten-year lease in such a transaction would be considered a short-term lease.

The principal fallacy in lease terminology is the assumption that short-term and long-term leases collectively constitute an all-inclusive classification. Actually there are intermediate-term leases that properly could be called neither short-term nor long-term. These would include a great many of the everyday commercial leases that are made for ten to fifteen year periods.

No nomenclature has been developed for this type of lease. In this text, we will generally consider them in the short-term category because their covenants will be more closely akin to the covenants of a short-term than a long-term lease.

If any lease for less than 21 years is referred to as a long-term lease, it will be with the qualification that it pertains to the type of property involved—for instance, a ten-year lease (supra) on a one family dwelling.

Percentage Lease: a lease wherein the tenant is required to pay as rental a specified percentage of the gross income from sales made upon the premises.

Net Lease: a lease in which the tenant pays all or a substantial part of cost of operating and maintenance. There are various expressions used in the real estate business to describe the many variations in net lease transactions. For instance, if a lease provides for the tenant to pay *all* operating expenses, maintenance costs, insurance, real estate taxes, etc., it might be referred to as "100% net" or "net-net." If the lease provides for the tenant to maintain and operate the premises only, it might be referred to as "net-excepting for taxes, insurance and outside repairs."

Net Rental: rental paid under a net lease agreement.

Gross Lease: the antonym of net lease. One in which the owner pays taxes, insurance, maintenance, operating expense, etc. The gross lease today is confined largely to apartments and older commercial buildings. In other commercial properties there is generally a negotiated sharing of the cost of operation.

Escalation Clause: a lease covenant providing for the tenant to pay any increase in taxes and/or operating expense above the amounts prevailing at the time of the execution of the lease agreement. The usual escalation clause also provides for a decrease in rental if there is a decline in real estate taxes or operating expenses.

Primary and Secondary Rentals: a lease covenant under which a rental is divided into two categories. The primary rental is a fixed amount usually based upon a definite percentage of property value as established at the time of the execution of the lease agreement. The secondary rental, which would be prorated according to the space which a tenant might occupy in a building, covers the expense of taxes, repairs and insurance, water, heat, etc. The secondary rental agreement achieves the same result as an escalator clause.

Short-Form Lease: when either of the parties wishes to record a lease agreement but does not want the rentals and covenants exposed to the public eye, a short-form document is sometimes used which recites the fact that a lease has been made between the parties covering certain premises for a specified term. It would then stipulate somewhat as follows: "This lease has been made upon the rents, terms, covenants and conditions contained in a certain collateral agreement or lease between the parties hereto and bearing even date herewith."

Assignment: an instrument by which a lessee transfers his interest to a third party. For all practical purposes, an assignment is synonymous with a sublease.

Extension: an agreement by which a lease is made effective for an additional period of time beyond its expiration date—usually synonymous with renewal.

Renewal Option: a lease covenant giving the lessee the right to extend the lease for an additional period of years on specified terms.

Security: a sum of money, or equivalent, deposited by the lessee with the lessor or a trustee, as guarantee for performance under the lease terms.

Concession: an allowance, usually in the form of rent abatement, made to the lessee by the lessor. Concessions are made for a variety of reasons—to induce a tenant to sign a lease; as consideration of additional expenses of the tenant, as, for example, moving expenses, rental obligations on lease of premises which tenant is vacating, and so on.

Bonus: generally refers to payment made by lessee to the lessor as additional consideration.

10.2 DIALOGUE ON LEASING

Q *What is the difference between renting and leasing?*

A Renting may be by oral or written agreement; termination of the agreement usually corresponds to the length of time between the making of rental payments. A lease is a contract between consenting parties that one may have the exclusive use of the property of another for an agreed time at an agreed price. The lease contract should be registered on the title to the property so that anyone wishing to make an offer of purchase for the property may know what is attached to it and the first available date that the lease will have expired and the owner is free to dispose of it.

Q *What is an apartment building?* (For condominiums see page 96)

A An apartment building is owned by an entity such as a person, persons, a partnership, or a corporation. The owner is responsible for the complete management and maintenance of the building and the outside grounds, such as lawns, gardens, snow sweeping and outside lighting, and such things as:

  a) The heating, lighting, cleaning, and maintenance of public halls, stairs, elevators, basement locker areas, laundry rooms, parking areas and so on

b) Plumbing and all mechanical units, incinerator rooms, swimming pools, and recreation areas
c) Ensuring that all house rules are observed by all tenants
d) Insurance of the total building and for public liability (the latter covers the insured against any hurt or harm occurring to anyone while in the owner's building)
e) Allocation of locker space to all tenants
f) Janitorial and management services
g) Security-guard services

The owner takes into account the interest and risk on his (or her) invested capital, maintenance, and managerial fees. He then sets a competitive rental for his individual suites. Those with the better outlooks command the better rentals.

10.3 DIALOGUE ON LEASEBACK

Q *Define leaseback.*

A The parties in a leaseback contract are an already successful business, a bank (or loan company), and an insurance company. With the high cost of land, building and financing, this form of contract becomes more attractive. It works in the following manner:
 a) Assume that *Family Grocers*, a successful company, wishes to open a new branch in a developing area.
 b) It discusses the proposition with *Alert Insurance Company*, which supports the suggestion to build.
 c) *Family Grocers* secures a short-term loan from the bank, and erects a building to its own specifications.
 d) *Family Grocers* sells the property to *Alert Insurance Company* for cash.
 e) Alert Insurance Company leases the premises to Family Grocers on a leaseback contract.
 f) *Family Grocers* pays off the bank, pays municipal taxes, insurances, maintains the property including the parking area, and observes all provisions of the leaseback contract.

Advantages
 a) *Family Grocers* has another outlet for its business, and has more working capital for its inventory. The company receives 100 percent of the value of the property in cash; with a conventional mortgage it

might only receive 80 percent or so. The company has a business expense tax claim for the rental paid to *Alert Insurance Company*.

b) The *Alert Insurance Company* has excellent security. It is investing policyholders' funds, and by law is restricted to secure investments.

c) The bank has made a profit on its short-term loan, which is paid off in full. Thus, every party benefits.

10.4 DIALOGUE ON APARTMENTS

Q *What is the difference between an apartment building and a condominium?*

A An apartment building is owned by an entity. The owners are responsible for the total building and the land on which it stands, but each apartment of a condominium is called a unit, and the unit holders are collectively responsible for all those things in the common area that would ordinarily be the responsibility of an individual owner.

10.5 DIALOGUE ON CONDOMINIUMS

Q *What are the responsibilities of a condominium unit holder?*

A A unit holder in a condominium is responsible for the maintenance of all that is encompassed by the periphery walls of his own area, and is jointly responsible for all other areas (known as common areas) of the building both inside and outside, with all other unit holders. Condominiums are registered as corporations and as such may sue and be sued. If a unit holder defaults on his municipal taxes, the municipality may foreclose on the individual's unit but not on any other.

The main difference between an apartment building and a condominium complex is that the condominium is run by an elected council, which is a council within the municipal council. The bylaws of a condominium are enforceable and are registered on the title. A condominium council is elected annually to run the building, when the financial statements are read and debated, and new resolutions are accepted for debate. Some condominiums, through bad management, go bankrupt; on the other hand, many condominiums are managed very successfully. Some assess themselves a monthly rate that will leave a balance for corporate investment each year. In this way, a fund is built up to meet any expensive, urgent repairs such as roofing or plumbing repairs in the common areas. Common areas are all those areas other than those owned by individual unit holders—e.g., hall, recreation room, parking areas, game rooms, incinerator rooms, lawns, and gardens. When a condominium building has built up a reserve for emergency expenses it makes a valid selling point for unit holders wishing to sell their title. Condominiums can also be used for office buildings and warehouses.

10.6 DIALOGUE ON TIMESHARING CONDOMINIUMS

Q *What is timesharing in condominiums?*
A This usually occurs in resort areas, where several persons join together in the purchase of a condominium apartment called a unit. For example, if a condominium unit in Florida is to be sold for $120,000, four parties may join together and each subscribe $30,000 for one-quarter ownership in the unit. They then decide who shall occupy the unit at times agreeable to all. They may also want to rotate their times of occupancy so that each in turn can enjoy the best of the seasonal weather. They may mutually agree upon appointing a property manager to supervise the unit and rent it at a stated price per week. The revenue going into a separate fund will take care of the agent's fees, the municipal taxes, heat and air-conditioning, and such renewals as linen, crockery, and light fixtures. The agent may attend the annual general meeting and exercise his or her own judgment on how to vote, or vote by proxy according to instructions given by owners. Some timesharers exchange their times with people in other countries of Europe, South America or Mexico. The concept of timesharing is now international.

Disadvantages
a) The absentee landlord may be subject to the ravages of vandals.
b) There is the problem of the maintenance of the building, especially concerning such mechanical devices as the elevator, controlled entrance doors, laundry facilities, and the enforcement of house rules.
c) Other unit holders may not be compatible or "good neighbors."
d) One or more of the joint owners may leave personal recreational equipment in the unit or in the storage areas, to the exclusion of other parties to the agreement.
e) One of the parties to the agreement may die.

There should always be a clear partnership agreement in timesharing arrangements (see Key-Man Insurance, Article 1.3).

Advantages

a) The arrangement makes available a permanent holiday accommodation, with inflation frozen as of the date of purchase of the unit.
b) There is satisfaction knowing that the other parties will take care of the unit.
c) There is freedom for the parties agreeing to rent the unit for certain weeks of the year, with the revenue being placed in an account ready to pay the municipal taxes, management fee, repairs within the unit, and assessment for the maintenance of common areas.

For a full treatise on the subject of partnerships, see Articles 1.4 and 1.5. It is important that all parties know both their duties and their responsibilities. In reality, a partnership agreement is a written constitution of private law between consenting parties, and there should be an article or articles that will provide a remedy for any difference between the participating entities.

10.7 DIALOGUE ON COOPERATIVES

Q *What is the difference between a condominium and a cooperative?*

A Condominium unit (apartment) owners have an indefeasible right to their own units. On the other hand, with a cooperative, the total building is owned by all shareholders. If one apartment occupant defaults on his municipal taxes, the municipality may sue the whole cooperative for the amount in default. In short, every cooperative shareholder is jointly with all others responsible for everything to do with the building. Each cooperative shareholder owns a percentage according to the amount of shares held in every stick, stone, lawn, swimming pool, elevator, and all amenities in the common areas and in each other's suites (see Cooperatives, Article 1.8).

REVIEW QUESTIONS

1. What is the difference between leasing and renting?
2. Define leaseback.
3. Give five advantages of owning a condominium unit compared to renting an apartment.
4. What is timesharing ownership of a condominium? Give five advantages and five disadvantages for parties owning such a unit.

11 INSURANCE

11.1 DIALOGUE ON INSURANCE TERMS

Q *What is an insurance agent?*
A This is an insurance company employee who writes up insurance policies.

Q *What is an insurance broker?*
A An insurance broker is an agent who places his client's business with any one of several insurance companies. He advises his client of the company offering the best value (coverage) per dollar of insurance premium paid. He should process claims that the insured may make.

Q *What is the difference between a stock company and a mutual insurance company?*
A A stock company is a corporation that operates statistically and scientifically for profit to its shareholders.

A mutual insurance company is a corporation, owned and operated by its policyholders, wherein regular premiums are received from which claims (losses) are paid. Profits are returned by way of bonuses to policyholders.

Q *What is mandatory insurance?*

A This is insurance prescribed by law, such as automobile insurance and workers' compensation insurance. (The latter is required of employers to cover employees against injury, disability, or death while at work.)

Q *What is personal insurance?*

A Personal insurance includes life, hospital, accident, sickness, and disability insurance.

Q *Is there any method of compensating for inflation in insurance?*

A Yes. Arrangements may be made to make quarterly, half-yearly, or annual adjustments to increase premiums and the policy coverage. The cost of the insurance coverage may be paid monthly, quarterly, half-yearly, or in a lump sum.

Q *What is an endorsement or rider?*

A It is an addition to a contract covering more perils (risks) than the original policy, for which an increased premium will be charged to cover the additional risks.

Q *What is a broad form of policy?*

A This is one that covers a greater number of risks. The more perils covered, the greater the cost of the premium.

Q *What is an annuity?*

A It is an insurance policy which, upon maturity, assures the annuitant (beneficiary) of a stated income for a period of time, or for life.

Q *What are exclusions?*

A These are provisions in a contract, limiting the scope of the coverage. Certain perils and conditions that are not covered by insurance are listed on the policy. They should be read carefully.

Q *What is a nonforfeiture option?*

A If, on a policy, the insured fails to make further premium payments, the value of the policy may have an immediate cash surrender value; or it may be converted into a fully paid-up policy of a lesser amount, to become due and payable at the original date; or it may be rewritten for a continuing smaller premium with a correspondingly smaller benefit. The advantage of a nonforfeiture policy is that upon the suspension of further payments, all is not necessarily lost.

Q *What is an underwriter?*

A It is that department of an insurance company dealing with the agency and the procuring and processing of business; the managerial department that deals with routine conduct of the business; or the actuarial and scientific department that analyzes and determines the

11.1 DIALOGUE ON INSURANCE TERMS

degree of risk in insuring unusual perils for which there is no actuarial date (such as insuring the fingers of a concert violinist). In marine insurance, where a successful claim is likely to be enormous, such as for the total loss of a fully laden oil tanker, several insurance companies may each underwrite a percentage of the total risk.

Q *What is mortgage insurance?*
A Some lending institutions cover the mortgagor against default of payments on the part of the mortgagee. The premium is usually a single charge calculated as a percentage of the loan. Such a charge is amortized along with the loan repayments.

Q *What is a beneficiary?*
A It is the named party to whom an insurance claim is paid.

Q *What is an adjuster?*
A This is the person who assesses the replacement value in dollars for anything lost, damaged, or stolen. The insurance company may employ its own adjusters. Some persons are professional adjusters and work on a freelance basis.

Q *What is term life insurance?*
A Term life is an insurance benefit payable upon proof of the death of the insured. The proof would be positive upon the production of the policy with an attached copy of the death certificate. A copy of a death certificate may be obtained from the local Bureau of Vital Statistics in the area of the deceased.

Q *What is fidelity insurance?*
A This insures against defalcation (theft or misappropriation of funds) by employees. The document is called a Fidelity Bond. When an insurance company has paid out on a fidelity bond, it has the same right as the insured to recover stolen property from the offender. This is known as subrogation (the right of a party to succeed to the right of another).

Q *What is meant by subrogation?*
A Subrogation is putting a party in the place of another in respect to a legal right or claim.

Q *What is insurable interest?*
A If you sell your house for $80,000 with a down payment of $20,000 and the balance to be paid to you by amortization (equal monthly payments over a period of years), and under the terms of the sale you state that the purchaser shall keep the house completely covered by fire insurance for its full worth, for the total period, you then have insurable interest. The policy will state that in the case of claim, you, the vendor, shall have first

claim on the insurance policy, "as your interest may appear." If, for example, $42,000 is still owed you, your claim would be 42/80ths and the purchaser would receive 38/80ths of the proceeds of the claim.

Q *What is an insurance premium?*

A The amount paid or agreed to be paid as consideration for a contract of insurance.

11.2 UPDATING INSURANCE

It is improbable that an insurance agent can assure a profit for a contractor, but by his counsel he may obviate a loss.

An agent should be frequently consulted and made aware of any major changes in the company. A good time to consult is after the business income tax has been filed and the annual inventory taken.

Listed below are areas that require consultation:

a) All inventory times
b) Changes in key personnel (See Article 3.1)
c) During inflation or deflation periods
d) Upon purchase of new equipment
e) Whenever building progress reports are rendered to the architect
f) Regarding subtradesmen's perils
g) For F.O.B. (free on board) consignments

When inventories are taken, insurance coverage should be made to the latest stock values. Changes in managerial staff require updating with new names, and old ones must be expunged. Inflation or deflation changes the value of inventory, the salary wage bill, and public liability insurance. The purchase of new equipment requires new insurance. For example: A heavy and expensive piece of equipment was covered by all-risk insurance F.O.B. Calgary. It was lost through carelessness at the bottom of a deep lake, 1,000 miles away from that city. The replacement of a new machine was made at Calgary. The insurer suffered in three ways:

a) Shipping costs of the new equipment from Calgary to the scene of the operation
b) Overheads
c) Downtime (crew idle time)

Q *What does F.O.B. mean?*

A It stands for "free on board." This is a commercial arrangement whereby goods are loaded on board at a specified place, free of transport charges to the purchaser at that particular point. The terms of contract cover delivery, terms relating to quantity to be delivered, and times and places of delivery. F.O.B. usually relates to waterborne carriers. If the goods are F.O.B. Chicago and are consigned to a purchaser in New York City, the ownership of the goods (to be purchased) takes place in Chicago, at which point the purchaser is responsible for freightage and insurance.

Q *What does F.O.R. mean?*

A It stands for "free on rail". This commercial arrangement is similar to F.O.B., but F.O.R. relates to wheeled vehicles instead of waterborne carriers.

Q *What is a subpoena?*

A A subpoena is a government or court order requiring a person to present himself or deliver things to a court at a stated time and place.

Q *What is an affidavit?*

A It is a written declaration under oath sworn before a notary public or magistrate.

Q *What does champerty mean?*

A Champerty is an arrangement by a third party to carry on a suit, at his/her expense, for share of eventual proceeds from the action (if any). Local research should be made as to the legality of such an action.

11.3   PERSONAL PROPERTY INVENTORY

The following pages have been excerpted from the brochure entitled *Personal Property Inventory*, supplied by SAFECO Insurance Company of America, and is reproduced here with permission.

People lose thousands of dollars annually through fire and theft. Look around your home. In the living room alone, how many items would you overlook if everything were gone? Would you have to depend on your memory in filling out your insurance claim?

This booklet, with its room-to-room format, is designed to help you take a fast and accurate inventory of your home's contents. If you don't know the purchase price of an item, try to determine how much it would cost to replace it. You may wish to have some of your valuable articles professionally appraised.

Other inventory aids are the camera and tape recorder. Take photographs of the full room and close-ups of individual items. Extra details, such as model and serial number, can be recorded on a tape. All inventory records should be kept safe from fire and theft, and away from the premises.

We urge you to take your inventory as soon as possible. Only *you* know how much you could lose if you postpone the project.

Bedroom and Bath #1

Article	Qty	Date Purchased	Purchase Price	Replacement Cost
Bed, Headboard				
Spring, Mattress				
Dresser				
Chest				
Vanity Table				
Vanity Accessories				
Bench				
Lamps				
Tables				
Chaise Lounge				
Chairs				
Mirrors				
Pictures				
Draperies				
Curtains, Blinds				
Rugs				
Carpets				
Blankets, Quilts				
Spreads				
Sheets				
Pillow Cases				
Pillows				
Clothes Hamper				
Shower Curtain				
Bath Towels				
Hand Towels				
Bath Mats				
Medicine				
Drugs				
Hairdryers				
Electric Curlers				
Razors				
Subtotal				

Bedroom and Bath #2

Article	Qty.	Date Purchased	Purchase Price	Replacement Cost
Bed, Headboard				
Spring, Mattress				
Dresser				
Chest				
Vanity Table				
Vanity Accessories				
Bench				
Lamps				
Tables				
Chaise Lounge				
Chairs				
Mirrors				
Pictures				
Draperies				
Curtains, Blinds				
Rugs				
Carpets				
Blankets, Quilts				
Spreads				
Sheets				
Pillow Cases				
Pillows				
Clothes Hamper				
Shower Curtain				
Bath Towels				
Hand Towels				
Bath Mats				
Medicine				
Drugs				
Hairdryers				
Electric Curlers				
Razors				
Subtotal				

Living Room

Article	Qty	Date Purchased	Purchase Price	Replacement Cost
Sofas				
Davenports				
Studio Couches				
Lounge Chairs				
Occasional Chairs				
End Tables				
Coffee Tables				
Table Accessories				
Desks				
Desk Accessories				
Shelves, Wall Units				
Wall Hangings				
Clocks				
Pictures				
Mirrors				
Benches				
Chests				
Lamps				
Pillows, Cushions				
Fireplace Accessories				
Draperies				
Curtains, Blinds				
Rugs				
Carpets				
Subtotal				

Summary

Area	Total Purchase Price	Total Replacement Cost
Living Room		
Dining Room		
Family Room, Library		
Bed & Bath #1		
Bed & Bath #2		
Bed & Bath #3		
Bed & Bath #4		
Clothing, Men		
Clothing, Women		
Clothing, Children		
Kitchen & Pantry		
Appliances, Utility		
Music, Audio Visual		
Leisure, Hobbies		
Yard, Garage		
Valuables		
Valuables		
GRAND TOTAL		

Name _____

Address _____

Date of Inventory _____

11.4 HOMEOWNERS WARRANTY (HOW)

The following material has been excerpted from a booklet entitled *Insurance/Warranty Documents*, published by Home Owners, Warranty Corporation and is reproduced here with the permission of the copyright holder.

Limited Warranty

Identity of Warrantor. Your Builder is the warrantor under this Warranty. Home Owners Warranty Corporation ("HOW") developed the Warranty Program under which this warranty has been issued and administers the Program on behalf of participating builders.

To Whom Given. This Warranty is extended to you as the purchaser of the home identified on the cover page of this Warranty and automatically to any subsequent owners.

Coverage During First Year. Your Builder warrants that, for one year beginning on the commencement date, the home will be free from defects due to noncompliance with the Approved Standards attached to this Warranty.

Coverage During Second Year. Your Builder warrants that during the second year after the commencement date:

(1) The home will be free from Major Structural Defects. A "Major Structural Defect" is actual physical damage to the following designated load-bearing portions of the home caused by failure of such load-bearing portions which affects their load-bearing functions to the extent that the home becomes unsafe, unsanitary or otherwise unlivable.

1. Foundation systems and footings;
2. Beams;
3. Girders;
4. Lintels;
5. Columns;
6. Walls and partitions;
7. Floor systems; and
8. Roof framing systems.

Repair of a Major Structural Defect is limited (1) to the repair of damage to the load-bearing elements of the home themselves which is necessary to restore their load-bearing ability; and (2) to the repair of those items of the home damaged by the Major Structural Defect which make the home unsafe, unsanitary or otherwise unlivable.

(2) The plumbing, electrical, heating, cooling and ventilating systems of the home, exclusive of fixtures, appliances or items of equipment, will be free from defects due to noncompliance with the Approved Standards. Defects in fixtures, appliances and items of equipment whether or not part of the plumbing, electrical, heating, cooling or ventilating systems are not covered. (See the Approved Standards for definition.)

Coverage for Common Elements in Condominiums. Common elements serving condominium units are also covered by this Warranty. "Common Elements" means any portion of a condominium structure (including, but not limited to, any passageways, rooms, or other spaces) which are provided for the common use of the residents of the structure. It also means part of a plumbing, electrical, heating, cooling or ventilating system serving two or more condominium units and outbuildings containing parts of such a system.

Common elements are covered for the same length of time as similar items which are part of an individual unit, but the commencement date of the Warranty period of common elements is determined by the common elements commencement date as stated on the cover page of this Warranty.

Remedy. If a defect occurs in an item which is covered by this Warranty, your Builder will repair, replace, or pay you the reasonable cost of repairing or replacing the defective item. Your Builder's total liability under this Warranty is limited to the purchase price of the home stated on the cover sheet of this Warranty. The choice among repair, replacement, or payment is your Builder's.

Your Builder and HOW have agreed that if he does not perform under this Warranty, HOW as the administrator of the Builder's warranty, will meet the Builder's warranty obligation, subject to a one-time $250 charge to you.

Steps taken to correct defects shall not act to extend the time of this Warranty.

Other Insurance or Warranties. In the event your Builder or HOW repairs or replaces, or pays the cost of repairing or replacing, any defect covered by this Warranty for which you are covered by other insurance or warranties, you must, upon request by your Builder or HOW, assign the proceeds of such insurance or warranties to your Builder or HOW to the extent of the cost to your Builder or HOW of such repair, replacement or payment.

Other Rights. This Warranty gives you specific legal rights. You may also have other legal rights which vary from state to state. This Warranty does not affect any rights of you or your Builder under any other express or implied warranty.

Exclusions

The following are not covered by this Warranty:

a. Defects in outbuildings including detached garages and detached carports (except outbuildings which contain the plumbing, electrical, heating, cooling or ventilation systems serving the home); swimming pools and other recreational facilities; driveways; walkways; patios; boundary walls; retaining walls; bulkheads; fences; landscaping (including sodding, seeding, shrubs, trees, and plantings); off-site improvements, or any other improvements not a part of the home itself.

b. After the first year, concrete floors of basements and attached garages that are built separate from foundation walls or other structural elements of the home.

c. Damage to real property which is not part of the home covered by this Warranty and which is not included in the purchase price stated on the cover page of this Warranty.

d. Any damage to the extent it is caused or made worse by:

— Negligence, improper maintenance or improper operation by anyone other than your Builder or HOW or their employees, agents, or subcontractors; or

— Failure by you or by anyone other than your Builder or HOW or their employees, agents or subcontractors to comply with the Warranty requirements of manufacturers of appliances, equipment or fixtures; or

— Failure by you, the purchaser, to give notice to your Builder or HOW of any defects within a reasonable time; or

— Changes of the grading of the ground by anyone other than your Builder, HOW, or their employees, agents, or subcontractors; or

— Changes, alterations, or additions made to the home by anyone after your initial occupancy, except those performed by your Builder or HOW under their obligations under this program; or

— Dampness or condensation due to the failure of you, the purchaser, to maintain adequate ventilation.

e. Any loss or damage which you, the purchaser, have not taken timely action to minimize.

f. Any defect in, or caused by, materials or work (including, but not limited to, items shown on any "Addendum to the Application for HOW Protection") supplied by anyone other than your Builder, HOW or their employees, agents, or subcontractors.

g. Normal wear and tear or normal deterioration.

h. Loss or damage not caused by a defect in the construction of the home by your Builder, or his employees, agents or subcontractors, but resulting from accidents, riot and civil commotion, or Acts of God including, but not limited to: fire, explosion, smoke, water escape, changes which are not reasonably foreseeable in the level of the underground water table, windstorm, hail, lightning, falling trees, aircraft, vehicles, flood, mudslides, earthquake and volcanic eruption.

i. Any damage caused by soil movement for which compensation is provided by legislation or which is covered by other insurance.

j. Insect damage.

k. Any loss or damage which arises while the home is being used primarily for nonresidential purposes.

l. Failure of your Builder to complete construction of the home.

m. Any condition which does not result in actual physical damage to the home.

n. Bodily injury or damage to personal property.

How to Make A Claim

Request for Warranty Service. *If you have a complaint, first send a clear and specific written complaint to your Builder.* Ordinarily, your Builder will supply the warranty service provided in this Warranty without the need for direct involvement by HOW.

Request for Warranty Performance. If you believe your Builder has not performed as provided in this Warranty, you may submit your Request directly to HOW. You should make any such request by mailing the attached "Request for Warranty Performance" form to HOW at the mailing address shown on the cover page of this document, or by sending a letter specifically demanding such performance and identifying yourself, your Builder, the defect, and the remedy you seek.

Time of Notice of Claim. You must give written notice of a defect in any item under this Warranty to HOW no later than 30 days after the warranty coverage on that item expires. If such notice is not received by HOW by that deadline, any claims for the defect will be rejected.

Dispute Settlement. Upon receiving your "Request for Warranty Performance" HOW will notify your Builder and ask him to respond to your complaint. If your Builder disagrees with your complaint, HOW will arrange for informal dispute settlement between you and your Builder by a neutral third party. Your Builder will be bound by such third party decision when accepted by you (see "Acceptance of Decision" below).

Under the Magnuson-Moss Warranty Act and under this Warranty, you may not file suit against your Builder or HOW until your claim has been submitted to informal dispute settlement and a decision has been reached or you have waited 40 days for a decision following your submission of a Request for Warranty Performance, whichever comes first. State or federal laws may permit you to file suit without waiting, despite this paragraph.

Acceptance of Decision. If you accept the decision you must sign and return to HOW at the mailing address shown on the cover page of this Warranty, within 45 days after the date of decision, an "Acceptance of Decision" form by which you agree to accept the decision in full satisfaction of your claim. Your Builder will then be bound to perform as required in the decision. Neither HOW nor your Builder is responsible for damage caused or made worse by your delay in accepting the decision.

The time allowed by the decision for performance by your Builder will be measured from the date it receives your "Acceptance of Decision" form and will be extended automatically if weather, strikes, or other matters not within its control interfere with the performance.

Rejection of Decision. After you receive the decision you must decide whether or not to accept it. If you do not accept the decision within 45 days, your Builder is under no obligation to perform in accordance with the decision.

Release. When your Builder or HOW finishes repairing or replacing the defect or pays you the costs of doing so, you must sign and deliver to your Builder or HOW a full release of all legal obligations with respect to the defect.

Condominium Claims. If the Claim involves a common element in a condominium, it may be made only by an authorized representative of the condominium association.

Other Claimants. Any other person to whom this Warranty is extended shall submit and pursue, by the same procedures, any claims that he may have.

Miscellaneous

Assignment of Manufacturer's Warranties. The Builder is required by contract with HOW to assign to you all manufacturers' warranties on items he has provided as part of the home.

Independence From Purchase Contract. This Warranty is independent of the contract between you and your Builder for the construction of the home and/or its sale to you. Contract disputes which are not warranty disputes are not eligible for informal dispute settlement under this Warranty. Nothing contained in that contract or any other contract between you and your Builder can restrict or override the provisions of this Warranty. You and your Builder may contract for additional standards or requirements, but any such agreement between you and your Builder will not be binding under this Warranty.

Notices. All notices to your Builder, to you, or to HOW must be sent by mail, postage prepaid, to the recipient at the address shown on the cover page of this Warranty or to whatever other address the recipient may designate in writing.

General Provisions. Should any provision of this Warranty be deemed by a court of competent jurisdiction to be unenforceable, that determination will not affect the enforceability of the remaining provisions. This Warranty is to be binding upon your Builder, and the purchaser, their heirs, executors, administrators, successors and assigns. Use of one gender in the Warranty includes all other genders; and use of the plural includes the singular, all as may be appropriate. This Warranty is to be covered by and construed in accordance with the laws of the state in which the home is located.

Amendments. This Warranty cannot be changed or altered in any way.

Request for Warranty Performance

TO THE OWNER:

Before using this form, send a clear and specific written request for warranty work to your Builder. After you have contacted your Builder and he has not responded as provided in your Home Warranty, complete the following and mail to HOW along with a copy of your initial complaint to the Builder. If some of the requested information is unknown to you, please indicate. Written notice of a defect in any item under the Warranty must be received by HOW no later than 30 days after the warranty coverage of the item expires.

_____
Name of Owner(s)

_____   _____   _____
Street Address   City, State   Zip

_____   _____
Home Phone (Area Code & No.)   Bus. Phone (Area Code and No.)

_____   _____
Home Warranty Agreement Number   Date of Home Warranty Agreement

_____
Name of Builder

_____   _____   _____
Street Address   City, State   Zip

_____
Phone (Area Code & No.)

Describe Defects:

Remedy Sought:

(Use additional sheets, if necessary)

We hereby notify HOW Corporation that we have requested our Builder to perform warranty work, but the Builder has not responded as provided in the Home Warranty Agreement.

_____ _____
Signature   Date

Major Structural Defect Insurance Policy

In consideration of the premium received and subject to the provisions in this policy or added by endorsement, INA Underwriters Insurance Company ("Insurer") does insure against loss caused by Major Structural Defects for the Policy Term stated on the Declarations page.

I. **What is Covered**

   A. This policy covers Major Structural Defects in the Home which first occur during the Policy Term. If the Home is a condominium unit, the policy also covers Major Structural Defects in common elements which first occur during the Policy Term for common elements. The common elements covered are those which first comprise the building in which the Home is located and which the Home shares in common with other units in the building.

   B. A "Major Structural Defect" is actual physical damage to the following designated load-bearing portions of the Home caused by failure of such load-bearing portions which affects their load-bearing function to the extent that the Home becomes unsafe, unsanitary or otherwise unlivable:

   1. Foundation systems and footings;
   2. Beams;
   3. Girders;
   4. Lintels;
   5. Columns;
   6. Walls and partitions;
   7. Floor systems; and
   8. Roof framing systems.

II. **What the Insurer Will Do**

   A. Subject to the Policy Limits and the Deductible provided in this policy, if a Major Structural Defect is covered by this policy, the Insurer will repair or replace that defect or will pay the Purchaser the reasonable actual cost of such repair or replacement. The choice as to repair, replacement or payment to the Purchaser shall be solely that of the Insurer.

   B. The repair of a Major Structural Defect is limited (1) to the repair of damage to the load-bearing portions of the Home themselves which is necessary to restore their load-bearing ability; and (2) to the repair of those items of the Home damaged by the Major Structural Defect which make the Home unsafe, unsanitary or otherwise unlivable.

III. **Deductible**

Coverage under this policy is subject to a 1% deductible per claim. This means that out of each claim covered under this policy, the Purchaser must first pay 1% of the original purchase price of the Home toward the cost of repairing or replacing covered Major Structural Defects, and that, if the Insurer chooses to pay the Purchaser instead of performing the repair or replacement work, the Insurer will pay the Purchaser the reasonable actual cost of repair or replacement, less the 1%.

IV. **Policy Limits**

The Insurer's total liability for all Major Structural Defects arising during the term of this policy is limited to the "Amount of Insurance" shown on the Declarations page less all amounts paid by the Builder or on behalf of the Builder under the Home Warranty which the Builder issued on the Home. Any payments made by the Insurer on account of defects in the common elements in a condominium structure shall be pro rated among the units within such structure and applied to reduce the amount of total Insurer Liability under the Major Structural Defect Insurance Policy for each such unit.

V. **Exclusions**

The following are excluded from the coverage of this policy:

A. Defects in outbuildings including detached garages and detached carports (except outbuildings which contain the plumbing, electrical, heating, cooling or ventilation systems serving the Home); swimming pools and other recreational facilities; driveways; walkways; patios; boundary walls; retaining walls; bulkheads; fences; landscaping (including sodding, seeding, shrubs, trees, and plantings); off-site improvements, or any other improvements not a part of the Home itself.

B. After the first year, concrete floors of basements and attached garages that are built separate from foundation walls or other structural elements of the Home.

C. Damage to real property which is not part of the Home covered by this policy and which is not included in the purchase price stated on the cover page of the Warranty issued by the Builder on the Home.

D. Any damage to the extent it is caused or made worse by:
 1. Negligence, improper maintenance or improper operation by anyone other than your Builder or its employees, agents, or subcontractors; or
 2. Failure by you or by anyone to comply with the Warranty requirements of manufacturers of appliances, equipment or fixtures; or
 3. Failure by you, the Purchaser, to give notice to your Builder of any defects within a reasonable time; or
 4. Changes of the grading of the ground by anyone other than your Builder or its employees, agents, or subcontractors; or
 5. Changes, alterations, or additions made to the Home by anyone after your initial occupancy, except those performed by your Builder under its obligations under the Builder's Home Warranty; or
 6. Dampness or condensation due to the failure of you, the Purchaser, to maintain adequate ventilation.
E. Any loss or damage which you, the Purchaser, have not taken timely action to minimize.
F. Any defect in, or caused by, materials or work supplied by anyone other than your Builder, its employees, agents, or subcontractors.
G. Normal wear and tear or normal deterioration.
H. Loss or damage not caused by a defect in the construction of the Home by your Builder, or its employees, agents, or subcontractors, but resulting from accidents, riot and civil commotion, or Acts of God including, but not limited to: fire, explosion, smoke, water escape, changes which are not reasonably foreseeable in the level of the underground water table, windstorm, hail, lightning, falling trees, aircraft, vehicles, flood, mudslides, earthquake and volcanic eruption.
I. Any damage caused by Soil Movement for which compensation is provided by legislation or which is covered by other insurance.
J. Insect damage.
K. Any loss or damage which arises while the Home is being used primarily for nonresidential purposes.
L. Failure of your Builder to complete construction of the Home.
M. Any condition which does not result in actual physical damage to the Home.

N. Costs of shelter, transportation, food, moving, storage, or other incidental expenses related to relocation during repair.
O. Bodily injury or damage to personal property.
P. Any claim reported to the Insurer after an unreasonable delay or later than 30 days after the expiration of the Policy Term.

VI. Resale

Each successor in title to the Home, including any mortgagee in possession, is automatically entitled to coverage under this policy for its unexpired term. There is no limit to the number of such successions during the term of this policy.

VII. How to Make a Claim

A. All claims under this policy must be pursued through the Insurer, not through the Builder.
B. Should a Major Structural Defect first occur during the Policy Term, the Purchaser must notify Insurer in writing of the claim on forms provided by the Insurer or its authorized representative. The notice fully describing the defect must be given within a reasonable time after the Major Structural Defect arises, and in any event no later than 30 days after the expiration of the Policy Term. Claims reported after an unreasonable delay or more than 30 days after the expiration of the Policy Term are not covered.
C. The Insurer will not be obligated to pay a claim unless it receives a full and unconditional release from the Purchaser of all rights and causes of action the Purchaser may have with respect to that claim.

VIII. Condominiums

If the Home is a condominium unit, the Purchaser may, at his option, file and pursue any claim directly on his own behalf or through any representative designated by the condominium association to file and pursue such claims. However, any portion of a claim involving common elements may only be made through such a representative.

IX. Rights of Mortgagees

The Insurer will, where practicable, make payment for any claim for $1,000 or more to the Purchaser and the mortgagee as their respective interests may appear. The mortgagee will be bound by the adjustment of any claim made with the Purchaser.

X. **General**
A. If the Insurer's performance of any of its obligations is delayed by any event not resulting from the Insurer's own conduct, the Insurer will be excused from performing until the effects of that event are remedied. Examples of such events are Acts of God or the common enemy, war, riot, civil commotion, sovereign conduct, or acts of persons who are not parties to this policy.
B. All notices required under this policy must be sent with first class postage prepaid to the intended recipient's address shown on the Declarations page, or to whatever new address the intended recipient has designated by giving such notice.
C. This policy is governed by the laws of the jurisdiction in which it is issued. If any provision of this policy is contrary to any law to which it is subject, that provision is hereby amended to conform to that law.
D. No change in this policy will be valid unless in the form of an endorsement attached to the policy and approved by an executive officer of the Insurer.
E. In interpreting this policy, use of one gender will include all other genders, and use of the singular will include the plural.

XI. **Definitions**
For the purposes of this policy, the following terms apply:
A. "Builder" – Is the person, corporation, partnership or other entity which is registered with the Home Owners Warranty Corporation and which obtained this policy on behalf of the Purchaser.
B. "Home" - Is the single-family dwelling on which this policy is issued, except that: "Home" also includes:
 1. A two- to four-plex structure which may be conveyed as a single unit, and
 2. The common elements which comprise the building in which a condominium unit is situated and which it shares in common with other units in the building.
C. "Purchaser" – Is the first person to whom the Home is sold by the Builder, and his successors in title. Purchaser also includes a person who receives a lease-hold interest of at least 50 years in the Home and a mortgagee in possession. Purchaser does not include the Builder or any firm under common control with the Builder.
D. "Soil Movement" – Subsidence, expansion or lateral movement of the Soil (excluding flood or earthquake).

Table of Contents
Approved Standards

SECTION	SUBJECT	SECTION	SUBJECT
I	Introduction	V	Coverage During the First Year
II	Home Owner Responsibilities	VI	Coverage During the Second Year
III	Exclusions	VII	Coverage During Years Three Through Ten
IV	Definitions	VIII	HOW Quality Standards

I. Introduction

The Home Owners Warranty Corporation (HOW) and your registered HOW builder have provided your new home with a ten year protection plan; a plan, backed by the HOW Home Warranty and Insurance Documents, that is extended to you and to subsequent purchasers of your home during the period that the Home Warranty and Insurance are in force.

Please read this carefully. It is intended to acquaint you with the extent of coverage and the responsibilities HOW and your builder have assumed. Also note that coverage on certain items varies within the 10-year period and some items rely on proper maintenance by you, the Home Owner, to prevent damage and ensure proper functioning of your home and its various systems. The Information in Section VIII, the Quality Standards, provide the basis for determining the validity, under the HOW Program, of coverage of deficiencies or defects that may occur.

The HOW Approved Standards also require that homes be built in compliance with local building codes. In local areas where no building codes are used, or where the existing codes are found unacceptable, one of the following will apply:

(A) The Minimum Property Standards of the U.S. Department of Housing and Urban Development (HUD);
(B) HOW approved codes to cover building, mechanical, plumbing, and electrical (See Appendix A);
(C) The codes of a nearby HOW approved jurisdiction.

In each case, the HOW Corporation will approve the applicable code and inspection system, or establish an inspection system to monitor adherence to the acceptable codes.

Your Builder is also required to construct your home in compliance with any Special Standards that HOW develops for any region of the country.

The Quality Standards (Section VIII) list defects that may be found in new homes, and outline the extent of the Warrantor's responsibility for correcting each of the defects. These standards are intended to specify performance standards for home construction and to determine the validity of home owner complaints related to defective workmanship, materials, and systems during the initial warranty period.

When minimum performance standards or specific tolerances for construction items have not been given in these Quality Standards, builders shall construct homes in accordance with accepted industry practice for materials and workmanship. The validity of any home owner complaint for defects for which a standard has not been enumerated herein shall be determined on the basis of accepted industry practice and the settling of any dispute concerning such complaint shall be conducted accordingly.

II. Home Owner Responsibilities

Your new home requires an active maintenance effort on your part to reduce the likelihood of damage due to neglect, improper maintenance, or abnormal use. One of the more typical problems encountered by new home owners is water damage to exterior walls and basements. Damage of this sort may be caused by the location and type of home owner-installed trees and shrubbery, or failure of the home owner to maintain the proper drainage away from the home. It is your responsibility to maintain, in this instance, a proper grade around the home that will ensure the continued movement of surface water away from the home.

Excessive entrance of water around the foundation can cause soil movement and serious damage. Excessive water entrance and subsequent damages caused by the home owner changing the grade, not properly maintaining it, or cultivating and landscaping areas near the foundation will not be considered an eligible claim.

Various regional areas of the country have local maintenance problems. Home owners are encouraged to discuss specific maintenance responsibilities with their builders.

Additional home owner responsibilities are included herein under specific topics in Section VIII, Quality Standards.
NOTE: Damage caused or made worse by home owner negligence, improper maintenance and/or operation will not be covered.

III. Exclusions

Certain exclusions are listed in the Home Warranty and Insurance Documents which state that the following items are not covered:

a. Defects in outbuildings, including detached garages and detached carports (except outbuildings which contain the plumbing, electrical, heating, cooling, ventilation or mechanical systems serving the home); swimming pools and other recreational facilities; driveways; walkways; patios; boundary walls, retaining walls, bulkheads; fences; landscaping (including sodding, seeding, shrubs, trees, and plantings); off-site improvements; or any other improvements not a part of the home itself.

b. After the first year, concrete floors of attached garages and basements that are built separate from foundation walls or other structural elements of the home.

c. Bodily injury, damage to personal property, or damage to real property which is not included in the purchase price stated on the cover page of this Warranty.

d. Any damage to the extent it is caused or made worse by:
— Negligence, improper maintenance or improper operation by anyone other than your Builder or HOW, or their employees, agents, or subcontractors; or
— Failure by you or by anyone other than your Builder or HOW, or their employees, agents or subcontractors to comply with the Warranty requirements of manufacturers of appliances, equipment or fixtures; or
— Failure by you, the purchaser, to give notice to your Builder or HOW of any defects within a reasonable time; or
— Changes of the grading of the ground by anyone other than your Builder, HOW, or their employees, agents, or subcontractors; or
— Changes, alterations, or additions made to the home by anyone after your initial occupancy, except those performed by your Builder or HOW under their obligations under this program.

e. Any loss or damage which purchaser has not taken timely action to minimize.

f. Any defect in, or caused by, materials or work (including, but not limited to, items shown on any "Addendum to the Application for HOW Protection") supplied by anyone other than your Builder, HOW, or their employees, agents, or subcontractors.

g. Normal wear and tear or normal deterioration.

h. Loss or damage not caused by a defect in the construction of the home by your Builder, or his employees, agents, or subcontractors, but resulting from accidents, riot and civil commotion, or Acts of God including, but not limited to: fire, explosion, smoke, water escape, glass breakage, changes which are not reasonably foreseeable in the level of the underground water table, wind storm, hail, lightning, falling trees, aircraft, vehicles, flood, mudslides, earthquake, and volcanic eruption.

i. Any damage caused by soil movement for which compensation is provided by legislation or which is covered by other insurance.

j. Insect damage.

k. Any loss or damage which arises while the home is being used primarily for nonresidential purposes.

l. Failure of your Builder to complete construction of the home.

m. Any condition which does not result in actual physical damage to the home.

Additionally, the HOW Warranty may have an Addendum to the Application for HOW Protection, attached to indicate all items supplied by others and therefore excluded from the HOW Warranty (See f. above). For example, work performed by the purchaser or persons other than the Builder on such items as interior or exterior painting, floor coverings, finishing of recreation rooms, grading and landscaping and other similar items are not covered by the HOW Warranty, and the Approved Standards are not applicable to those items.

IV. Definitions

1. **Appliances, Fixtures and Equipment:** The term, "Appliances, Fixtures and Equipment" (including their fittings, attachments, controls and appurtenances) shall include, but not be limited to:

Furnaces, boilers, oil tanks and fittings, humidifiers, air purifiers, air handling equipment, ventilating fans, air conditioning equipment, water heaters, pumps, stoves, refrigerators, garbage disposals, compactors, dishwashers, automatic door openers, washers and dryers, bathtubs, sinks, toilets, faucets and fittings, lighting fixtures, and circuit breakers. The initial HOW Warranty coverage period for appliances, fixtures and equipment (including their fittings, attachments, controls and appurtenances) is one year, regardless of manufacturers' warranties on specific items. The HOW Warranty and manufacturers' warranties, however, may be voided by the Owner's negligence or improper maintenance or service.

2. **Systems:** The term "systems" (exclusive of appliances, fixtures and equipment, as specified above) means the following:
   (A) **Plumbing Systems**—gas supply lines and fittings, and water supply, waste and vent pipes and their fittings; septic tanks and their field drains; water, gas and sewer service piping, and their extensions to the tie-in of a public utility connection, or on-site well and sewage disposal system.
   (B) **Electrical System**—all wiring, electrical boxes, switches, outlets and connections up to the public utility connection.
   (C) **Heating, Ventilating, Cooling and Mechanical Systems**—all ductwork, steam, water, and refrigerant lines, registers, convectors, radiation elements and dampers.

The HOW Warranty period for systems (excluding appliances, fixtures, and equipment) is two years.

V. Coverage During the First Year

During the first year of HOW's Ten-Year Protection Plan, your home is warranted against the following:
- Faulty workmanship and materials;
- Defects in appliances, fixtures and equipment, (See definitions, Section IV);
- Defects in wiring, piping and ductwork in the electrical, plumbing, heating, cooling, ventilating and mechanical systems; and,
- Major Structural Defects.

NOTE: New homes, no matter how carefully constructed, go through a period of normal settlement and shrinkage. During this period, hairline cracks, some wood shrinkage and warping and other minor matters may occur, much of which is unavoidable. Warrantor will assume no responsibility for these minor defects.

VI. Coverage During the Second Year

For the Second Year of the Protection Plan your home is warranted against the following:
- Defects in the electrical, plumbing, heating, cooling, ventilating and mechanical systems (See definitions, Section IV) exclusive of appliances, fixtures and equipment attached thereto; and,
- Major Structural Defects.

VII. Coverage During Years Three Through Ten

From the beginning of the third year until the end of the tenth year, your home is insured against Major Structural Defects only.

VIII. HOW Quality Standards — Topic Index

The Quality Standards list specific items (defects) within each separate area of coverage. The first section covers Workmanship and Materials; the second section covers Systems; and the third covers Major Structural Defects.

The Quality Standards are expressed in terms of performance standards. For easy comprehension, the format is designed as follows:
1. **Possible Deficiency**—a brief statement, in simple terms, of problems that may be encountered.
2. **Performance Standard**—a performance standard relating to a specific deficiency.
3. **Responsibility**—a statement of the corrective action required of the Warrantor to repair the deficiency; or a statement of Home Owners' maintenance responsibilities.

Workmanship and Materials, First Year Only

Site Grading
Concrete
Masonry
Wood & Plastic
Thermal and Moisture Protection
Doors and Windows
Finishes
Specialties
Equipment
Mechanical
Electrical

Systems; First and Second Year

Mechanical
Electrical

Major Structural Defects

Workmanship and Materials: First Year Only

Topic: Site Work	Coverage: 1st Year Only	Area: Workmanship and Materials
Site Grading		
Possible Deficiency	Settling of ground around foundation, utility trenches or other areas.	
Performance Standard	Settling of ground around foundation walls, utility trenches or other filled areas shall not interfere with water drainage away from the home.	

Responsibility	If the Builder has provided final grading: upon request by the Owner, Warrantor shall fill settled areas affecting proper drainage, one time only, during the first year Warranty period. Owner shall be responsible for removal and replacement of shrubs or other landscaping affected by placement of such fill.
Site Drainage	
Possible Deficiency	Improper drainage of the site.
Performance Standard	The necessary grades and swales shall have been established by the Builder to insure proper drainage away from the home. Standing or ponding water shall not remain for extended periods in the immediate area of the house after a rain (generally no more than 24 hours), except that in swales which drain other areas, or in areas where sump pumps discharge, a longer period can be anticipated (generally no more than 48 hours). The possibility of standing water after an unusually heavy rainfall should be anticipated by the Home Owner. No grading determination shall be made while there is frost or snow on the ground, or while the ground is saturated.
Responsibility	The Builder is responsible only for initially establishing the proper grades and swales. Owner is responsible for maintaining such grades and swales once they have been properly established by the Builder.
Topic: Concrete	**Coverage: 1st Year Only** **Area: Workmanship and Materials**
Expansion and Contraction Joints	
Possible Deficiency	Separation or movement of concrete slabs within the structure at expansion and contraction joints.
Performance Standard	Concrete slabs within the structure are designed to move at expansion and contraction joints.
Responsibility	None.
Cast-In-Place Concrete	
Possible Deficiency	Basement or foundation wall cracks.
Performance Standard	Shrinkage cracks are not unusual in concrete foundation walls. Such cracks greater than 1/8 inch in width shall be repaired.
Responsibility	Warrantor will repair cracks in excess of 1/8 inch width.
Possible Deficiency	Cracking of basement floor.
Performance Standard	Minor cracks in concrete basement floors are normal. Cracks exceeding 3/16 inch in width or 1/8 inch in vertical displacement shall be repaired.

Responsibility	Warrantor will repair cracks exceeding maximum tolerances by surface patching or other methods as required.
Possible Deficiency	Cracking of slab in attached garage.
Performance Standard	Cracks in garage slabs in excess of 1/4 inch in width or 1/4 inch in vertical displacement shall be repaired.
Responsibility	Warrantor will repair cracks exceeding maximum tolerances by surface patching or other methods as required.
Possible Deficiency	Uneven concrete floors/slabs.
Performance Standard	Except for basement floors or where a floor or portion of floor has been designed for specific drainage purposes, concrete floors in rooms designed for habitability shall not have pits, depressions or areas of unevenness exceeding 1/4 inch in 32 inches.
Responsibility	Warrantor will correct or repair to meet the Performance Standard.
Possible Deficiency	Cracks in concrete slab-on-grade floors with finish flooring.
Performance Standard	Cracks which rupture the finish flooring material shall be repaired.
Responsibility	Warrantor will repair cracks, as necessary, so as not to be readily apparent when the finish flooring material is in place. (See also "Finishes.")
Possible Deficiency	Pitting, scaling or spalling of concrete work covered by Warranty.
Performance Standard	Concrete surfaces shall not disintegrate to the extent that the aggregate is exposed and loosened under normal conditions of weathering and use.
Responsibility	Warrantor will take whatever corrective action necessary to repair or replace defective concrete surfaces. Warrantor is not responsible for deterioration caused by salt, chemicals, mechanical implements and other factors beyond its control.
Possible Deficiency	Settling, heaving, or separating of stoops, steps, or garage floors.
Performance Standard	Stoops, steps or garage floors shall not settle, heave, or separate in excess of 1 inch from the house structure.
Responsibility	Warrantor will take whatever corrective action is required to meet the Performance Standard.

Possible Deficiency	Standing water on stoops.
Performance Standard	Water should drain from outdoor stoops and steps. The possibility of minor water standing on stoops for a short period after rain can be anticipated.
Responsibility	Warrantor shall take corrective action to assure drainage of steps and stoops.
Coverage: 1st Year Only	**Area: Workmanship and Materials**

Topic: Masonry
Unit Masonry

Possible Deficiency	Basement or foundation wall cracks.
Performance Standard	Small cracks not affecting structural stability are not unusual in mortar joints of masonry foundation walls. Cracks greater than 1/8 inch in width shall be repaired.
Responsibility	Warrantor will repair cracks in excess of 1/8 inch by pointing or patching. These deficiencies shall be reported and repairs made during the first year Warranty period.
Possible Deficiency	Cracks in masonry walls or veneer.
Performance Standard	Small hairline cracks due to shrinkage are common in mortar joints in masonry construction. Cracks greater than 3/8 inch in width are considered excessive.
Responsibility	Warrantor will repair cracks in excess of Performance Standard by pointing or patching. These repairs shall be made during the first year Warranty period. Warrantor will not be responsible for color variation between old and new mortar.
Coverage: 1st Year Only	**Area: Workmanship and Materials**

Topic: Wood and Plastic
Rough Carpentry

Possible Deficiency	Floors squeak or subfloor appears loose.
Performance Standard	Floor squeaks and loose subfloor are often temporary conditions common to new home construction, and a squeak-proof floor cannot be guaranteed.
Responsibility	Warrantor will correct the problem only if caused by an underlying construction defect.
Possible Deficiency	Uneven wood floors.
Performance Standard	Floors shall not have more than 1/4 inch ridge or depression within any 32 inch measurement when measured parallel to the joists. Allowable floor and ceiling joist deflections are governed by the Approved building code.

Responsibility	Warrantor will correct or repair to meet Performance Standard.
Possible Deficiency	Bowed walls.
Performance Standard	All interior and exterior walls have slight variances on their finished surfaces. Bowing of walls should not detract from or blemish the wall's finished surface. Walls should not bow more than 1/4 inch out of line within any 32 inch horizontal or vertical measurement.
Responsibility	Warrantor will repair to meet Performance Standard.
Possible Deficiency	Out-of-plumb walls.
Performance Standard	Walls should not be more than 1/4 inch out of plumb for any 32 inch vertical measurement.
Responsibility	Warrantor will repair to meet the Performance Standard.
Finish Carpentry (Interior)	
Possible Deficiency	Poor quality of interior trim workmanship.
Performance Standard	Joints in moldings or joint between moldings and adjacent surface shall not result in open joints exceeding 1/8 inch in width.
Responsibility	Warrantor will repair defective joints, as defined. Caulking is acceptable.
Finish Carpentry (Exterior)	
Possible Deficiency	Poor quality of exterior trim workmanship.
Performance Standard	Joints between exterior trim elements, including siding and masonry, shall not result in open joints in excess of 3/8 inch. In all cases the exterior trim, masonry and siding shall be capable of performing its function to exclude the elements.
Responsibility	Warrantor will repair open joints, as defined. Caulking is acceptable.
Topic: Thermal and Moisture Protection **Coverage: 1st Year Only** **Area: Workmanship and Material**	
Waterproofing	
Possible Deficiency	Leaks in basement.
Performance Standard	Leaks resulting in actual trickling of water shall be repaired. Leaks caused by improper landscaping installed by Owner, or failure of Owner to maintain proper grades are not covered by the Warranty. Dampness of the walls or floors may occur in new construction and is not considered a deficiency.

Responsibility Warrantor will take such action as necessary to correct basement leaks except where the cause is determined to result from Owner action or negligence.

Insulation

Possible Deficiency Insufficient insulation.

Performance Standard Insulation shall be installed in accordance with applicable energy and building code requirements.

Responsibility Warrantor will install insulation in sufficient amounts to meet Performance Standard.

Louvers and Vents

Possible Deficiency Leaks due to snow or rain driven into the attic through louvers or vents.

Performance Standard Attic vents and/or louvers must be provided in order to properly ventilate your house.

Responsibility None.

Roofing and Siding

Possible Deficiency Ice build-up on roof.

Performance Standard During prolonged cold spells, ice build-up is likely to occur at the eaves of a roof. This condition occurs when snow and ice accumulate and gutters and downspouts freeze up.

Responsibility Prevention of ice build-up on the roof is an Owner maintenance item.

Possible Deficiency Roof or flashing leaks.

Performance Standard Roofs or flashing shall not leak under normally anticipated conditions, except where cause is determined to result from ice build-up or Owner actions or negligence.

Responsibility Warrantor will repair any verified roof or flashing leaks not caused by ice build-up or Owner actions or negligence.

Possible Deficiency Standing water on flat roof.

Performance Standard Water shall drain from flat roof except for minor ponding immediately following rainfall or when the roof is specifically designed for water retention.

Responsibility Warrantor will take corrective action to assure proper drainage of roof.

Possible Deficiency Delamination of veneer siding or joint separation.

Performance Standard	All siding shall be installed according to the manufacturer's and industry's accepted standards. Separations and delaminations shall be repaired or replaced.
Responsibility	Warrantor will repair or replace siding as needed unless caused by Owner's neglect to maintain siding properly. Repaired area may not match in color and/or texture. For surfaces requiring paint, Builder will paint only the new materials. The Owner can expect that the newly painted surface may not match original surface in color.

Sheet Metal

Possible Deficiency	Gutters and/or downspouts leak.
Performance Standard	Gutters and downspouts shall not leak but gutters may overflow during heavy rain.
Responsibility	Warrantor will repair leaks. It is the Home Owner's responsibility to keep gutters and downspouts free of leaves and debris which could cause overflow.
Possible Deficiency	Water standing in gutters.
Performance Standard	When gutter is unobstructed by debris, the water level shall not exceed 1 (one) inch in depth. Industry practice is to install gutters approximately level. Consequently, it is entirely possible that small amounts of water will stand in certain sections of gutter immediately after a rain.
Responsibility	Warrantor will correct to meet Performance Standard.

Sealants

Possible Deficiency	Leaks in exterior walls due to inadequate caulking.
Performance Standard	Joints and cracks in exterior wall surfaces and around openings shall be properly caulked to exclude the entry of water.
Responsibility	Warrantor will repair and/or caulk joints or cracks in exterior wall surfaces as required to correct deficiencies once, during the first year Warranty period. Even properly installed caulking will shrink and must be maintained by the Home Owner during the life of the home.

Topic: Doors and Windows	Coverage: 1st Year Only	Area: Workmanship and Materials

Wood and Plastic Doors

Possible Deficiency	Warpage of exterior doors.

Performance Standard	Exterior doors will warp to some degree due to temperature differential on inside and outside surfaces. However, they shall not warp to the extent that they become inoperable or cease to be weather resistant or exceed National Woodwork Manufacturers Association Standards (1/4 inch, measured diagonally from corner to corner.)
Responsibility	Warrantor will correct or replace and refinish defective doors, during the first year Warranty period.
Possible Deficiency	Warpage of interior passage and closet doors.
Performance Standard	Interior doors (full openings) shall not warp in excess of National Woodwork Manufacturers Association Standards (1/4 inch).
Responsibility	Warrantor will correct or replace and refinish defective doors to match existing doors as nearly as possible, during the first year Warranty period.
Possible Deficiency	Shrinkage of insert panels show raw wood edges.
Performance Standard	Panels will shrink and expand, and may expose unpainted surface.
Responsibility	None.
Possible Deficiency	Split in door panel.
Performance Standard	Split panels shall not allow light to be visible through the door.
Responsibility	Warrantor will, if light is visible, fill split and match paint or stain as closely as possible, one time in first year Warranty period.

Glass

Possible Deficiency	Broken glass.
Performance Standard	None.
Responsibility	Broken glass not reported to the builder prior to closing is the Home Owner's responsibility.

Garage Doors on Attached Garage

Possible Deficiency	Garage doors fail to operate properly, under normal use.
Performance Standard	Garage doors shall operate properly.
Responsibility	Warrantor will correct or adjust garage doors as required, except where the cause is determined to result from Owner actions or negligence.
Possible Deficiency	Garage doors allow entrance of snow or water.

Performance Standard	Garage doors shall be installed as recommended by the manufacturer. Some entrance of the elements can be expected under abnormal conditions.
Responsibility	Warrantor will adjust or correct garage doors to meet manufacturer's recommendations.

Wood, Plastic and Metal Windows

Possible Deficiency	Malfunction of windows.
Performance Standard	Windows shall operate with reasonable ease, as designed.
Responsibility	Warrantor will correct or repair as required.
Possible Deficiency	Condensation and/or frost on windows.
Performance Standard	Windows will collect condensation on interior surfaces when extreme temperature difference and high humidity levels are present. Condensation is usually the result of climatic/humidity conditions, created by the Home Owner within the home.
Responsibility	Unless directly attributed to faulty installation, window condensation is a result of conditions beyond the Warrantor's control. No corrective action required.

Weatherstripping and Seals

Possible Deficiency	Air infiltration around doors and windows.
Performance Standard	Some infiltration is normally noticeable around doors and windows, especially during high winds. Poorly fitted weatherstripping shall be adjusted or replaced. It may be necessary for the Owner to have storm doors and windows installed to provide satisfactory solutions in high wind areas.
Responsibility	Warrantor will adjust or correct poorly fitted doors, windows, or poorly fitted weatherstripping.

Topic: Finishes   **Coverage: 1st Year Only**   **Area: Workmanship and Materials**

Lath and Plaster

Possible Deficiency	Cracks in interior wall and ceiling surfaces.
Performance Standard	Hairline cracks are not unusual in interior wall and ceiling surfaces. Cracks greater than 1/8 inch in width shall be repaired.
Responsibility	Warrantor will repair cracks exceeding 1/8 inch in width as required; one time only, during the first year Warranty period. (See also "Painting.")

Gypsum Wallboard

Possible Deficiency Defects which appear during first year of Warranty such as nail pops, blisters in tape, or other blemishes.

Performance Standard Slight "imperfections" such as nail pops, seam lines and cracks not exceeding 1/8 inch in width are common in gypsum wallboard installations and are considered acceptable.

Responsibility Warrantor will repair only cracks exceeding 1/8 inch in width, one time only, during the first year Warranty period. (See also "Painting.")

Ceramic Tile

Possible Deficiency Ceramic tile cracks or becomes loose.

Performance Standard Ceramic tile shall not crack or become loose.

Responsibility Warrantor will replace cracked tiles and re-secure loose tiles unless the defects were caused by the Owner's action or negligence. Warrantor will not be responsible for discontinued patterns or color variations in ceramic tile.

Possible Deficiency Cracks appear in grouting of ceramic tile joints or at junctions with other material such as a bathtub.

Performance Standard Cracks in grouting of ceramic tile joints are commonly due to normal shrinkage conditions.

Responsibility Warrantor will repair grouting if necessary; one time only, during the first year Warranty period. Warrantor will not be responsible for color variations or discontinued colored grout. Regrouting of these cracks is a maintenance responsibility of the Home Owner within the life of the home.

Finished Wood Flooring

Possible Deficiency Cracks developing between floor boards.

Performance Standard Cracks in excess of 1/8 inch in width shall be corrected.

Responsibility Warrantor will repair cracks in excess of 1/8 inch within the first year Warranty period, by filling or replacing, at Warrantor's option.

Resilient Flooring

Possible Deficiency Nail pops appear on the surface of resilient flooring.

Performance Standard Readily apparent nail pops shall be repaired.

Responsibility — Warrantor will correct nail pops which have broken the surface. Warrantor will repair or replace, at Warrantor's option, resilient floor covering in the affected area with similar material. Warrantor will not be responsible for discontinued patterns or color variations in the floor covering.

Possible Deficiency — Depressions or ridges appear in the resilient flooring due to subfloor irregularities.

Performance Standard — Readily apparent depressions or ridges exceeding 1/8 inch shall be repaired. The ridge or depression measurement is taken as the gap created at one end of a six-inch straightedge placed over the depression or ridge with three inches of the straightedge on one side of the defect, held tightly to the floor.

Responsibility — Warrantor will take corrective action as necessary, to bring the defect within acceptable tolerance so that the affected area is not readily visible. Warrantor will not be responsible for discontinued patterns or color variations in floor covering.

Possible Deficiency — Resilient flooring loses adhesion.

Performance Standard — Resilient flooring shall not lift, bubble or become unglued.

Responsibility — Warrantor will repair or replace, at Warrantor's option, the affected resilient flooring as required. Warrantor will not be responsible for discontinued patterns of color variation of floor covering, or for problems caused by Owner neglect or abuse.

Possible Deficiency — Seams or shrinkage gaps show at resilient flooring joints.

Performance Standard — Gaps shall not exceed 1/16 inch in width in resilient floor covering joints. Where dissimilar materials abut, a gap not to exceed 1/8 inch is permissible.

Responsibility — Warrantor will repair or replace, at Warrantor's option, the affected resilient flooring as required. Warrantor will not be responsible for discontinued patterns or color variation of floor covering, or for problems caused by owner neglect or abuse.

Painting

Possible Deficiency — Exterior paint or stain peels, deteriorates or fades.

Performance Standard — Exterior paints or stains should not fail during the first year Warranty period. However, fading is normal and the degree is dependent on climatic conditions.

Responsibility — If paint or stain is defective, Warrantor will properly prepare and refinish affected areas, matching color as close as possible. Where finish deterioration affects the majority of the wall area, the whole area will be refinished.

Possible Deficiency	Painting required as corollary repair because of other work.
Performance Standard	Repairs required under this Warranty shall be finished to match surrounding areas as closely as practicable.
Responsibility	Warrantor will finish repair areas as indicated.
Possible Deficiency	Deterioration of varnish or lacquer finishes.
Performance Standard	Natural finishes on interior woodwork shall not deteriorate during the first year of ownership. However, varnish type finishes used on the exterior will deteriorate rapidly and are not covered by the Warranty.
Responsibility	Warrantor will retouch affected areas of natural finish interior woodwork, matching the color as closely as possible.
Possible Deficiency	Mildew or fungus on painted surfaces.
Performance Standard	Mildew or fungus will form on a painted surface if the structure is subject to abnormal exposures (i.e., rainfall, ocean, lake, or river front).
Responsibility	Mildew or fungus formation is a condition Warrantor cannot control and is a Home Owner maintenance item, unless it is a result of non-compliance with other sections of the Quality Standards.

Wall Covering

Possible Deficiency	Peeling of wall covering
Performance Standard	Peeling of wall covering shall not occur.
Responsibility	Warrantor will repair or replace defective wall covering applications.
Possible Deficiency	Edge mis-matching in pattern of wall covering.
Performance Standard	None.
Responsibility	None.

Carpeting

Possible Deficiency	Open carpet seams.
Performance Standard	Carpet seams will show. However, no visible gap is acceptable.
Responsibility	Warrantor will correct.

Possible Deficiency	Carpeting becomes loose, seams separate or stretching occurs.
Performance Standard	Wall to wall carpeting, installed as the primary floor covering, when stretched and secured properly shall not come up, become loose, or separate from its point of attachment.
Responsibility	Warrantor will re-stretch or re-secure carpeting as needed, if original installation was performed by Builder.
Possible Deficiency	Spots on carpet, minor fading.
Performance Standard	Exposure to light may cause spots on carpet and/or minor fading.
Responsibility	None.

Special Coatings

Possible Deficiency	Cracks in exterior stucco wall surfaces.
Performance Standard	Cracks are not unusual in exterior stucco wall surfaces. Cracks greater than 1/8 inch in width shall be repaired.
Responsibility	Warrantor will repair cracks exceeding 1/8 inch in width, one time only, during the first year Warranty period.

Topic: Specialties   **Coverage: 1st Year Only**   **Area: Workmanship and Materials**

Louvers and Vents

Possible Deficiency	Inadequate ventilation of attics and crawl spaces.
Performance Standard	Attic and crawl spaces shall be ventilated as required by the approved building code.
Responsibility	The Builder shall provide for adequate ventilation. Warrantor will not be responsible for Home Owner alterations to the original system.

Fireplaces

Possible Deficiency	Fireplace or chimney does not draw properly.
Performance Standard	A properly designed and constructed fireplace and chimney shall function properly. It is normal to expect that high winds can cause temporary negative draft situations. Similar negative draft situations can also be caused by obstructions such as large branches of trees too close to the chimney. Some homes may need to have a window opened slightly to create an effective draft, if they have been insulated and weatherproofed to meet high energy conservation criteria.

Responsibility	Warrantor will determine the cause of malfunction and correct, if the problem is one of design or construction of the fireplace.
Possible Deficiency	Chimney separation from structure to which it is attached.
Performance Standard	Newly built fireplaces will often incur slight amounts of separation. Separation shall not exceed 1/2 inch from the main structure in any 10 foot vertical measurement.
Responsibility	Warrantor will determine the cause of separation and correct if standard is not met. Caulking is acceptable.
Possible Deficiency	Firebox paint changed by fire.
Performance Standard	None.
Responsibility	None. Heat from fires will alter finish.
Possible Deficiency	Cracked firebrick and mortar joints.
Performance Standard	None.
Responsibility	None. Heat and flames from "roaring" fires will cause cracking.

Topic: Equipment Coverage 1st Year Only **Area: Workmanship and Materials**
Residential Equipment

Possible Deficiency	Surface cracks, joint delaminations and chips in high pressure laminates on vanity and kitchen cabinet countertops.
Performance Standard	Countertops fabricated with high pressure laminate coverings shall not delaminate.
Responsibility	Warrantor will replace delaminated coverings to meet specified criteria. Warrantor will not be responsible for chips and cracks noted following first occupancy.
Possible Deficiency	Kitchen cabinet malfunctions.
Performance Standard	Warpage not to exceed 1/4 inch as measured from face frame to point of furthermost warpage with door or drawer front in closed position.
Responsibility	Warrantor will correct or replace doors or drawer fronts.
Possible Deficiency	Gaps between cabinets, ceiling or walls.
Performance Standard	Acceptable tolerance 1/4 inch in width.
Responsibility	Warrantor will correct to meet Performance Standard.

Topic: Mechanical	Coverage: 1st Year Only	Area: Workmanship and Materials

Water Supply System

Possible Deficiency: Plumbing pipes freeze and burst.

Performance Standard: Drain, waste and vent, and water pipes shall be adequately protected, as required by applicable code, during normally anticipated cold weather, and as defined in accordance with ASHRAE design temperatures, to prevent freezing.

Responsibility: Warrantor will correct situations not meeting the code. It is the Home Owner's responsibility to drain or otherwise protect lines and exterior faucets exposed to freezing temperatures.

Plumbing

Possible Deficiency: Faucet or valve leak.

Performance Standard: No valve or faucet shall leak due to defects in material or workmanship.

Responsibility: Warrantor will repair or replace the leaking faucet or valve.

Possible Deficiency: Defective plumbing fixtures, appliances or trim fittings.

Performance Standard: Fixtures, appliances or fittings shall comply with their manufacturer's standards.

Responsibility: Warrantor will replace any defective fixture or fitting which does not meet acceptable standards, as defined by the manufacturer.

Possible Deficiency: Noisy water pipes.

Performance Standard: There will be some noise emitting from the water pipe system, due to the flow of water. However, water hammer shall be eliminated.

Responsibility: Warrantor cannot remove all noises due to water flow and pipe expansion. Warrantor will correct to eliminate "water hammer."

Possible Deficiency: Cracking or chipping of porcelain or fiberglass surfaces.

Performance Standard: Chips and cracks on surfaces of bathtubs and kitchen sinks can occur when surface is hit with sharp or heavy objects.

Responsibility: Warrantor will not be responsible for repairs unless damage has been reported to Builder prior to first occupancy.

Heating

Possible Deficiency Inadequate heating.

Performance Standard Heating system shall be capable of producing an inside temperature of 70°F, as measured in the center of each room at a height of 5 feet above the floor, under local outdoor winter design conditions as specified in ASHRAE handbook. Federal, state or local energy codes shall supersede this standard where such codes have been locally adopted.

Responsibility Warrantor will correct heating system to provide the required temperatures. However, Owner shall be responsible for balancing dampers, registers and other minor adjustments.

Refrigeration

Possible Deficiency Inadequate cooling.

Performance Standard Where air-conditioning is provided, the cooling system shall be capable of maintaining a temperature of 78°F, as measured in the center of each room at a height of 5 feet above the floor, under local outdoor summer design conditions as specified in ASHRAE handbook. In the case of outside temperatures exceeding 95°F, a differential of 15°F from the outside temperature will be maintained. Federal, state, or local energy codes shall supersede this standard where such codes have been locally adopted.

Responsibility Warrantor will correct cooling system to meet temperature conditions, in accordance with specifications.

Condensation Lines

Possible Deficiency Condensation lines clog up.

Performance Standard None.

Responsibility Condensation lines will clog eventually under normal use. This is a Home Owner maintenance item. Builder shall provide unobstructed condensation lines at time of first occupancy.

Evaporative Cooling

Possible Deficiency Improper mechanical operation.

Performance Standard Equipment shall function properly at temperature standard set.

Responsibility Warrantor will correct and adjust so that blower and water system operate as designed.

Air Distribution

Possible Deficiency	Noisy ductwork.
Performance Standard	When metal is heated it expands and when cooled it contracts. The result is "ticking" or "crackling" which is generally to be expected.
Responsibility	None.
Possible Deficiency	Oilcanning.
Performance Standard	The stiffening of the ductwork and the gauge of the metal used shall be such that ducts do not "oilcan". The booming noise caused by "oilcanning" is not acceptable.
Responsibility	Warrantor will correct to eliminate this sound.

Topic: Electrical Coverage: 1st Year Only Area: Workmanship and Materials

Electrical Conductors, Fuses, and Circuit Breakers

Possible Deficiency	Fuses blow or circuit breakers (excluding ground fault interruptors) "kick out".
Performance Standard	Fuses and circuit breakers shall not activate under normal usage.
Responsibility	Warrantor will check wiring circuits for conformity with local, state, or approved national electrical code requirements. Warrantor will correct circuitry not conforming to code specifications.

Outlets, Switches and Fixtures

Possible Deficiency	Drafts from electrical outlets.
Performance Standard	Electrical junction boxes on exterior walls may produce air flow whereby the cold air can be drawn through the outlet into a room. The problem is normal in new home construction.
Responsibility	None.
Possible Deficiency	Malfunction of electrical outlets, switches or fixtures.
Performance Standard	All switches, fixtures and outlets shall operate as intended.
Responsibility	Warrantor will repair or replace defective switches, fixtures and outlets.

Service and Distribution

Possible Deficiency	Ground fault interruptor trips frequently.
Performance Standard	Ground fault interruptors are sensitive safety devices installed into the electrical system to provide protection against electrical shock. These sensitive devices can be tripped very easily.

Responsibility	Builder shall install ground fault interruptor in accordance with approved electrical code. Tripping is to be expected and is not covered, unless due to a construction defect.

Systems: First and Second Year

Topic: Mechanical	Coverage: 1st and 2nd Year	Area: Systems

Water Supply System

Possible Deficiency	Water supply system fails to deliver water.
Performance Standard	All on-site service connections to municipal water main and private water supply shall be the Builder's responsibility. Private systems shall be designed and installed in accordance with all approved building, plumbing and health codes.
Responsibility	Warrantor will repair if failure is the result of defective workmanship or materials. If conditions beyond Warrantor's control disrupt or eliminate the sources of the supply the Warrantor has no responsibility.

Septic Tank System

Possible Deficiency	Septic system fails to operate properly.
Performance Standard	Septic system shall be capable of properly handling normal flow of household effluent. Septic system shall be designed and installed to comply with state, county or local code regulations.
Responsibility	Warrantor will repair if failure is the result of defective workmanship or materials. Warrantor will not be responsible for malfunctions which occur through Owner negligence or abuse or from conditions that are beyond Warrantor's control, such as freezing, soil saturation, increase in water table, excessive use, etc. Owner shall be responsible for septic system maintenance.

Plumbing

Possible Deficiency	Leakage from any piping.
Performance Standard	No leaks of any kind shall exist in any soil, waste, vent or water pipe. Condensation on piping does not constitute leakage, and is not covered.
Responsibility	Warrantor will make repairs to eliminate leakage.
Possible Deficiency	Stopped up sewers, fixtures and drains.
Performance Standard	Sewers, fixtures and drains shall operate properly.

Responsibility — Warrantor will not be responsible for sewers, fixtures and drains which are clogged through the Owner's negligence. If a problem occurs, the Owner should consult Warrantor for a proper course of action. Where defective construction is shown to be the cause, Warrantor will assume the cost of the repair; where Owner negligence is shown to be the cause, the Owner shall assume all repair costs.

Possible Deficiency — Refrigerant lines leak.

Performance Standard — Refrigerant lines shall not develop leaks during normal operation.

Responsibility — Warrantor will repair leaking refrigerant lines and re-charge unit, unless damage was caused by Owner.

Topic: Mechanical   **Coverage: 1st and 2nd Year**   **Area: Systems**
Air Distribution

Possible Deficiency — Ductwork separates or becomes unattached.

Performance Standard — Ductwork shall remain intact and securely fastened.

Responsibility — Warrantor will re-attach and re-secure all separated or unattached ductwork.

Topic: Electrical   **Coverage: 1st and 2nd Year**   **Area: Systems**

Possible Deficiency — Failure of wiring to carry its designed load.

Performance Standard — Wiring should be capable of carrying the designed load for normal residential use.

Responsibility — Warrantor will check wiring for conformity with local, state, or approved national electrical code requirements. Warrantor will repair wiring not conforming to code specifications.

Major Structural Defects: 1st Year Through 10th Year

A "Major Structural Defect" is actual physical damage to the following designated load-bearing portions of the home caused by failure of such load-bearing portions which affects their load-bearing functions to the extent that the home becomes unsafe, unsanitary or otherwise unlivable:

1. Foundation systems and footings;
2. Beams;
3. Girders;
4. Lintels;
5. Columns;

6. Walls and partitions;
7. Floor systems; and
8. Roof framing systems.

Repair of a Major Structural Defect is limited (1) to the repair of damage to the load-bearing elements of the home themselves which is necessary to restore their load-bearing ability; and (2) to the repair of those items of the home damaged by the Major Structural Defect which make the home unsafe, unsanitary or otherwise unlivable.

Damage to the following non-load bearing elements do not constitute a major structural defect (See Note 1).
 a. Roof shingles and sheathing;
 b. Dry wall and plaster;
 c. Exterior siding;
 d. Brick, stone or stucco veneer;
 e. Subfloor and flooring materials;
 f. Wall tile or other wall coverings;
 g. Non-load bearing partitions;
 h. Concrete floors in attached garages and basements that are built separate from foundation walls or other structural elements of the home;
 i. Electrical, heating, cooling, ventilation, mechanical, and plumbing systems; appliances, equipment, fixtures, paint, doors, windows, trim, cabinet, hardware and insulation.
NOTE 1: In the event of a Major Structural Defect occurring in the first year of coverage, repairs will also include correction of items necessary to bring the home into compliance with the Approved Standards.

The unsafe, unsanitary, or otherwise unlivable criteria, under Major Structural Defect is limited only to the repair of plumbing, waste, gas, oil and electric lines, ductwork, heating systems, and other items that affect the health or safety of the occupants of the home, which were damaged by the Major Structural Defect.

Appendix A — Model Codes

Building Codes

- BOCA Basic Building Code, Building Officials & Code Administrators International, Inc.
- National Building Code, American Insurance Association
- Standard Building Code, Southern Building Code Congress
- Uniform Building Code, International Conference of Building Officials
- One and Two Family Dwelling Code, Under the Nationally Recognized Model Codes

Mechanical Codes

- Uniform Building Code, Volume II, Mechanical, International Conference of Building Officials
- BOCA Basic Mechanical Code Building Officials & Code Administrators International, Inc.
- Standard Mechanical Code, Southern Building Code Congress

Plumbing Codes

- Standard Plumbing Code, Southern Building Code Congress
- Uniform Plumbing Code, International Association of Plumbing & Mechanical Officials
- BOCA Basic Plumbing Code, Building Officials & Code Administrators International, Inc.

Electrical Codes

- Electrical Code for One and Two Family Dwelling, National Fire Protection Association
- National Electrical Code, National Fire Protection Association

11.5 LIMITED WARRANTY: HOME WARRANTY AGREEMENT

The following specimen certificate of participitation Home Warranty Insurance Policy is presented as a guide as to what is available for home purchasers by way of insurance of the quality of the property.

The following material has been excerpted from a booklet entitled *Approved Standards*, published by Home Owners, Warranty Corporation and is here reproduced with the permission of the copyright holder.

11.5 LIMITED WARRANTY: HOME WARRANTY AGREEMENT

THIS CERTIFICATE ISSUED PURSUANT TO A HOME WARRANTY AGREEMENT BETWEEN BUILDER AND PURCHASER OF THE HOME DESCRIBED BELOW PROVIDED INSURANCE UNDER MASTER—HOME WARRANTY INSURANCE POLICY NO. 1978 HW OF INA UNDERWRITERS INSURANCE COMPANY, COVERING THE HOME OWNERS WARRANTY CORPORATION, HOME OWNERS REGISTRATION CORPORATION, PARTICIPATING LOCAL COUNCILS AND THE BUILDERS REGISTERED WITH SUCH COUNCILS, ET AL, IN ALL 50 UNITED STATES, TERRITORIES, POSSESSIONS AND THE DISTRICT OF COLUMBIA.

CERTIFICATE OF PARTICIPATION
IN HOME WARRANTY INSURANCE POLICY NO. 1978 HW
ISSUED BY INA UNDERWRITERS
INSURANCE COMPANY
Los Angeles, California

Amount of Insurance Coverage: $ Certificate No.

TO: Builder's Name:

  Address:

ASSIGNED TO:

  Purchaser's Name:

  Address:

MORTGAGEE:

  Name:

  Address:

This certifies with respect to the "Home" situated on the land located and described as (NOTE: Insert address and lot and block number or other legal description of the property sufficient to identify the Home):

purchased by the person(s) whose name(s) and address appear above has been constructed or caused to be constructed by the "Builder", whose name and address appear above and who is registered in the "National Council Register" maintained by the Home Owners Warranty Corporation, a District of Columbia Corporation, that:

(a) upon assignment and delivery of this "Certificate" to the "Purchaser", the warranties contained in the "Home Warranty Agreement" become operative as of the commencement date for the "Initial Warranty Period" which is   provided that the commencement date for common elements, if any, shall be   and,

(b) Purchaser has qualified for "Insurance Coverage" on the Home, not exceeding the Amount of Insurance Coverage shown above, for a period of ten (10) years from such commencement date or dates subject only to the provisions of the Home Warranty Agreement and the Terms and Conditions of this Certificate appearing below. Certified to as of the   day of   19

INA UNDERWRITERS
INSURANCE COMPANY

Bertram C. Stedman
SECRETARY

John C. Minnium
President

Copyright, INA Underwriters Insurance Company 1978

TERMS AND CONDITIONS

I. DEFINITIONS

For purposes of this Certificate, the terms defined in this Article shall have the meaning hereby assigned to them respectively:

A. "Approved Standards"—The building standards adopted by Local Council, with approval of National Council, and in force at commencement of construction of the Home, for the geographic area in which the Home is situate, which standards consist of (1) structural, mechanical and electrical standards and (2) quality standards.

B. "Builder"—The person, corporation or partnership which conveys title to the Home to Purchaser or which, by contract with Purchaser, builds a Home on land of Purchaser.

C. "Certificate"—This Certificate of Participation, including the terms and conditions, which extends to Purchaser the benefits of the Master Policy.

D. "Final Settlement"—The completion of the transaction whereby (a) the Home is irrevocably conveyed by Builder to Purchaser (unless it has been built on land owned by Purchaser, in which case only clause (b) shall apply) and (b) the full proceeds to which Builder is entitled (above any secured deferred portion of the agreed purchase price) are paid to it.

E. "HOME"—Any dwelling unit not previously occupied (except under an agreement granting Purchaser an option to purchase) in which Purchaser receives an ownership or long-term (having a term of at least 50 years) leasehold interest, excluding dwellings constructed solely for lease. The Home DOES include (a) a condominium unit, as defined in the Master Deed for such condominium project (provided, however, that all units in the condominium are eligible for coverage under the Master Policy and Builder has committed itself to make such coverage available for all units), together with (b)(i) only those common elements which comprise the building in which the condominium unit is situate, and which it shares in common with other units in the building and (ii) the plumbing, heating, electrical and cooling systems serving such unit. The Home DOES NOT include permanent out buildings (except, in the case of condominiums, those which house plumbing, heating, electrical or cooling systems serving the unit), swimming pools and other recreational facilities, driveways, walkways, patios, boundary walls, retaining walls not necessary for structural stability of the Home, landscaping, fences, nonpermanent construction materials or off-site improvements.

F. "Initial Warranty Period"—The periods during which the warranties of Builder are in effect, commencing as of the date or dates set forth on page 1 in paragraph (a) of this Certificate.

G. "Insurance Coverage"—The benefits available to Purchaser under the Master Policy subject to the provisions of the Home Warranty Agreement and this Certificate.

H. "Insurer"—INA Underwriters Insurance Company, its successors and assigns.

I. "Local Council"—The organization which has entered into a License Agreement with National Council and is authorized to administer the national home warranty program within the specified geographic area in which the Home is located.

J. "Major Construction Defect"—Actual damage to the load-bearing portion of the Home (including damage due to Soil Movement as defined below) which affects its load-bearing function and which vitally affects or is imminently likely to produce a vital effect on the use of the Home for residential purposes.

K. "Master Policy"—Home Warranty Insurance Policy, Number 1978 HW issued by Insurer to National Council.

L. "National Council"—Home Owners Warranty Corporation, a District of Columbia corporation, its subsidiaries, successors and assigns.

M. "National Council Register"—A register of approved Builders maintained by National Council.

N. "Purchaser"—Any person for whom a Home is built or the first person to whom a Home is sold for occupancy by him or his family as a Home and his successors in title to the Home and/or mortgagee in possession. Purchaser does not mean any development company, associate or subsidiary company of Builder or any person or organization to whom the Home may be sold or otherwise conveyed by Builder for subsequent resale, letting or any purpose other than occupancy as a Home.

O. "Soil Movement"—Subsidence, expansion or lateral movement of the soil (excluding flood and earthquake).

II. THE INSURANCE COVERAGE

A. INITIAL WARRANTY PERIOD. Insurer will, at its sole option, either (i) repair, (ii) replace, or (iii) pay to Purchaser the reasonable cost of such repair or replacement of any warranted defects to the Home arising during the Initial Warranty Period and covered in the Home Warranty Agreement, as determined through conciliation or by an arbitration award, but only if Builder cannot or for any reason does not honor such conciliation or arbitration award; provided that this coverage under the Master Policy shall not include the first $50.00 of the total of claims filed by Purchaser for the first two years following the commencement date.

B. THIRD THROUGH TENTH YEAR. Insurer will, at its sole option, either (i) repair, (ii) replace, or (iii) pay to Purchaser the reasonable cost of such repair or replacement of any Major Construction Defects arising during the period from the third through the tenth year from the beginning date of the Initial Warranty Period, PROVIDED that the Insurance Coverage shall not include:

(i) any claim for a Major Construction Defect unless written notice of such defect shall have been given by Purchaser to Local Council as soon as practicable after such defect in the Home first appears. In any case, the right to file such a claim expires thirty (30) days after the end of the ten year term commencing with the first day of the Initial Warranty Period;

(ii) any claim caused by Soil Movement for which compensation is provided by legislation or which is covered by other insurance;

(iii) any loss or damage which Purchaser, wherever feasible, has not taken timely action to minimize;

(iv) failure of Builder to complete construction or Builder's non-compliance with the Purchase Contract for the Home except with respect to such items, if any, on the Inspection Schedule attached to the Home Warranty Agreement as constitute non-compliance with the Approved Standards; or

(v) loss or damage caused by matters described in paragraphs III B (1) through (14) of the Home Warranty Agreement.

The protection of this Certificate from the third through the tenth year, inclusive, is intended to cover damage due only to Major Construction Defects. Protection during those years does not cover damages due

11.5 LIMITED WARRANTY: HOME WARRANTY AGREEMENT

to minor structural defects or to defects not in the structure such as faulty equipment or finishings, nor will it cover imperfections in structure which may exist but which do not result in substantive actual loss or damage.

C. MORTGAGEE CLAUSE. Notwithstanding paragraphs A. and B. above, where the Insurer shall become responsible to pay the reasonable costs of repair or replacement for Major Construction Defects arising at any time during the 10-year period of protection and amounting to $1000 or more, Insurer shall make such payment to the purchaser and the mortgagee named on page 1 hereof (or successor mortgagees who have notified the Insurer in writing of their security interest in the Home on or prior to the date of payment of the claim) as their respective interests may appear.

A mortgagee shall be fully and completely bound by any conciliation or arbitration between Insurer and Purchaser relating to such Major Construction Defects.

III. MAXIMUM LIABILITY

The aggregate liability under one or more claims covered by this Certificate shall not exceed the amount of Insurance Coverage set forth on page 1 of this Certificate.

IV. HOW A CLAIM IS MADE

A. CLAIMS ARISING DURING THE INITIAL WARRANTY PERIOD.

(1) Purchaser must file a typewritten or legibly written complaint with Builder and seek redress from Builder for the defects claimed.

(2) If Purchaser is not satisfied with Builder's response, he may file with Local Council a written application for conciliation listing the claimed defects on forms provided by Local Council. Such claim shall be accompanied by an inspection deposit of $25.00 — which shall be refunded if Local Council shall find the claim has substantial merit.

(3) Upon such filing, Local Council shall attempt to effect a conciliation with Builder and Purchaser in accordance with procedures established by Local Council.

(4) If Purchaser and Builder cannot reach a conciliation, Local Council shall notify the parties and, upon request by either Purchaser or Builder accompanied by a $75.00 deposit by the requesting party, arrange arbitration as to the existence of the defect or defects claimed and the nature and cost of repair or replacement, which arbitration shall be conducted in accordance with the Expedited Home Construction Arbitration Rules of the American Arbitration Association or through other arbitration rules and procedures adopted by Local Council and approved by National Council as substantially equivalent. The Expedited Home Construction Arbitration Rules may provide for a payment to the American Arbitration Association of $15.00 by any party requesting postponement. All or a portion of the arbitration deposit, and, if not previously refunded, the inspection deposit, shall be refunded to the party initiating arbitration, by the other party, if the arbitrator finds the request for arbitration has substantial merit.

(5) If the arbitrator finds warranted defects in the Home, Builder shall repair or replace, or, at its sole option, pay to Purchaser the cost of repairing or replacing the defects within sixty (60) days following such finding.

(6) If Builder fails to so perform, Local Council through National Council shall arrange for Insurer to make payment under the Master Policy in the amount found by the arbitrator to be necessary to pay the cost of repairing or replacing the defects and to cover the cost of any refund to Purchaser of the arbitration deposit.

(7) Purchaser, as a condition precedent to such payment, shall transfer all his rights hereunder as to such claim against Builder to Insurer. Further, Purchaser shall deliver to Local Council a fully executed release for such claims or rights, if any, against Insurer, Local Council and National Council.

B. CLAIMS ARISING AFTER THE INITIAL WARRANTY PERIOD.

(1) After the Initial Warranty Period, Purchaser must pursue claims through Local Council, not Builder.

(2) Should Purchaser suffer a Major Construction Defect, Purchaser shall, as soon as possible thereafter, file with Local Council, on forms provided by Local Council, a claim fully describing the defect. Such claim shall be accompanied by an inspection deposit of $50.00 which shall be refunded if Local Council finds the claim has substantial merit.

(3) If Local Council finds, by conciliation procedures, all or a portion of the claim to be invalid, and Purchaser is not satisfied with such findings, then upon Purchaser's request accompanied by payment of an arbitration deposit of $75.00 (which amount, together with the inspection deposit if not previously refunded, shall be refunded if the arbitrator shall find the complaint has substantial merit), Local Council shall arrange for arbitration as to the existence of the Major Construction Defect claimed and the nature and cost of repair or replacement which arbitration shall be conducted in accordance with the Expedited Home Construction Arbitration Rules of the American Arbitration Association or through other arbitration rules and procedures adopted by Local Council and approved by National Council as substantially equivalent. Subject to the provisions of paragraph D below, the decision of the arbitrator shall be final and binding upon Purchaser, Insurer, Local Council and National Council.

C. ENFORCEMENT OF CLAIMS.

If for any reason Local Council shall not proceed to obtain for Purchaser payment under the Master Policy sufficient to comply with the decision of the arbitrator, Purchaser shall so notify National Council in writing and if National Council shall not obtain for Purchaser payment under the Master Policy within 30 days of receipt of such notice, the decision of the arbitrator may be submitted to a court of appropriate jurisdiction for enforcement.

D. LIMITATION ON ARBITRATION AWARD.

In no event shall the award of the arbitrator exceed the scope of the remedies specified in Article III hereof.

E. ALTERNATE ARBITRATION PROCEDURES.

(1) Either party to the arbitration of a dispute under the Expedited Home Construction Rules of the American Arbitration Association involving a claim in excess of $10,000 may, prior to commencement of the arbitration proceeding, ask for and obtain an increase in the number of arbitrators to three (3) upon payment (in addition to the $75.00 deposit) of $150.00 which shall not be refundable; or

(2) By mutual written consent of both parties to a dispute and written notice to Local Council, the dispute may be arbitrated pursuant to the Construction Industry Arbitration Rules of the American Arbitration Association. Said rules contain a different fee schedule and procedures and provide for the final apportionment of fees between the parties by the arbitrator or arbitrators in the award.

INSURANCE

V. CONDOMINIUMS
Anything in this Certificate to the contrary notwithstanding, Purchaser may, at his option, file and pursue claims involving condominium Homes either directly on his own account or through a representative designated by the condominium association to file such claims, provided that where the claim involves an element common to more than the subject Home, or a structural deficiency involving more than one Home, the claim may only be made by a representative designated by the condominium association to file such claims.

VI. GENERAL
A. In the event that the performance by Builder, Local Council, National Council or Insurer of any of their obligations or undertakings hereunder shall be interrupted or delayed by any occurrence not occasioned by the conduct of Builder, Local Council, National Council or Insurer, whether such occurrence be an act of God or the common enemy or the result of war, riot, civil commotion, sovereign conduct, or the act or conduct of any person or persons not party or privy hereto, then Builder, Local Council, National Council or Insurer shall be excused from such performance for such period of time as is reasonably necessary after such occurrence to remedy the effects thereof.

B. Should this Certificate be lost, multilated, stolen or destroyed, Local Council shall cause a duplicate Certificate to be issued. All rights and obligations of Purchaser under this Certificate shall be automatically transferred to any subsequent Purchaser upon transfer of title to the Home.

C. All notices hereunder shall be sent by mail, postage prepaid, as follows:

(1) if to Purchaser or Builder, at the respective address for Purchaser or Builder shown on page 1 of this Certificate;
(2) if to Local Council, at the name and address set forth below;
or
(3) if to National Council, at 15th and M Streets, N.W., Washington, D.C. 20005;
or, in each case, at such other address as Purchaser, Builder, Local Council or National Council, as the case may be, may designate in writing.

D. Use of one gender shall include all other genders; use of the singular shall include the plural; and use of the plural shall include the singular; all as may be appropriate.

E. The Master Policy is in the possession of National Council and may be inspected at any time during regular business hours. Facsimilies thereof are in the possession of Local Council and may be inspected by Purchaser at any time during business hours at the office of Local Council appearing below.

F. This agreement shall also include items designated below as endorsements.

VII. ENDORSEMENTS
"Home" shall include two (2) to four (4) family structures provided that at least one of the units in the structure is initially occupied by Purchaser.

"Home" shall include dwelling units which, prior to initial sale, were rented on a temporary basis.

"Builder" shall also include the person, corporation or partnership which builds a Home on land of a third party for subsequent conveyance to Purchaser.

Name and Address of Local Council:

HOW-16 7/78

11.6 EXPERIENCE RATING*

Contractors and others, when their premium level at normal manual rates reaches a practical level (very roughly, $750 policy minimum), become eligible for experience rating; that is, calculation of individual credits or debits applied to manual rates, dependent upon the ratio of premiums to losses over a given number of years. These rating plans vary a good deal with the kind of coverage involved. In principle, they are similar, however; all are closely scrutinized by state insurance departments, intrastate and interstate rating authorities, and independent rating organizations.

Manual rates contemplate a certain average level of losses and, by mathematical formula, a comparision is made of actual losses reported over roughly three years compared with expected levels. Weights or credibility

---

*Articles 11.6, 11.7, 11.8 have been excerpted from *Insurance for Contractors* by Walter T. Derk, published by Fred S. James, 230 West Monroe, Chicago, Ill., 60606 and is reproduced with the permission of the copyright holder.

factors are allowed to minimize the effect of single catastrophe losses so that the small contractor who reports just one serious case does not pay an astronomical premium for eternity. In general, a frequency of claims will count more in experience rating than will severity, but this effect decreases as premium volume increases.

11.7 CERTIFICATES OF INSURANCE ... NO CLERICAL DETAIL

Today's insurance climate suddenly makes the previously humdrum task of requesting and policing certificates of insurance vitally important. No longer can you assume that your subcontractor or supplier has insurance even though the paperwork has been delayed. He may not have coverage at all, either because no one is willing to write it, or because he feels he cannot afford to pay the premium.

While you are most often in the position of providing someone else with a certificate of insurance, it is equally important that you be aware of the need to require certificates from *your* subcontractors and suppliers. Some firms have their own version of the printed form and these require close examination to determine exactly what is provided. Unfortunately, some of these forms seem to raise more questions than they answer. For this reason, don't be shy about asking your insurance representative for his appraisal of both the certificates and the specifications they purport to meet.

In general, you should look to your subcontractors and suppliers for the same coverage and limits required of you under contract specifications. To give you the greatest degree of protection, the existence of Workers' Compensation, Employers' Liability, Comprehensive General Liability, and Comprehensive Automobile Liability policy forms should be verified by certificates issued at your request. All should allow for fifteen or more days' advance written notice of any cancellation or material change affecting coverage. Specific mention should be made of Contractual Liability coverage and Products-Completed Operations Liability coverage, Explosion, Collapse, and Underground Damage, Broad Form Property Damage Liability, etc., where applicable. Despite widespread use of A.I.A. standard general conditions, it is rare to encounter a certificate of insurance which confirms the contractor's full, correct coverage on the initial submittal. The need to correct this duplication of work and needless delay—often delay of the project itself—is obvious; it is always less expensive to do something right the first time.

Most questions stem from missing or inadequate confirmation of:

(1) Contractual liability insurance applicable to the hold-harmless clause in question (always subject to normal policy conditions and exclusions)

(2) Completed operations liability

(3) Personal injury liability, including deletion of the employee exclusion otherwise applicable to that coverage extension

(4) Missing proof of *Owners'/Architects'/Engineers'* Protective *L*iability insurance as may have been specified

(5) Explosion, collapse, or underground damage coverage

(6) Limits of liability insufficient to meet specifications

(7) Notice of cancellation provisions.

Some owners and contractors have inadvertently compounded the problem by preparing their own certificate of insurance forms with required Bodily Injury and Property Damage limits printed or pretyped right on such form when they are submitted for completion. Imagine the confusion, then, when one insurance company is called upon to certify limits of $500/1,000,000 on such a form when it actually covers only $250/500,000, with the contractor carrying a separate $1 million Umbrella Excess layer through another company.

Many insurance companies have now adopted a uniform Accord certificate of insurance form. We endorse its use, but recommend asking for advance notice of cancellation or material change, preferably by certified mail in this day of dubious postal reliability. If refused, the contractor has done all he can by the purchase of insurance, although he may contractually be committed to provide notice of such cancellation.

We strongly urge against including any stipulation to provide notice of *non-renewal*, as well. The certificate-holder can easily maintain a clerical suspense file to ask for a new certificate prior to expiration of the policies shown, whereas putting the burden on insurance companies is totally impractical. Aside from the hundreds of thousands of forms issued by insurance companies and their agents each year, renewal negotiations often continue well beyond the time required for such notification, and the only solution—automatic notice of non-renewal in every case—would be misleading, chaotic and ridiculously expensive to everyone concerned, including the certificate-holder.

Where you require a hold-harmless agreement from a subcontractor or anyone else, proof of insurance applicable to that contract should be furnished by a certificate. Mere mention of a Comprehensive policy form is not sufficient, since there is nothing automatic about the Contractual Liability coverage provided by most such policies. Where any doubt exists about the matter, your insurance representative should be consulted and the certificates sent on to him for examination and comment.

There is no point in requiring that the indemnification clause be typed on the insurance company's certificate form; their rules generally prohibit doing so because the insurance company is not a party to your contract with an owner or general contractor. They can only attest to the existence of insurance covering bodily injury (or personal injury) and property damage legal liability arising out of an occurence, as defined, subject to all the terms, conditions, definitions, exclusions and limitations inherent in all liability policies. To require more is an exercise in futility.

Complying with these recommendations is vital to good business practice. If your insurance carrier has to come in and defend or pay a claim caused by your subcontractor or supplier, that cost will be reflected in your future premiums. Workers' Compensation laws make you liable for payment of statutory benefits to an injured employee of an independent contractor who carries no insurance, therefore such payroll will be included in your premium audit. Acceptance of your own risk by underwriters is predicated upon the assumption that you will secure such certificates routinely.

11.8 COVERAGE CHECK LIST

Without implying that any contractor, large or small, should necessarily buy all of the following basic coverages and optional extensions or that doing so will guarantee a good insurance program, we list here most of what is commonly available as a checklist. You or your insurance representative shold periodically examine current and renewal policies to determine which of these are presently insured, how much additional premium needed extensions would cost, and which, if any, to buy:

General Liability

- ☐ 1. Comprehensive Policy Form
- ☐ 2. Contractual Liability—Blanket Broad-Form Coverage
- ☐ 3. Deletion of Selected Contractual Liability Exclusions
- ☐ 4. Completed Operations—Products Liability Coverage
- ☐ 5. Vendor's Liability Protection Via Manufacturers' Policies
- ☐ 6. Limits of Liability Consistent With Automobile Policy

156 INSURANCE

☐ 7. Host Liquor Liability Coverage

☐ 8. Additional Insureds—Employees

☐ 9. Additional Insureds—Lessors, Trusts Including Beneficiaries

☐ 10. Employee Benefit Liability Coverage

☐ 11. Personal Injury Liability Coverage Including Employees' Claims

☐ 12. Fire Legal Liability Coverage Or Waiver Of Subrogation For Leased Premises

☐ 13. Property Damage Liability Coverage—Explosion, Collapse, Or Underground Damage

☐ 14. Broad Form Property Damage Liability Coverage

☐ 15. Owned Or Non-Owned Watercraft Liability Coverage

☐ 16. Owned Or Non-Owned Aircraft Liability Coverage

☐ 17. World Wide Coverage

☐ 18. Joint Venture Coverage

☐ 19. Adequate Notice Of Cancellation

Automobile Liability

☐ 1. Comprehensive Policy Form

☐ 2. Medical Payments Coverage

☐ 3. Uninsured Motorists Coverage

☐ 4. Use Of Other Automobiles Coverage—Broad Form/Limited Form

☐ 5. No-Fault Benefits

☐ 6. Non-Ownership Liability—Partnerships

☐ 7. Limits Of Liability Consistent With General Liability Policy

☐ 8. Complete And Accurate Schedule of Vehicles

☐ 9. Foreign Auto Coverage
☐ 10. Joint Venture Coverage
☐ 11. Adequate Notice Of Cancellation

Automobile Physical Damage

☐ 1. Fleet Automatic Coverage
☐ 2. Fire
☐ 3. Theft
☐ 4. Combined Additional Coverage
☐ 5. Malicious Mischief And Vandalism
☐ 6. Comprehensive Coverage
☐ 7. Collision
☐ 8. Towing
☐ 9. Foreign Coverage, If Required
☐ 10. Leased Equipment Coverage, Avoidance Of Duplication With Lessor
☐ 11. Complete And Accurate Schedule Of Vehicles, Values
☐ 12. Adequate Notice Of Cancellation

Workmen's Compensation and Employers' Liability

☐ 1. Increased Limits—Employers' Liability
☐ 2. All States Endorsement—Broad Form
☐ 3. Separate Coverage As Required In Monopolistic Fund States
☐ 4. Status Of Executive Officers Or Partners
☐ 5. Longshoremen's And Harbor Workers', Jones Act, Or Federal Employers' Liability Coverage
☐ 6. Additional Medical Coverage Endorsement

☐ 7. Voluntary Compensation Coverage Endorsement

☐ 8. Status Of Domestic Employees Sent Outside The U.S.A.

☐ 9. Foreign Coverage

☐ 10. Foreign Voluntary Compensation Excess Of Benefits Paid Locally

☐ 11. Repatriation Expense Coverage

☐ 12. D. C. Benefits, Maryland And Virginia Employees

☐ 13. Joint Venture Coverage

☐ 14. Adequate Notice Of Cancellation

Umbrella Excess Liability

☐ 1. Accurate Schedule Of Underlying Primary Policies

☐ 2. Underlying Policy Limit Requirements

☐ 3. Employee Benefit Liability Coverage

☐ 4. Status Of Following-Form Excess Limitations:
   (a) "Care, Custody, Or Control" Property Damage
   (b) Contractual Liability
   (c) Explosion, Collapse, Underground Property Damage
   (d) Other

☐ 5. Fire Legal Liability Coverage

☐ 6. Aircraft, Watercraft Liability

☐ 7. Primary Defense Coverage Not Provided By Underlying Policies

☐ 8. World Wide Coverage

☐ 9. Joint Venture Coverage

☐ 10. Adequate Notice Of Cancellation

Material, Equipment, And/Or Installation Floaters

- [ ] 1. "All-Risk" Perils
- [ ] 2. On Premises Coverage
- [ ] 3. Material In Transit
- [ ] 4. On Job Site Coverage
- [ ] 5. Rented Equipment
- [ ] 6. Deductible Features
- [ ] 7. Report Of Insurance Values Requirements

Builder's Risk Insurance

- [ ] 1. Responsibilities Of Contractor To Provide
- [ ] 2. "All-Risk" Versus Specified Perils
- [ ] 3. Deductible Features, Responsibilities

Directors' & Officers' Liability

- [ ] 1. Investigation Of Availability, Practicality

General

- [ ] 1. Complete And Accurate List Of Entities To Be Insured
- [ ] 2. Up-To-Date List Of Locations Covered

REVIEW QUESTIONS

1. Define mandatory insurance.
2. What is an endorsement rider?
3. Define underwriter.
4. What are the duties of an insurance underwriter?
5. Define Homeowners Warranty (HOW) Agreement.
6. Define experience rating.

12 ARBITRATION

12.1 ARBITRATION

In Britain and the United States, arbitration has been, for many years, an accepted means of settling a wide range of disputes. The procedure has been in use in Britain since the seventeenth century. In the United States, the American Arbitration Association now handles over 50,000 cases annually. In Canada there are a number of "chapters" (see page 166). Many countries are signatories to the United Nations New York Convention of 1958.

The following booklets and publications may be obtained from the American Arbitration Association, 140 West 51st Street, New York, N.Y., 10020:

a) *Expedited Home Construction Arbitration Rules*
b) *A Manual for Home Construction Arbitration Rules*
c) *Construction Industry Mediation Rules*

State and provincial governments can provide (at nominal cost) copies of the Arbitration Act.

The American Arbitration Association is a public-service, nonprofit, nongovernmental organization, dedicated to the resolution of disputes of all kinds through the use of arbitration, mediation, conciliation, democratic elections, and other voluntary methods. Membership in the Association is open to all individuals and organizations interested in voluntary arbitration.

12.2   MEDIATION CLAUSE

Parties may refer to construction industry mediation rules in their contract:

> If a dispute arises out of, or relating to, this contract, or a breach thereof, and if some dispute cannot be settled through direct discussions, the parties may agree to first endeavor to settle the dispute in an amicable manner by mediation under Voluntary Construction Mediation Rules of the American Arbitration Association, before having recourse to arbitration or a judicial forum.

12.3   CONCILIATION

The word "conciliation" means "to render accord (by a third unbiased party)," or "to reconcile differences between contesting parties without recourse to arbitration or a judicial forum."

12.4   AMERICAN ARBITRATION ASSOCIATION

The following material has been excerpted from literature supplied by the American Arbitration Association, and is reproduced here with permission.

12.4 AMERICAN ARBITRATION ASSOCIATION

THERE is a legal alternative for resolving disputes without going to court—it is called **arbitration**—and there is a national organization that specializes in this process.

The **American Arbitration Association** is a not-for-profit, public service organization that provides private dispute settlement services. These services include the administration of arbitration, mediation, elections, and other voluntary methods of conflict resolution. The AAA also conducts research to improve and expand these processes; sponsors educational programs to encourage their use; and issues publications to disseminate information about them.

The Association was established in New York City in 1926 by leaders of the financial, business, and legal communities. Today, the AAA offers its services through 24 regional offices throughout the country, and more than 50,000 persons serve as impartial arbitrators.

Every year, the AAA administers thousands of disputes. These conflicts involve insurance claims, business matters (including international trade), construction problems, disputes in the textile and apparel industries, labor-management relations, medical malpractice, community relations, the environment, fair campaign practices, and other areas of conflict.

From the time a disagreement arises, voluntary dispute-resolution processes can be applied to resolve the difficulty. These processes can prevent labor strife, lessen hostility in the community, preserve business relationships, alleviate court congestion, and provide relief to the taxpayer.

Arbitration

AND OTHER SYSTEMS OF DISPUTE SETTLEMENT

Arbitration is the submission of a dispute by two or more parties to an impartial third party, who, by prior agreement, makes a decision that is legally binding and enforceable. Some of the benefits of arbitration are
- Choice of independent arbitrators
- Specialized expertise of arbitrators
- Impartial forums
- Low cost
- Privacy
- Custom-made procedures
- Expeditious proceedings
- Finality of awards.

Arbitration offers disputing parties an alternative to the court system. For more than fifty years, the AAA has helped parties resolve their differences out of court by providing assistance to parties at every step of the settlement process.

The AAA does not decide cases, but supplies the independent arbitrators who do. It also furnishes full administrative services at reasonable fees. Each case is arbitrated under specific rules and procedures and its processing is planned to proceed smoothly from initiation to final settlement. Normally, one administrator will be assigned to a case and see it through.

As its name suggests, arbitration is the chief method used by the AAA for the voluntary final settlement of disputes, but fact-finding, conciliation, and mediation are also employed, either separately or in conjunction with the arbitration process itself.

The AAA's trained staff is readily available to provide technical assistance and resource information on arbitration procedures and other dispute-settlement systems. The AAA staff will also consult and assist in the design of dispute resolution procedures for particular groups, organizations, or industries.

Election Services

The AAA provides impartial administration of elections, including balloting for officers, boards of directors, and delegates; contract ratifications, referendums, and representation issues; and stockholder proxy counts. Among organizations using these election services are
- Labor unions
- Corporations
- Trade associations
  - Savings and loan associations
  - Community groups
    - Teacher organizations.

Experts will assist you in designing specific election procedures to suit your organization's needs. Voting is conducted by mail or at polling sites; results are tabulated manually or by computer. Above all, the impartiality and the secrecy of an election are maintained.

Education AND Training

The Department of Education and Training conducts workshops, seminars, and conferences throughout the country. Developments in case law, recent court decisions, and new techniques are emphasized. It offers skill-building programs for those industries and groups that rely heavily on arbitration. Some of the seminars and workshops covered in these areas are
- Labor-management relations (both public and private)
- Business
- Construction
  - Uninsured motorist and no-fault insurance
    - International trade
      - Medical malpractice.

In addition, the AAA will plan and develop in-house training programs upon request.

The Arbitration Clause

Arbitration is voluntary and depends upon the agreement of the parties to arbitrate. An arbitration clause in a contract will expedite settlement discussions. Millions of contracts now call for arbitration of controversies. The AAA has developed a standard arbitration clause that can easily be inserted in a commercial contract:

> Any controversy or claim arising out of or relating to this contract, or the breach thereof, shall be settled by arbitration in accordance with the Rules of the American Arbitration Association, and judgment upon the award rendered by the Arbitrator(s) may be entered in any Court having jurisdiction thereof.

When this wording is found to be appropriate, it is not necessary to apply to the AAA for permission to use this clause.

The Submission Agreement

If the contract does not contain an arbitration clause, it is still possible to arbitrate under AAA administration if both parties agree.

Collective Bargaining Agreements

In collective bargaining contracts, the parties may obtain the benefits of administered arbitration by referring to the Voluntary or the Expedited Labor Arbitration Rules of the American Arbitration Association, or by otherwise authorizing the Association to act in connection with unresolved grievances.

Publications

Among the periodicals that are available to AAA members or subscribers are
- A journal containing authoritative articles on arbitration
- A quarterly report to lawyers on major issues in arbitration law
- A review of court decisions involving arbitration
- Three award-reporting services that summarize decisions in private industry, in schools, and in government, and a fourth that summarizes no-fault insurance awards.

The AAA also publishes bulletins, books, and specialized pamphlets on arbitration practice and on other forms of dispute settlement. In addition, films on labor arbitration and mediation in the private and public sectors are available.

AAA Membership

Corporations, unions, law firms, trade and educational associations, academic institutions, governmental agencies, organizations of all kinds, and individuals who are interested in voluntary dispute settlement may join the AAA as contributing members. Members are informed about the latest developments in private dispute settlement. They have ready access to AAA's Eastman Arbitration Library in New York City and to collections at regional offices throughout the country. Individualized service at research facilities in New York is provided. Members also receive selected AAA publications as a result of their membership and special rates on all AAA publications and educational programs. Membership dues and contributions help support and develop AAA's research, library, publication, and educational activities. Contributions are tax deductible. It is, of course, not necessary to be a contributing member of the AAA to bring a case to arbitration.

RETURN TO: American Arbitration Association
140 West 51st Street
New York, New York 10020

or

The AAA regional office nearest to you (see back panel)

Please send me more information about the American Arbitration Association and its services.

Arbitration Procedures & Rules: ☐ Accident Claims ☐ Commercial ☐ Construction ☐ Labor
☐ International ☐ Community ☐ Other_____

☐ Election Services ☐ Publications & Films ☐ Training Programs (specify type)_____
☐ AAA Membership Information ☐ Annual Report

PLEASE PRINT OR TYPE

Name_____ Title_____

Organization_____ Telephone_____

Address_____

City/State_____ Zip Code_____

12.5 THE ARBITRATORS' INSTITUTE OF CANADA

The following material has been excerpted from the Canadian Arbitration Journal, a publication of the Arbitrators Institute of Canada, whose function is comparable to that of the American Arbitration Association.

II.

THE ROLE OF ARBITRTION TO RESOLVE AN IMPASSE IN NEGOTIATION OF SUBSTANTIVE TERMS

During the negotiation of the substantive terms of a contract, the parties attempt to define the details of the contract in order to regulate their relationship with a great deal of predictability. Predictability, however, becomes increasingly more difficult in long-term agreements due to changes arising from developing technology, the dynamic circumstances of the market or an alteration in the situation of the parties. Further, contracts very often extend beyond national boundaries; a political atmosphere and changing economic conditions can greatly affect the ability of the parties to comply with their responsibilities or to exercise rights under the agreement. Negotiating an agreement, therefore, under these conditions is almost similar to negotiating an agreement about the weather.

The terms of the contract very often are simply impossible to make precise. Arbitration will allow the parties to create a mutually beneficial contract for the present, leaving it to arbitration to deal with the various elements of unpredictability. For instance, the party who owns a patent can enter into long-term licencing agreement, leaving it to arbitration as to how the royalties would be measured after a certain period of time or on the occurence of a certain event. Arbitration offers an element of flexibility. It permits the parties to be put in a state of continuing negotiation, and with an assurance that, in case of an unforeseen impasse, and objective and impartial solution would be found.

It should also be noted that at negotiation the parties are more willing to give-and-take; once the contract is made, this relationship has the tendency to become permanent, indeed hardening into a non-negotiable right or duty. A concession given by one party and received by the other at the time of negotiation invites a psychological condemnation of being a loser for one party and of over-confidence of being a winner, for the other. Conceptually, however, a long term relationship cannot and should not always be taken as definitive. Contractual relationships respecting these properties, like a long-term relationship called marriage, must not create winners or losers.

Aside from the scope of the contract, the compensation that is payable, the life of the contract, the accounting practice in the calculation of com-

12.5 THE ARBITRATOR'S INSTITUTE OF CANADA   167

pensation, sharing in development cost, distribution arrangement, and so. on, can be left to arbitration so that the consensus on fundamentals would not be frustrated by a failure to reach precise positions on these variable terms. If the parties find it worthwhile to establish a long-term collaboration by entering into a long-term contract, then their natural expectation that commercial benefit will result from this collaboration should be adequate to establish such collaboration. Arbitration provides a guarantee that good-faith dealing and fair resolution will preclude disaster or undue advantage to either party. An added bonus to this obvious advantage offered by arbitration is the fact that the resolution of the impasse is ultimately reached through an amicable device, thus preserving mutual confidence and an undeteriorated relationship.

The appeal of arbitration as a technique in negotiation is especially noticeable in cases of problems arising through changing circumstances, and particularly by the emergence during the life of an agreement of non-negotiated issues. In an ordinary contract case, an unforeseen circumstance could enable one party to termine the contract on the ground that its purpose had been frustrated. The rules respecting the doctrine of frustration, however, are so stringent that they create simply a one-way street remedy, namely, the avoidance of the agreement. For this reason, they do not offer the possibility of restoring the harmonious collaboration of the parties that existed before the occurence of the circumstance. Gross inequities brought about by government action or by unexpected events need not require as a response an irreversible avoidance of the contract and thus terminate the working relationship of the parties. Arbitration can be invoked to redress such inequities. Thus, unforeseen developments need not create an impasse at negotiation, and need not create a fear of financial ruin.

The parties can be confident that non-negotiated issues can emerge during the life of the contract without disruptive effect if arbitration is a feature of the agreement and the arbitration is given wide terms of reference. If issues arise during the life of the contract on which the parties must take different positions, the pressure on them is less overpowering since at that later time the parties would be better informed to deal with them than at the time of contracting. In dealing with them at this later time, the atmosphere will likely be analogous to, if not better than, the atmosphere at the time of negotiation. The device provided by arbitration will, in these cases, remedy human shortcomings that are inherent in the performance, of long-term and complex contracts and which are sought to be anticipated at the time of negotiation. Contracts respecting these rights simply go beyond the natural capacity of lawyers and the parties to anticipate the vicissitudes that can befall such rights and the parties. Arbitration is a suitable escape from a pressure to take a position at the time of contracting when the parties and their lawyers are unaware of the future factors that will affect the present business decision. In brief, "the use of an arbitration clause in negotiation to provide a present agreement to resolve unsettled or unsettable issues is means for securing substancial agreement of the parties without the common misapprehension that attaches to long or complex agreements and to provide that the substancial agreement can be effectuated regardless of changing conditions. In this respect, the negotiation stage is related to the resolution of unforeseeable questions or disputes over changed circumstances during the life of the agreement." [2]

III.

THE ROLE OF ARBITRATION TO RESOLVE AN IMPASSE IN DRAFTING THE AGREEMENT

The drafting of an agreement is simply the translation into a written document the terms of a bargain to which the parties have in fact agreed. In most cases, the drafting of an agreement is a simple matter and can be expressed in general terms. In an ordinary contract, the unique practice, custom and language of commerce involved in the transaction often complete or supplement the terms of the agreement. In the drafting of agreements that have interprovincial or transnational reach, on the other hand, the language, custom and practice relevant to the transaction can vary from place to place. For this reason, conflicting usages often preclude completing the agreement. The terms of the agreement are, as a rule of contract law in the Anglo-American legal system, conclusive. The drafting of the agreement by the lawyers of the parties often take the form of negotiation after the negotiation. The choice of specific terminologies can narrow or broaden a right or obligation beyond what the parties themselves have truly understood. The cast of the sentence, the form of a proviso, and the general structure of the agreement itself may create a contractual order that the courts, upon litigation, can impose. Since the lawyers in these cases are drafting an agreement, not so much that the position of their client would be sustained by a court, but rather so that the parties will avoid going to court, prediction and specificity of language is their goal in drafting. As earlier stated, however, predictability is not always easy to attain. More importantly, language has its own limitations that descriptive precision of the bargain is just as unattainable in the drafting of the agreement.

It is therefore inevitable that during the negotiation of language an impasse between lawyers and, ultimately, the parties, occurs in the drafting of the agreement. It is, of course, folly to permit linguistic limitations, unpredictability and inflexibility to make an end of a meticulously negotiated bargain. A resort to arbitration can terminate the impasse. It only remains for the parties to articulate the general objective or substance of a certain term, and leave it to arbitration to compensate for the inadequacies created by language, unpredictability and inflexibility. In this manner, a general formula, coupled with arbitration, becomes a built-in-mechanism for adjustment.

The merit of resorting to arbitration in such cases is strengthened by the fact that at a certain point an attempt at precision can be counterproductive. Complex, abstract and contingent factors can only be articulated by complex, hypothetical and heavily qualified clauses. Such clauses can work, not so much as instruments of conflict avoidance, but as sources of conflict.

IV.

THE ROLE OF ARBITRATION AS A SUBSTITUTE TO COURT LITIGATION

The ongoing relationship of the parties may be a reason for the choice of arbitration. This is obvious in employer-employee relationships, where grievance arbitration and bargaining arbitration have become institutionalized.

In many matters of contract, merely because the parties have a disagreement does not require them to be at war with each other. There is a need for ongoing relationship. The parties are not opposed in any sense; they enter into a joint venture for mutual economic benefit. For this reason, the maintenance of trust and good business dealings is similar to that which exists in an employer-employee relationship. Accordingly, the combative atmosphere of court litigation and the coercive finality of a court decision often are unsuitable to the establishment of joint, cooperative ventures.

The adversary process in court litigation tends to force the parties to view the result as a matter of victory and loss by the disputing parties. In both the psychological and sociological aspects of the controversy, court litigation makes both parties losers in that a commercially profitable, ongoing business venture is conclusively condemned.[3]

If the contract has transnational character, it is often difficult to remove national bias. The moral authority of the arbitration is almost always acceptable to the parties; such moral authority is necessarily doubtful in Court because of the national bias of the Court. I believe that a perceived National bias has significantly impeded industrial cooperation between an industrialized country, on the one hand, and a developing country, on the other, and even between two developed countries. The perceived national bias encumbers the ability of the courts to dispense that concept of justice that the parties expect.

In any event, the uniquely national character of the proceeding creates apprehension on the non-national party. The foreign language, the strange customs, the peculiar procedure, the stigma of mystery of the court—all these combine to create the belief that the parties are litigating on unequal terms. Sanders stressed these factors as follows:

> "A party may be reluctant to bring his case regardless of how strongly he is convinced of his own rights—before the judge in a faraway country whose rules of procedure are different from those prevailing in his own country. Doubts may also arise whether the

judge, to whom he is a foreigner, may be inclined to turn the scale to the other side, his compatriot. More important however is that not only are the rules of procedure prevailing in the foreign court unfamiliar to the foreign claimant, but so is the substantive law of that country. Of course, the choice of law in the contract itself could oblige the foreign judge to apply the national law of the claiment but—as observed from experience—the judge may be very much inclined to apply his own national law, that he knows best of all, the moment he sees the slightest ground for doing so. The claimant in a court proceeding finds himself then in a foreign court whose rules of procedure may differ substantially from the rules prevailing in court proceedings in his own country where he may be confronted with the application of a foreign national law, also unknown to him." [4]

NEW YORK CONVENTION, 1958

I'd like to turn to, perhaps, an unrelated matter, and that is to the matter of enforcement. As most of you know, the New York Convention of 1958 has been adhered to by most industrial nations. Canada has not adhered to the New York Convention and here we have a case where the Federal authorities pass the ball to the Provincial authorities and the Provincial authorities pass it back to the Federal authorities. It sounds very much like the law of law, "the tennis ball keeps going across the net." But in any event, the fact of the matter is that the New York Convention has not been implemented by legislation in this country. Now what does that mean? In my view, that inhibits the work that you are seeking to achieve because there is doubt in the minds of businessmen outside of this country as to whether or not the arbitral award will be enforced within the Canadian jurisdiction. Now it is true that there is great resort to arbitration today by non-Canadian nationals both in the American Arbitration Association, and I believe here, but there is still the area of doubt as to enforceability. The implementation of the New York Convention would remove that doubt and I urge this group to continue the work that it has started in that direction.

The freedom of the parties to choose an arbitration tribunal clothed with an expertise on the subject matter of the controversy is a feature that the parties cannot always find in case of court litigation.

A judge is often unaware of the businessman's position and the technical intricacies of the subject matter. A judge sitting on the bench has no knowledge or background in such matters, and, at the trial, has to be schooled into this sophisticated art through a cumbersome and expensive divice of examination and cross-examination of expert witnesses. Indeed, even the presence of an expert witness is somewhat neutralized by the formal court procedure and the lack of the same communication wave length with the judge. [5] Expertise creates trust and confidence. One author, Pearson, has obvserved:

12.5 THE ARBITRATOR'S INSTITUTE OF CANADA

"People trust Judges to be uncorrupt and very intelligent and perfectly fair. But that is not the same as being confident in their decision. If the dispute arises from a textile trade transaction and the Judge has to have all the trade terminology explained to him, the businessman whose money is at stake is apt to feel 'If there was someone I could trust who really knew the trade, I'd rather have his decision than be judged by this learned man who is taking his first lesson in textiles.' This is where the Chambers of Commerce and Trade Associations do a most useful job in setting up panels of arbitrators who really can be trusted and are trusted, even by losers."[6]

Arbitration introduces into the tribunal not only men who have skills, but also a relevant business sense and expertise. This tribunal would not only find it less difficult to deal with a complex question respecting these matters but also to articulate a solution that is responsive to the controversy.

Expertise can expedite the resolution of the controversy, thus avoiding the unduly long delay that is endemic to courts. It is, of course, true that often one party does not want speed in the resolution of the dispute.[7] For reasons only known to him, he will put stumbling blocks in the way of a decision. In such a situation, I am convinced that an arbitration tribunal has at its disposal available tools to facilitate the conclusion of the controversy. It must also be pointed out that party-inspired delays can be encouraged by the very nature of a court proceeding and the adversary nature of litigation. The proceedings in court are encumbered by formality, rules of evidence that have been devised for a jury that does not always have the capacity to discriminate between the probative value of various species of evidence and by interlocutory motions before the trial of the case.

An arbitration tribunal is clearly insulated from these deficiencies. More importantly, the arbitration tribunal is not operating under a backlog that plagues the courts.

Arbitration offers also to the parties the resolution of a controversy that does not entail an impairment of the reputation of a party. Secrecy of privacy of arbitration offers to the parties the possibility of resolving their disputes between themselves without, so to say, "washing their linens in public." Arbitration is characterized by confidentiality, and this confidentiality of proceedings is sometimes worth to the parties more than winning a case in court. Lazarus describes the dispute between the owner of a refinery and the contractor when the foundations and sections of a wall of refinery building were cracked.

"The privacy of the proceedings was worth more than winning the award to the cement company. Even though its product had been upheld as perfect in content, the company would have suffered badly if a long damage suit were tried in the courts and if the public had read only one side of the story. In addition, the building was done in an area where millions of dollars worth of contracts for cement work were annually let by the state government. Privacy also prevented the problem from becoming a subject for political accusations."[8]

It should also be noted that the arsenal of remedies traditionally available to a court in contract litigation are sometimes characterized by overkill or underkill, and therefore unresponsive to the requirements and interest of the parties. The objective of the judicial proceeding is primarily, if not exclusively, a search for remedial measure rather than a means of conflict resolution. This makes the parties perpetual antagonists because of the winner-take-all nature of the solution. The court may award damages, recession and a specific performance, as developed by the traditional contract law principles. These conventional remedies often follow a falling out of the parties rather than one which would prevent such falling out. Arbitration, on the other hand, offers the possibility to the parties of ironing out their dispute before reaching such a critical point in their relationship. An arbitration award can, in other words, take the form of a declatory judgement so that the parties can have a conflict resolution before breach rather than a conflict resolution following the breach of a contract.[9]

These various considerations show that the courts are not necessarily designed to umpire all the problems of businessmen. While it is true that the idea of remedy is to place the aggrieved party in the same position as he would be were there no breach, more often than not an award of damages may be a very pale substitute for an effective, continuing relationship.[10]

V.
CONCLUSION

The advantages of arbitration, compared with other methods of resolving disputers are numerous. Its role as a machinery to facilitate agreements on substantive terms of a contract, to draft the wording of the contract and to adjust the contract to changing circumstances has not been fully utilized. I hope that businessmen and lawyers are made more aware of this role of arbitration.

NOTES:

1. 108 Forbes Magazine at 21-23, July 1, 1971, quoted in Holtzmann, Arbitration Clauses—Valuable Methods for Solving Business Problems Arising in Long-Term Business Arrangements: An Overview, (1973) The Business Lawyer 585, at 588.

2. Aksen, Legal Considerations in Using Arbitration Clauses to Resolve Future Problems Which May Arise During Long Term Business Agreements, (1973) The Business Lawyer 595, at 539-600.

3. See Carlston, Psychological and Sociological Aspects of Judicial and Arbitration Process, in International Arbitration, Liber Amicorum for Martin Domke at 44 (Sanders ed. 1967).

12.5 THE ARBITRATOR'S INSTITUTE OF CANADA

4. International Commercial Arbitration, 20 Neths. Int. L.R. 37 quoted in O'Keefe, Arbitration in International Trade at 247-248.

5. "(The judge) is merely a lawman and he does not know how business is carried on. It has got to be explained to him how it is done. I remember in 'tejimandi' contracts it took days and days to explain to an English judge the modus operandi while a businessman would know it within minutes, what is 'tejimandi'." Merchant, The Role of Commercial Arbitration, Proceedings of the Training Course on Commercial Arbitration, quoted in O'Keefe, supra at 25.

6. See Pearson, Arbitration and the Business Man, in International Arbitration, Liber Amicorum for Martin Domke 208, at 211 (Ed. Sanders 1967).

7. See Pearson, Arbitration and the Business Man, in International Arbitration, Liber Amicorum for Martin Domke at 208 (Ed. Sanders 1967).

8. O'Keefe, Arbitration in International Trade 27 (1975).

9. Aksen, Legal Consideration in Using Arbitration Clauses to Resolve Future Problems Which May Arise During Long-Term Business Agreements, (1973) The Business Lawyer 595, at 601.

10. Id. at 597.

REVIEW QUESTIONS

1. What advantage does arbitration offer to contending parties, other than resorting to a judicial forum?
2. What advantage is provided by including a mediation clause in a building contract?
3. List seven advantages of submitting a dispute to arbitration instead of a judicial court of law.
4. What is the address of the American Arbitration Association regional office nearest you?
5. What is the address of the Arbitrators' Institute of Canada nearest you?

APPENDIX A
GLOSSARY OF LEGAL TERMS*

Abandonment: To release claim or forfeit rights—as in the case of a homestead.

Abeyance: Pending or temporarily suspended. Such as an action held in abeyance.

Abstract of judgment: Record of a court's judgment. Creates lien when recorded.

Abstract of title: A digest or summary of documents or records affecting title to property.

Acceleration clause. Provision sometimes inserted in a mortgage or trust deed note causing it to become payable at once, in a lump sum under certain conditions—such as in event property is sold, leased or payments not paid promptly.

Acceptance: Giving consent to an offer—as when seller signs an offer to purchase.

Accession: Acquiring title to unauthorized improvements to your land.

Accommodation paper: An act of trying to help a friend by cosigning his note at a finance company or bank.

---

*This glossary has been excerpted from *Practical Advice for Builders and Contractors*, by Edward E. Colby (Englewood Cliffs, N.J.: Prentice-Hall, Inc.) and is here reproduced with the permission of the copyright holder.

Accretion: Addition to your land as by deposits from a stream or lake.

Acknowledgment: A formal declaration before a notary public or other qualified officer, in signing a document, that it is your voluntary act.

Acquisition: The process by which property is procured—through purchase, inheritance, gift, foreclosure, etc.

Acre: An area of land containing 43,560 feet.

Act of God: A disaster inflicted by nature such as an earthquake, unusual flood, tornado, or hurricane. Sometimes a valid legal excuse for not performing a building contract.

Action to quiet title: A lawsuit to determine status of title to land. Often to remove a defect or cloud on the title.

Actual notice: Notice given by open possession and occupancy of property.

Administrator: A man appointed by a court to take charge of an estate of a deceased person who left no will. If a lady were appointed, she would be called the administratrix.

Adult: A person who has reached an age established by law to attain certain privileges, such as the right to vote, to enter into binding contracts, etc. Those persons of lesser age are minors.

Ad valorem: Based upon the value—property taxes for example.

Adverse possession: Openly holding possession of land under some claim of right which is opposed to the claim of another.

Affiant: One who makes a sworn statment, such as an affidavit.

Affidavit: A sworn statement in writing before an officer authorized to administer oaths.

Affirmation: A solemn declaration—usually by one opposed to oaths on religious grounds.

Agency: Act of representing a principal in the capacity of an agent.

Agent: One who is authorized to represent another person, as in a real estate transaction.

Agreement of sale: A written contract whereby buyer and seller agree on terms of the sale.

Alias: An assumed name.

Alien: A resident who is a citizen of a foreign country.

Alienate: Act of transferring title to property.

Alienation clause: Provision in a mortgage or trust deed providing for full payment if the property is sold.

Alluvium: Deposit of soil on or adjoining property, as by flow of a river or stream, or by tides.

American Stock Exchange: The second largest stock exchange in the United States. Their requirements are not as rigid as the New York Stock Exchange.

Amortize: Pay off debt in installments; or gradual recovery of an investment.

Annexation: Adding land to another unit, such as bringing a tract within the limits of a city.

Annuity: Money paid annually or in other agreed periods.

Anticipatory breach: An announced violation of contract that permits a lawsuit before the completion date of the contract.

Appraisal: An opinion as to value based upon facts and experience, by one skilled in such work.

Appurtenance: A thing or right which attaches to or becomes incident to the land, so as to become a part of the realty. A house, fence, etc. which, when the land is conveyed, goes with it without special mention in the deed.

Arbitration: A substitute for court proceedings to settle disputes between parties to a contract.

Architect: A professionally trained person who plans buildings and sometimes is employed to oversee their construction.

Assessed value: Value placed on property by the assessor as basis for the levy of taxes.

Assessment (special): Levy against particular properties for cost of improvements which particularly benefit them. (Sewers, sidewalks, drains, etc.)

Assessor: An official, usually county or city, who determines the value of property for tax purposes.

Assign: To endose over to another, such as a promissory note or lease.

Assignee: One to whom property or a right is transferred.

Assignor: One who assigns or transfers a property or right to another.

Assumption of mortgage or trust deed: Taking title to property and assuming personal liability for payment of existing notes for which the property is security.

Attachment: Seizure of property by court order in connection with a pending lawsuit.

Attorney in fact: A person to whom a power of attorney is given authorizing him to do all or specific acts for another.

Attractive nuisance doctrine: A theory of law that anything that attracts children and the child is injured does not require proof of negligence. It used to be the ice man and now could be a construction project.

Authorization to sell: Commonly called a listing by real estate brokers.

Authorized capital stock: The amount of common stock specified in the articles of incorporation.

Avulsion: Sudden removal of land by flowing water.

Award: The decision of the arbitrators. The same as a judge's ruling.

Balloon payment: Usually an extra large payment on an installment note at the time it is payable in full.

Bankruptcy: A federal court legal proceeding to aid those who are unable to pay their obligations when they fall due.

Bankruptcy petition: The required form to be filled out and filed in federal bankruptcy court by those who seek relief from financial problems.

Base and meridian: Principal survey lines in an area from which townships are numbered.

Bench mark: Permanent marker placed by surveyors at an important point, upon which local surveys are based.

Beneficiary: One who is a recipient of benefits from a trust, such as a lender of money secured by a trust deed.

Bequeath: To leave property by will.

Bequest: What is bequeathed by will—an inheritance.

Bid: An offer by a contractor to build a certain structure for a fixed price.

Bilateral contract: A contract by which both parties agree to perform certain acts.

Bill of sale: Signed document which transfers ownership of personal property.

Bills of lading: Paper evidence of title that represents the goods described in it.

Bills and notes: Abbreviation for a bill of exchange and a promissory note. A check is one of many examples of a bill of exchange that are used in daily business transactions.

Binder: A preliminary agreement for sale of real estate requiring a deposit, and providing for a formal deed or contract at some future date.

Blanket mortgage: A single lien covering two or more lots or parcels of land.

Board of directors: A group of persons who manage a corporation for all important matters.

Bona fide: In good faith—honest.

Bond (surety): A pledge to pay a sum of money in case of failure to

GLOSSARY OF LEGAL TERMS 179

fulfill obligations, inflicting damage, or mishandling funds. Usually written by a bonding company for a fee.

Bondable: An employee who is able to obtain a bond to protect the employer. Also a contractor who is able to do the same for his customer.

Bonds (corporate): Evidence of indebtedness of a corporation which is secured by its general assets.

Book value: The value of a property as carried on the owner's accounts.

Boot: A profit gained in exchange of properties, not reflected by cash, upon which income tax is not deferred.

Breach: Failure to perform a duty or fulfill an obligation.

Broker loan statement: A statement of charges to be made in connection with a loan, for information of borrower.

Building restrictions: Laws or ordinances requiring sound construction for protection of health and safety.

Bulk sales law: State law requiring that the sale of a business be advertised beforehand, for protection of creditors.

Business opportunity: A going business, including physical assets, good will, and perhaps a property lease.

Bylaws: Rules of internal management of a corporation within its corporate charter limits.

Capital gain: Profit from increase in value of an investment. If held more than six months, it becomes taxable at a lower rate.

Capitalization: In appraising, using a predetermined interest rate and the net earnings of a property as a basis of computing value.

Cashier's check: A check drawn by a bank on its own account and signed by the bank's official.

Caveat emptor: Means "Let the buyer beware." Dealing "at arms length." Used car dealer selling a jalopy "as is."

CD (certificate of deposit): A receipt for a time deposit of money left with a bank at an agreed rate of interest.

Certified check: A customer's check that is guaranteed by his bank to be good when presented for payment.

Certified financial statement: A statement of assets and liabilities confirmed by the person's or firm's certified public accountant.

Chain of title: Detailed account of all actions and events affecting a title to land as far back as the original government patent, if possible.

Change orders: A variation in the plans and specifications of the architect that require a written memo.

Chattel: Personal property; moveable property.

Chattel mortgage: A mortgage on personal property.

Closing statement: A final accounting in closing a transaction. Mandatory for real estate brokers.

Cloud on the title: Anything affecting clear title to property. Term usually used in connection with minor nuisance items that must be eliminated by quitclaim deed or quiet title lawsuit.

Collateral security: Additional sums or things of value posted to guarantee fulfillment of a principal contract.

Collusion: A secret arrangement to defraud someone.

Color of title: A title which appears to be good on the surface, but actually is not good.

Commercial acre: What remains of an acre after allowing for deductions for streets, alleys, etc. Something less than an acre.

Commercial paper: Notes assigned in the course of trade, bills of exchange, etc.

Commingling: Situation where husband or wife has confused separate property with community property to the extent it cannot be separated.

Common stock: A printed certificate that represents the complete ownership of a corporation.

Community property: That property acquired by husband and wife from time of the marriage onward as a result of their joint efforts.

Compaction: Tamping of filled ground to make it more suitable for building. Done extensively in subdividing of hilly ground.

Comparative analysis: Appraising a home or lot by comparing it with others of similar qualities with known recent sales prices.

Competent parties: Persons mentally fit; legally capable of entering into a contract.

Compound interest: Earnings on the original investment and the accumulated interest therefrom.

Condemnation: Ruling by a public agency that property is not fit for use. Also refers to taking of private property for public use by right of eminent domain, by paying the fair value.

Conditional sales contract: The purchase of personal property on contract, usually on the installment plan. Buyer does not receive a deed or title until he has made all payments called for by the contract.

Conditions: Limitations imposed in a deed.

Condominiums: Apartments or other types of properties in which the owner has fee title to the part actually occupied, with an undivided interest in the areas used by all occupants.

Conglomerate corporations: A group of companies that have been merged into a single ownership and are usually engaged in nonrelated businesses.

Consideration: Something of value to induce a person to enter into a valid contract. The consideration for a gift between husband and wife or parents and children can be love and affection.

Conspiracy: An agreement between two or more persons to commit an unlawful act.

Constructive notice: Notice given by the public records, as opposed to actual notice.

Contiguous: Adjoining, touching, as two contiguous parcels of land.

Contingent fee: A gambling fee by an attorney based upon favorable result of collecting money.

Contract: Agreement to do certain things, or not to do them.

Contractor: One who is licensed to build or erect a home, building, or other structure for another.

Contributory negligence: The fault or negligence of the claimant that weakens or defeats his claim against the alleged wrongdoer. One who enters a dark building under construction may be guilty of contributory negligence.

Conventional loan: A loan not guaranteed or insured by a governmental agency. Usually made by banks, insurance companies, and savings and loan associations for home mortgages.

Convertible stock: Designation where stock is changed into another class or into other obligations of the corporation.

Conveyance: Transfer of title from one person to another. This is accomplished by the use of a deed.

Cooperative apartments: Each occupant owns his apartment by receiving a share of stock and a lease from the cooperative apartment corporation.

Corner influence: In appraising, the additional value given to a corner lot due to its advantages, especially in business property.

Corporate charter: Articles of incorporation that give the corporation the right and power to do many things over a period of many years.

Corporate mergers: Usually, the larger corporation buys all or the controlling interest in a smaller corporation and controls its fate.

Corporate minutes: A detailed written record of what went on at meetings of the stockholders and also of the board of directors of a corporation.

Corporation: A legal creation authorized to act with the rights and liabilities of a person.

Cosigner: One who guarantees that if his friend who borrowed money does not pay as agreed that the good guy will get stuck.

Cost plus contract: An agreement that the owner will pay the cost of all labor and materials plus a certain profit to the contractor.

County records: A recording system for documents maintained by each county as provided by state law.

Covenant: Agreement in a deed to control the use and acts of future owners. Used also in other instruments such as leases and conditional sales contracts.

CPA (certified public accountant): A skilled professional accountant who has been licensed by his state after passing a difficult examination. He is to the accounting profession what the MD is to the medical profession.

Creditor's commmittee: A group of creditors who decide if the debtor's petition for an extension of time or compromise of his obligations shall be permitted. This is handled under Chapter XI of the federal Bankruptcy Act.

Damages: Compensation the court may award to a person who has been injured physically or financially by another.

D/B/A: Abbreviation for "doing business as," used in lawsuits to identify a trade name. John Jones, d/b/a Highway Motors.

Debentures: An unsecured note given by a corporation for money it has borrowed on a long term payback.

Declaration of homestead: Document recorded to declare a homestead under state law.

Declaration of restrictions: A list of restrictions to a tract imposed by a subdivider and recorded.

Decree: A decision by a court or others authorized to make decisions. Frequently mispronounced, as if spelled degree.

Dedication: Acceptance of land from an owner by a city or county for particular use by the public.

Deed: A written instrument which conveys title to real estate.

Deed of reconveyance: Deed given by trustee under deed of trust when loan is paid.

De facto and de jure corporations: A de facto corporation, although irregularly formed, exercises corporate rights under color of law. A de jure corporation is one which has been created in compliance with all legal requirements.

Default: Failure to perform a duty or keep a promise, such as to make payments on a note.

Defendant: Persons who are being sued in a civil lawsuit.

Deficiency judgment: A judgment awarded by a court against a person when after foreclosure the security for the loan does not realize enough money at a sale to pay the balance of the loan.

Delivery: Formal transfer of a deed to the new owner, without the right to recall it. Essential to a valid transfer of title.

Deposition: Sworn testimony by the way of questions and answers given outside of the courtroom in a pending lawsuit. Preliminary to the court trial.

Depreciation: Loss of value to property from any cause.

Devise: Gift of real estate by will.

Devisee: One who inherits property by will.

Discharge in bankruptcy: A document that legally excuses one from being forced to pay certain obligations listed in his bankruptcy schedule that are legally dischargeable.

Discounting bills: Paying bills promptly when due and thereby earning a discount. Builds up good credit.

Disgorge: A creditor who has been favored by a bankrupt debtor at the expense of all other creditors and he is ordered to return the tainted money to the trustee in bankruptcy.

Diversity of citizenship: A citizen of one state becoming legally involved with a citizen of another state.

Dividends: A payment of a portion of corporate profits to its stockholders. Also payment by a bank to its depositors as interest payment for use of their money.

Domicile: Place of residence. In court proceedings, residence is a matter of intent.

Dower: Interest of wife in her husband's estate after his death. Term not used much in community property states.

Draftsman: One who is trained in the skill of drawing plans. Frequently employed by architects for drawing plans and specifications.

Dummy director: A figurehead in the formation of a new corporation who has no duties to perform.

Duress: Unlawfully forcing someone to do an act against his will by use of force.

DWI (driving while intoxicated): Commonly called "drunk driving." One who is charged with the criminal offense of driving a motor vehicle while under the influence of alcohol to an extent prohibited by law.

Earnest money: A deposit of money given to bind an agreement or an offer.

Easement: The right or interest of one person in another's property.

Economic life: Life of a building during which it earns enough to justify maintaining it.

Egress: A means of leaving property without trespassing.

Emancipation of a minor: A legal proceeding to permit one under age to transact business as an adult.

Eminent domain: The right of government to take private property for public use, provided it serves a necessary public use and fair compensation is paid to the owner.

Encroachment: Building in whole or in part on another's property.

Encumbrance: A debt on property. Anything that burdens the title to property.

Endorsement: The signing on the back of check or note for the purpose of transfer.

Endorsement in blank: Signing to transfer rights to a check or note without qualification, making endorser equally responsible for payment.

Endorsement without recourse: Signing to transfer a check or note in this manner makes no guarantee to future holders.

Equitable owner: One who has hypothecated his property. He has conveyed title in trust perhaps, but retains the right to use and enjoy the property.

Equity (owner's): Value of owner's interest in property in excess of the liens against it.

Equity of redemption: Owner's right to redeem property after foreclosure sale for a period provided by law.

Escalator clause: Provision in a lease whereby the rents increase under certain conditions, such as every year, or based upon a periodical appraisal of the property.

Escheat: Process by which property reverts to the state for lack of private ownership. Bank accounts that lie dormant for a number of years, with no apparent owner alive, are subject to escheat laws.

Escrow: The depositing of papers and money with a third neutral party along with instructions to carry out an agreement, such as the transfer of title to a home.

Escrow holder: One who undertakes to carry out escrow instructions.

Estate: The interest of a person in property; as to real property, the degree, quantity, and extent of his interest.

Estate for life: Use of property only during the life of the person given the interest, after which it reverts to the original estate or others designated.

Estate tax (federal): A tax on estates of deceased persons in excess of an amount specified by law, with exemptions.

Estate at will: A lease which may be terminated at will by either party.

Estate for years: Another term for a lease or leasehold estate.

Estimator: A person who is skilled in the cost of construction to determine the amount the contractor should offer to build in his bid to the owner.

Ethics: A standard of moral practice and fair play.

Exchange agreement: A contract for the exchange of properties.

Exclusive listing: An authorization to sell which gives sole agency or right to sell to one real estate broker. He is entitled to his brokerage fee even if the owner finds his own buyer.

Execute: To sign and consent to carry out an agreement to completion.

Executor: Man named in a will to handle and dispose of an estate. If a woman is named for the same purpose, she is called executrix.

Exemption statutes: Laws that save property from creditors in connection with attachment or bankruptcy or other legal proceedings.

Expert witness: One who testifies in a lawsuit who is not directly involved in the dispute but is qualified by reason of experience or educational background.

Extras: Anything that is ordered by the owner after construction has started that was not included in the original contract.

Family corporation: One whose stock is owned and controlled by immediate members of a family with no stock available to the general public.

Federal Housing Administration (FHA): Federal government agency, which insures loans on residential property.

Federal Savings and Loan Association: A financial institution that is chartered by the Federal Home Loan Bank Board in Washington, D.C. and whose accounts are insured by an agency of the government.

Fee simple estate: Highest and best estate possible.

Felony: A serious crime punishable by a sentence of more than one year in a state penitentiary.

Fictitious name: A name which does not identify the person.

Fidelity bond: The dictionary says, "the quality or state of being faithful." A bond to protect the employer against employees who embezzle money.

Fiduciary relationship: A position of trust and confidence requiring loyalty.

Financing statement: A list of assets and liabilities which means a list of what you own and what you owe. Required by banks and other financial institutions before they will lend money.

Finder's fee: Money paid to a person who furnishes information helpful to arranging a loan or completing a deal.

First meeting of creditors: A bankruptcy court proceeding held in the courtroom of the Referee in Bankruptcy to question the bankrupt debtor.

Fixtures: Things that are attached to property and cannot be removed as ordinary personal property, as they become a part of the realty.

Foreclosure: The sale of pledged property to cover a defaulted debt.

Forfeiture: Loss of a deposit or earnest money for failure to perform.

Foundations: Nonprofit corporations that are formed for charitable or educational purposes.

Franchise: A right granted by a state to a newly formed corporation. Sometimes used to denote a food type of franchise sold by a national company, authorizing a purchaser to use its brand name and recipe.

Fraud: Causing loss of property due to use of deceit, cheating, false promises, etc.

Freeholder: Owner of land in fee.

Front foot: The measure of land along the street frontage. Used as a unit in pricing business property.

Garnishment: A court proceeding whereby a creditor attaches the wages or bank account of the debtor.

General lien: One which may attach to all property of a person, such as a judgement or a tax claim.

GI loans: The government guarantee of loans to veterans of various wars in connection with their purchase of a home with certain limitations.

Gift deed: A deed for which the consideration is love and affection, rather than money.

Gift tax (federal): A tax on gifts over a certain amount, with exemptions.

Going public: A corporation whose stock had previously not been made available to the general public and is now being offered to the public for the first time. Ford Motor Company stock was held by the Ford family for many years before going public.

Good will: The intangible value that a business has built up over a period of time.

Grant deed: Instrument used to convey title to land. Carries implied warranties.

Grantee: One who acquires title to property by deed.

Granting clause: Clause in deed stating "I grant" or "I convey." Essential to a valid deed.

Grantor: One who conveys title to property by deed.

Gross income: Total income from a business or property before deducting expenses.

Guarantee of title: An opinion on the condition of title based upon a search of the official records, and backed by a fund to compensate in case of oversight or negligence.

Harmless error rule: When a trial court judge commits an error and on appeal, the appellate court says that the trial court judge's error did not materially affect the defendant's rights or the law of the case.

Head of a family: One who is responsible for dependents. Not necessarily a married person.

Heirs: Those who by law obtain property upon death of another, either by will or by operation of law.

Holder in due course: One who in good faith takes a note for value and without knowledge of any defects, in the course of business.

Holding company: A super corporation which owns or controls such a dominant interest in one or more other corporations that it is able to dictate their policies.

Holographic will: A will entirely handwritten and signed by the testator or testatrix.

Homestead: A home upon which a declaration of homestead has been recorded. Gives certain protection against judgments.

Hypothecate: To pledge property as security for a debt, but retaining its use. As in connection with a trust deed loan.

Implied warranty: A warranty assumed by law to exist in an instrument although not specifically stated, as in a grant or warranty deed.

Impounds: Monthly payments by the mortgage borrower to pay for annual taxes and insurance premiums to mortgage company.

Improvements: Things built on land which become part of it.

Improvement acts: State laws providing for the installation of improvements in certain districts, such as street widening and paving, installation of sewer lines and storm drains, etc. The cost is usually assessed against the properties directly benefited.

Incompetent: One who is unable to manage his affairs because of feeblemindedness, senility, insanity, etc.

Indemnity: Guarantee against loss—as by an insurance policy. Same as a guarantor.

Indorsement: A name signed on the back of a check or note.

Ingress: A means of entering a property without trespassing.

Inherently dangerous: A type of danger that is an essential part of something, requiring special precautions to be taken to prevent injury.

Inherit: To obtain property as an heir.

Inheritance tax (state): Tax on estate of deceased resident.

Injunction: An order of a court to restrain against certain acts in connection with a pending lawsuit or one adjudicated.

Insolvent: Inability of a person to pay his debts. Where liabilities exceed assets.

Installment note: A note which provides for payment of a certain part of the principal at stated intervals.

Instrument: A document in writing creating certain rights to its parties or transferring them.

Interest: The rental charge for the use of money.

Interest table: A table giving the amount of annual interest on various sums of money at different rates of interest.

Interstate commerce: Involving two or more states in the United States.

Intestate: Death without leaving a will. The dead person is called a testator or testatrix, indicating male or female.

Intrastate commerce: Involving one state only.

Invitee: One who has a perfect legal right to be on the premises where the accident occurred.

Involuntary bankruptcy petition: A document filed by three or more creditors in federal bankruptcy court, claiming that the debtor person, firm, or corporation is unable to pay his/its bills when due and is therefore bankrupt.

Involuntary lien: A lien placed against property without the necessity of the owner's consent. Taxes and assessments are examples.

IOU (I owe you): A written acknowledgment of a sum of money owed to another, in spite of its informality. Similar to a note except that a note contains a promise to repay at a certain time.

Irrevocable: That which cannot be recalled or revoked.

Irrigation district: A district created by law to furnish water. It is a quasi-political district having governing features similar to counties and cities.

Joint note: A note signed by more than one person. All have equal responsibility for payment and must be sued together.

Joint and several note: Same as joint note, but makers may be sued either jointly or individually in event of default.

Joint tenancy: Equal ownership by two or more persons under four essential unities. It features right of survivorship. If one dies, his interest goes to the survivor or survivors.

Joint tenancy deed: A deed which names grantees as joint tenants. Very popular for married couples.

Judgment: A court's final decree. Often involves awarding a payment of money.

Judgment proof: Applies to persons who have no assets to satisfy a judgement for money.

Junior lien: A lien which is subordinate to another lien which has prior claim on the security. The prior lien holders can collect before the junior lien is satisfied.

Jurisdiction: The right given by law by which courts, commissions, etc. enter into and decide cases.

Key man insurance: Life insurance protection paid for by management to cover the cost of replacing a key man in the organization. Sometimes used as a fringe benefit for the key man.

Laches: Sleeping on your rights which results in failure to secure legal relief because of waiting too long.

Land contract: An agreement whereby land is sold, usually on an installment basis, and buyer does not receive a deed until the contract is paid out.

Land descriptions: A description of land recognized by law. One based on government survey or surveys based on it.

Landlord's lien: The landlord's right to hold the tenant's property as security for unpaid rent.

Last clear chance: The final opportunity to avoid the accident, even though the other party was on the wrong side of the road.

Latent defects: A defect being unknown and not discoverable by inspection.

Legalese: Slang definition of technical language used by certain judges and members of the legal profession.

Legal hybrid: A cooperative apartment because the stockholder-tenant possesses both stock in the corporation as well as a lease with the corporation.

Legal rate of interest: Varies in different states. Used to be about 6 percent or 7 percent; however, some states have increased the legal rates recently.

Lessee: A renter under a lease.

Lessor: A landlord or owner who has leased his property.

Letters of credit: A written authorization from your bank to other banks all over the world permitting you to draw money to be charged against your bank. Your bank will then charge your account.

Liable: Responsible under the law.

Licensee: A person who is authorized to be on the construction project. A license gives one the right to walk over another's land.

Lien: An encumbrance against property making it liable for a debt.

Life estate: Rights to use property for a lifetime only.

Limited partnership: A type of partnership with limited liability.

Line of credit: The amount of money your bank will permit you to borrow.

Liquid assets: Those readily convertible to cash.

Liquidate: To sell off property at best available price in order to secure cash.

Liquidated damages: Extent of damages agreed upon in a contract in event of default.

Lis pendens: A recorded notice to advise persons interested in certain property that a lawsuit is pending which may affect title to it.

Listing: A contract authorizing a real estate broker to buy, sell, or lease certain land under specified terms and conditions.

Litigants: All parties to a lawsuit.

Majority: The age at which a young man or lady becomes an adult, according to law.

Marginal releases: Entry on the margin of an official record book showing that a claim has been paid.

Marketable title: Title to real estate which is free and clear from any reasonable objections.

Market price: The going price of equivalent properties based upon recent sales.

Market value: The best price a piece of property would bring in dollars if freely advertised for sale for a reasonable time, to find a buyer who is fully informed on the possible uses of the property.

Master plan: A general plan for future physical development of a community.

Material fact: A fact, which if known to the parties, might seriously affect their decisions in a transaction.

Mechanic's lien: A lien right provided by law whereby persons who have furnished labor or materials may make legal claim against the property for their money.

Menace: Use of threats to induce one to enter into a contract.

Mesne profits: Mesne means intermediate. Profits from a property during a period when a rightful owner is wrongfully deprived of the earnings.

Metes and bounds: A method of describing the boundary lines of a parcel of land.

Miller Act: A federal law that protects all who furnish labor or materials used on a federal building project. Federal law prohibits the filing of a lien against the government, thus this substitute protection by way of the Miller Act.

Mineral, oil, and gas license: Special license to deal in such lands.

Minors: Young men and women who have not reached a legal age to vote or to enter into legal contracts. The laws of each state will vary.

Misdemeanor: A lesser crime than a felony. Sentences are to county jail for less than one year or a fine or both.

Money left on the table: Difference in money between the successful bidder on a highway construction job and the second low bidder.

Month to month tenancy: When rent is paid by the month. The usual arrangement for renting houses.

Moratorium: A law supending liability for paying a debt and granting more time for payment.

Mortality tables: Established procedures for determining life expectancy. Important in lawsuits to determine how long the claimant would have lived if he had not been struck by the car.

Mortgage: An instrument which makes property security for the payment of a loan.

Mortgagee: One who lends money secured by a mortgage.

Mortgagor: An owner who borrows money on a note secured by a mortgage.

Multiple listing: A cooperative listing for the sale of real estate taken by a real estate board, which permits any member of their group to find a buyer. Brokerage fees are then split.

Mutual consent: As essential to a valid contract.

Mutual funds: An organization that invests other persons' money and charges for its services. They claim to be experts in the field of investments.

Mutual mistake of fact: An error or misunderstanding of a material fact that exonerates both parties to a contract.

National bank: Chartered and authorized to engage in the banking business by the federal authorities. Each account is federally insured by an agency of the government.

Negligence: Doing something wrong or failing to do something that is required to be done.

Negotiable instrument: Those which are commonly transferred by endorsement in the course of trade—such as checks and drafts.

Negotiable note: One capable of being assigned in the ordinary course of business.

Net income: Remaining income from business or property after proper charges and expenses are deducted.

Net listing: One which provides that real estate agent gets his commission over and above a net sum to the seller.

Net worth: The difference between your assets and liabilities. What you own and what you owe.

New York Stock Exchange: The largest association of stockbrokers in the world, where trading in securities is accomplished under an organized system.

Nonpar value of stock: Corporate stock that is issued without placing value on the shares. Usually occurs in a family corporation.

Nonprofit corporation: A company that is organized for purposes other than earning money. It could be educational or charitable. Happens to some construction firms on an involuntary basis.

Notary public: Person authorized by law to take acknowledgements and oaths.

Notice of abandonment: Notice filed when work is discontinued on an unfinished job.

Notice of completion: Document filed to give public notice that a building job is completed.

Notice of default: Notice filed by owner of a trust deed with the county recorder that borrower has defaulted and foreclosure proceedings may be started.

Notice of intended sale: A notice to be recorded when a business is sold, to give notice to creditors and to the public.

Notice of nonresponsibility: A notice provided by law, which when recorded, is designed to relieve an owner from liability for work or materials used on his property without his authorization.

Notice to quit: A three-day notice to a delinquent tenant to pay up or surrender possession of the premises.

NSF checks: Abbreviation for "Not Sufficient Funds." Returned by the issuer's bank because there is not enough money on deposit to cover the check. The popular slang expression is "a hot check."

NSL (no stockholders liability): A state corporation that limits the liability of its stockholders to the original amount they contributed to the new corporation.

Obligee: The owner of the property and the building to be constructed is called the "obligee" under the bond issued by the bonding company.

Obligor: The bonding company that issues the construction bond is called the "obligor."

Off-sale license: State liquor license issued to sellers of "packaged goods" to be taken from the premises.

Offset statement: Statement of an owner or lien holder as to present status of a lien—the remaining principal balance on the note, interest due, etc.

On-sale license: License to sell alcoholic beverages for consumption on the premises, such as a cocktail bar or beer hall.

Open listing: A nonexclusive listing given to one or more real estate brokers. It may be oral or written, and the first agent to get owner's acceptance to an offer earns the commission.

Option: A written instrument which, for a consideration, gives one the right to buy or lease a property within a stated time on the terms set forth.

Optionee: One who secures an option right.

Optionor: An owner who gives an option.

Oral: Verbal or spoken; not in writing.

Original or prime contractor: The contractor who contracts with the owner to do the overall building job for an agreed price.

Origination fee: A charge made by a financial institution in connection with starting a new loan.

Outlawed claim: A claim is outlawed or barred by the statute of limitations where the claimant delays bringing suit beyond the time limit allowed by law.

Over the counter: Corporate stocks that are not listed on any stock exchange, but are sold by stock brokers "over the counter." The companies involved are usually smaller and it is not always easy to sell stock over the counter because the buyers are not as numerous as when stock is sold through a large stock exchange.

Overhead: The standard expenses of operating a place of business that are not chargeable to a particular part of the work.

Owner's equity: What a property is worth over and above the liens against it.

Paid-in capital: The amount of cash with which the new corporation is going to start its business.

Parol evidence: Oral or verbal.

Partial release clause: Clause in a mortgage or trust deed which provides for removal of certain property from the effect of the lien upon payment of an agreed sum. Subdividers must have these if their tract is subject to a "blanket lien."

Partial satisfaction: An acknowledgement in writing that a part of a claim or judgment has been paid. Usually filed with the clerk of the court.

Partnership: A contract between two or more persons to unite their property, labor or skill, or some of them, in prosecution of some joint or lawful business and to share profits and losses in certain proportions.

Party wall: One built on the dividing line of property for use of both owners.

Par value: The value placed on new stock about to be issued. This is determined by its incorporators.

Patent: An original conveyance of lands by the federal government. Title is granted by letters patent.

Payor and payee: The payor pays the sum due on a note, and the payee receives the money.

Percentage lease: A lease providing for rental based on the dollar volume of business done. Usually based on gross sales with an agreed minimum rental.

Performance bond: A guarantee that the contractor will perform the contract and also pay all bills for labor and material.

Personal property: Moveable property; that which is not real property.

Plaintiff: One who brings a civil lawsuit.

Plan of arrangement: A written proposal filed in federal bankruptcy court by an insolvent debtor for an extension of time and a compromise payment of his obligations.

Plans and specs: Abbreviation for "plans and specifications." These are usually prepared by an architect and are vital to the construction of any structure.

Pledge: A deposit of personal property to secure a debt.

Points: In the money lending business, a point is one percent of the amount of the loan. Bonuses and commissions are often expressed in "points."

Police power: The power vested in the state to enact and enforce laws for the order, safety, health, morals and general welfare of the public.

Postnuptial property settlement agreement: A written agreement between husband and wife, after their marriage, specifying their property rights for the past and future.

Power of attorney: Authority given in writing by one person for another to act for him.

Power of sale: A right given to a trustee to sell property under deed of trust if the borrower defaults.

Preferential payment: Money paid by an insolvent debtor to a creditor in violation of bankruptcy law because it was made within four months of the filing of his bankruptcy petition. The money has to be returned to the trustee in bankruptcy for benefit of all the creditors.

Preferred stock: Corporate stock that is entitled to priority over common stock in the distribution of profits.

Prenuptial property settlement agreement: Written contract between husband and wife to be, before their marriage, dividing and agreeing to their ownership of property in the event of death or divorce.

Prepayment penalty: A charge for paying off a mortgage balance ahead of schedule where the mortgage so specifies.

Prescription: A means of obtaining title to property by long open possession under some claim, in defiance of owner's rights.

Presumption: A fact assumed by law which must be proved to the contrary.

Prima facie: On its face; presumptive.

Primary mortgage market: Making original loans.

Principal: One who employs an agent.

Prior in time is prior in right: Rights established by prompt recording, ahead of others who failed to record their lien or mortgage or other instrument promptly.

Priority: Being first in rank, time, or place.

Privity of contract: Lack of agreement, understanding, or connection between the parties involved in the dispute.

Probate court: A special court that handles estates of persons who have died. Also all disputes that involve estates.

Probate sale: Sale to liquidate the estate of a deceased person.

Promissory note: Written promise to pay a sum of money at a definite future time.

Proof of claim: A special form that is filed in probate or bankruptcy court to substantiate a claim for money claimed to be owed by the decedent or bankrupt debtor.

Property: In general, anything capable of ownership.

Property management: A branch of the real estate business.

Property settlement agreement: A written agreement usually used in connection with a pending divorce action. It divides the property rights of the husband and wife as well as other matters.

Proration: In any transaction involving land, to divide taxes, interest, etc., proportionately between the parties, as in closing an escrow.

Proxy fights: A battle for control of a corporation by the owners of its stock granting to another the right to vote his stock.

Public liability insurance: Protection against claims for the injury or death of one or more persons.

Public utility: A private company giving public service, such as water, gas, or electricity.

Purchase money mortgage: One given as part of the purchase price when buying property. The note it secures is given to the seller instead of cash to meet the required downpayment.

Quasi-public corporation: A corporation which has been given certain powers of a private nature. The local gas company is given the right to exercise eminent domain.

Quiet title: A lawsuit to determine status of title; to remove a cloud on the title.

Quitclaim deed: Deed by which the grantor releases any claim or interest in a property he may possess. It says in effect, "Whatever interest, if any, I have, I give to you."

Quorum: The number of persons required to be present for corporate business to be legally transacted. For a stockholder's meeting, a quorum means a majority of the voting stock issued and not a majority of the actual bodies of the stockholders.

Range: A strip of land running north and south and six miles wide, established by government survey.

Reconveyance: Transfer of title to a former owner, as when a trustee under a deed of trust reconveys title when the note is paid in full.

Redemption: Reacquiring property lost through foreclosure within the prescribed time limit.

Referee in bankruptcy: An attorney who is appointed by the federal judges of his district to act as an official to preside over bankruptcy court. He is sort of a junior federal judge with limited power in his bankruptcy court.

Release clause: Provision in a trust deed or mortgage to release portions of the land from the lien upon payment of an agreed amount of money. Subdividers, who sell individual lots, are required to have these.

Request for notice of default: Acknowledged request filed with the county recorder by holder of a junior lien so he may be notified of actions of prior lien holders.

Rescission of contract: To set aside or annul a contract, either by mutual consent or by court order.

Reservation: A right withheld by a grantor when conveying property.

Residence: Sounds simple like where do you live. In the courtroom it can become very technical and very important. It is a matter of intent.

Res ipsa loquitor: Translated from Latin it means "the thing speaks for itself." A legal doctrine that eliminates the vital requirement of proof of negligence under certain circumstances.

Resolution: A written approval of the board of directors of a corporation authorizing its officials to take some action of importance. Examples could be, who is authorized to sign corporate checks or the purchase of real estate by a corporation, etc.

Restriction: A limitation on the use of property, usually imposed by a previous grantor.

Retainage: The portion of a percentage of the monthly payments made by the owner to the contractor for construction work completed. It is withheld until the construction contract has been completed.

Reversionary interest: The right of an estate or its residue after present possession is terminated, as with a life estate.

Right of first refusal: The choice of buying an interest or land itself under specified terms and conditions. If the right is not exercised, then the owner is privileged to sell to others.

Right of survivorship: The right of a joint tenant to the interest of a deceased joint tenant.

Right of way: An easement to pass over, or maintain services, on property or a particular part thereof.

Riparian right: Rights of a landowner to use the water on, under, or adjacent to his land.

Running description: Tracing the boundaries of a tract by giving distances, angles, and points around the edges. A metes and bounds description.

Sandwich lease: A sublease which is subject to an original lease, the sublessee having further sublet the property. He holds an "in between" lease.

Satisfaction: An instrument executed by a lien holder declaring that the debt has been paid. When recorded, it discharges the lien from the records.

Seal—corporation: A round metal device that contains the name of the corporation, the state of its incorporation, and the date it was incorporated. Required on all real estate matters.

SEC (Securities Exchange Commission): A federal agency that polices the sale of stocks and other securities to residents of states other than the home state of the corporation involved. Their requirements are tough; however, they effectively protect the gullible public from phony speculative investments.

Secondary mortgage market: The dealing in trust deeds and mortgages already in existence.

Section of land: A standard land measurement containing 640 acres, or one square mile.

Secured creditor: One who holds collateral as protection that his obligation will be paid. If the debtor does not pay as agreed, then the creditor can foreclose on the collateral.

Security device: An instrument or contract which results in real estate being made security for money owed, such as a trust deed, real property sales contracts, etc.

Security funds: Funds deposited by lessee to protect lessor if a default occurs. These are trust funds.

Separate property: That property which is owned and controlled separately by either husband or wife, as distinguished from community property.

Set-back ordinance: Local laws requiring owners, when building, to keep improvements a certain distance from lot boundaries.

Severalty ownership: Sole ownership—as by a single person.

Sheriff's deed: One given by the sheriff upon court order when property is sold to satisfy a judgment.

Signing by mark: Marking a mark or an *X* by a person unable to sign his name. The mark usually has to be witnessed by two persons.

Single person: One who has never married or whose marriage was annulled.

Solvent: Able to pay all debts when due.

Special assessment: A legal charge against property for improvements which particularly benefit it.

Special master: A person appointed by the judge to take charge of and sell property at a public sale and report the results of the sale to the court for necessary approval. It is usually an attorney.

Specific lien: A lien affecting one particular property.

Specific performance: Court order requiring a person to do what he has agreed to do in his contract.

Spouse: Either one of a married couple.

State chartered bank: A financial institution that is incorporated and approved by its own state. It is not subject to federal regulatory bodies.

Status quo: The existing state of affairs. In a dispute, leaving the parties in the same position they were in originally.

Statute: A law enacted by a legislative body.

Statute of frauds: A state law requiring certain agreements to be in writing to be enforceable at law.

Statute of limitations: A state law limiting the time in which certain court actions may be brought.

Statutory dedication: Surrendering land for public use when required by law; as for streets in a subdivision.

Stock certificates: Written or printed evidence of ownership of a certain number of shares or interest in a corporation.

Stockholder-shareholder: There is no difference between the two terms. One who owns stock in a corporation.

Stockholder's meeting: Meetings called by a corporation for the purpose of electing directors and transacting other business requiring the consent of the stockholders.

Stock option plan: Offers to key employees and officials of a corporation to buy stock at an agreed price on an optional basis. If the price of the stock goes up, you exercise your option; otherwise you forget it.

Stock splits: Dividing up of the outstanding shares of a corporation into a greater number of units. Sometimes done when the price of stock is too high for the average investor to buy.

Stop payment order: Written instructions to your bank not to pay a certain check that you issued but which has not yet been presented for payment.

Straight note: One payable in a lump sum and not in installments.

Subcontractor: A builder or contractor who enters into an agreement with the prime contractor to build some part of the entire structure. The plumber, electrician, roofer, heating, and air conditioning are typical examples.

Subdivision maps: When approved by the governing body and recorded, they are the basis for good legal description.

"Subject to" a mortgage: Language used when buyer does not assume personal liability for payment of a mortgage or trust deed note against a property he buys.

Sublease: A lease given when the original lessee in turn sublets.

Submission agreement: A written provision that if a dispute arises, which the parties are unable to settle, the matter will be referred to a board of arbitrators.

Subordination clause: Clause in a junior mortgage or trust deed enabling the first lien to keep its priority in case of renewal or refinancing.

Subpoena: A court order commanding a person to appear in court at a designated time and place. Failure to appear could constitute contempt of court.

Subrogation: The right to stand in another's shoes by by virtue of paying him money on his claim. This occurs when the insurance company pays for the repairs on your car and tries to collect its loss from the other party involved in the accident.

Substantial performance: When a certain portion of a construction contract has been completed. There is no set percentage of completion required; it will vary with the facts of each case.

Surety: One who becomes a guarantor for another person.

Tangible property: Personal property which has substance and can be manually delivered from one person to another.

Tax deed: One given when land is sold by the state for non-payment of taxes.

Taxes (real estate): A levy on property by political subdivisions, such as county, city, school districts to pay for government administration and services.

Tenancy in common: Ownership of equal or unequal undivided interests in property by two or more persons, without right of survivorship.

Tenancy at sufferance: Occurs when a lease expires and owner permits tenant to continue in possession on a temporary basis, usually one month at a time.

Tenant in partnership: Interest in property held as a partner.

Termites: Wood-devouring insects. Enemies of home owners.

Testator and testatrix: One who makes a will. Testator is a man, testatrix is a woman.

Third party beneficiary: A laborer, materialman, or subcontractor who is protected by a performance bond taken out by the general contractor, even though they are not named in the bond.

Tight money: A situation that exists when the demand for money is greater than the supply. Banks turn down applications for loans by good customers because they are temporarily out of loanable funds.

"Time is of the essence": Necessary provision in contracts. Contemplates prompt performance by the parties within the time limits set forth.

Title: Evidence of ownership and lawful possession.

Title insurance: Protection to a property owner against loss because of defective title. Policies are written by title companies and cover all usual hazards.

Title search: An accurate check of the courthouse records to determine if title to land has been affected by the filing of any instrument. This work is usually done by experienced personnel of the title companies.

Topography: The character of the land's surface, such as level or hilly.

Tort: A civil wrong other than a crime. An automobile accident claim is a good example.

Township: A unit of land six miles square, or thirty-six miles. Established by government survey.

Trade name: A name used by someone engaged in business, other than his own personal name. Jones Motor Company or Pacific Motor Company are both trade names for John Jones, the owner.

Treasury stock: Corporate stock that has been issued and paid for, but has later been reacquired by the corporation by purchase, donation, forfeiture, or other means.

Trespasser: One who enters upon the lands of another unlawfully.

Trust deed (deed of trust): A conveyance of title to a trustee to be held until a loan secured by a note is paid, at which time title is reconveyed.

Trust funds: Money that belongs to another that is being held for a particular purpose. Should be kept separate and apart from the holder's regular funds.

Trustee: A person or corporation which holds title in trust pending repayment of an obligation or the rendering of a service. In connection with trust deed, holds title until note is paid in full.

Trustee in bankruptcy: An official appointed by the Referee in Bankruptcy to take charge of the bankrupt person's estate.

Trustee's deed: One given by a trustee when foreclosed property is sold.

Trustor: Borrower on a trust deed note.

Turnkey job: An agreement to complete a structure for a fixed price.

Ultra vires: Acts of a corporation that are beyond its legal powers as provided in its charter.

Umpire: Not the baseball variety. A person selected by a board of arbitrators to decide the matter in controversy when the arbitrators are unable to agree.

Undivided interest: A partial interest in a whole property, merged with the interest of others.

Undue influence: Taking advantage of a person because of his weakness or distress.

Uniform commerical code: A comparatively new law requiring filings with the Secretary of State of security devices making personal property loans secured liens.

Uniform Simultaneous Death Act: Where husband and wife died in a joint disaster leaving community property, and evidence indicates that they died simultaneously, then one-half of the property goes to the husband's heirs and the other one-half to the wife's heir's.

Unilateral contract: One which imposes an obligation on one party only; exchange of a promise for an act.

Unissued stock: Corporate stock that has been authorized but has not been issued.

Unit owner: A person who buys an apartment in a condominium.

United States Supreme Court: The highest court in the United States. Its nine justices decide litigation that involves constitutional questions. They decide what matters their court will hear.

Unities: Essentials such as to a joint tenancy, the unities being time, title, interest, and possession.

Unlawful detainer: Failure of a tenant to vacate after being notified that he is in default.

Unsecured creditor: One who has extended credit without obtaining any collateral as security. Typical examples could be the drug store, the grocery store, the department store, the dress shop, and all of the public utilities.

Urban property: City property.

Urban renewal and redevelopment: Plan to improve substandard areas in populated communities.

Use tax: A sales tax on goods purchased from out of state.

Usury: Charging a high and illegal rate of interest.

VA loans: A mortgage loan made to a service veteran which is insured or guaranteed by the Veterans Administration.

Valuation: Appraising. Estimating the worth of property in money.

Vehicular traffic: Street or highway traffic.

Vendee: The buyer.

Vendor: The seller.

Verbal listing: A listing not reduced to writing.

Verification: Confirmation of the truth of a document by sworn statement.

Vest: To bestow upon, such as title to property.

Veterans Administration: A federal governmental agency which, among other services to veterans, insures or guarantees repayment of home loans borrowed by veterans.

Veterans tax exemption: A property tax exemption given to certain qualified veterans or their widows.

Void: Having no binding effect at law.

Voidable: That which may be declared void, but which is not void until so adjudged by a court.

Voluntary lien: A lien placed on property through the voluntary act of the owner, such as when he makes a mortgage loan.

Wage earner's plan: A petition filed in federal bankruptcy court by a debtor who is financially involved, for an extension of time in which to pay his debts in full. A sincere attempt to avoid an ordinary type of bankruptcy.

Waive: To relinquish; to surrender the right to require anything.

Warehouse receipt: A written instrument that represents that certain goods are in the hands of a warehouseman. It is a symbolical representation of the property itself.

Warranty deed: A deed which recites certain warranties that are guaranteed by the seller or grantor.

Waste: Abuse of property by a tenant or someone holding a temporary interest, such as a life estate, which results in a loss of value.

Water table: Depth of natural underground water from the surface.

Workmanlike manner: An artisan performing his chores in a skillful manner. The test is what type of work would be done in his own area and not in New York or Chicago.

Workmen's compensation insurance: Protection furnished by the employer for benefit of his employees in the event they are injured or killed on the job.

Writ: A written document issued by a court commanding a person to do certain acts, or sometimes to refrain from doing them.

Writing off a bad debt: Cancellation of a debt when the creditor is convinced that he cannot collect from the debtor. The creditor is then entitled to a tax credit due to his loss in writing off his chances to collect his money.

Writ of execution: A court order that property be attached and sold to pay a judgment.

Zoning: Control of the use of land by county or city authorities; power to limit property to specific use.

APPENDIX B
GLOSSARY OF REAL ESTATE TERMS*

Abandonment: A conveyance or recorded instrument used to terminate a homestead.

Absolute fee simple title: One that is unqualified; it is the best title one can obtain.

Abstract of title: A condensed history of the title, consisting of a summary of the various links in the chain of title, together with a statement of all liens, charges, or encumbrances affecting a particular property.

Acceleration clause: A clause in a mortgage, land purchase contract or lease stating that, upon default of a payment due, the balance of the obligation should at once become due and payable.

Access right: The right of an owner to have ingress and egress to and from his property.

Accretion: Addition to the land through natural causes—usually by change in water flow.

Acknowledgment: A formal declaration made before a notary public or other person empowered to perform the service, by the signatory to the instrument, as to the genuineness of the signature.

---
*From the book *Questions and Answers on Real Estate*, 8th ed. by Robert W. Semenow, © 1975 by Prentice Hall, Inc., Englewood Cliffs, NJ 07632.

Acre: A measure of land, 160 square rods (4,840 square yards, 43,560 square feet).

Administrator: A person appointed by court to administer the estate of a deceased person who left no will; that is, who died intestate.

Advance fee: A fee paid in advance of any service rendered in the sale of a property or in obtaining a loan.

Ad valorem: A tax according to a fixed percentage of its value.

Adverse possession: The right of an occupant of land to acquire title against the real owner, where possession has been actual, continuous, hostile, visible, and distinct for the statutory period.

Affiant: A person who has made an affidavit.

Affidavit: A statement of declaration reduced to writing, and sworn or affirmed to before some officer who has authority to administer an oath or affirmation.

Agent: One who represents another from whom he has derived authority.

Agreement of sale: A written agreement whereby the purchaser agrees to buy certain real estate and the seller agrees to sell upon terms and conditions set forth therein.

Air rights: The ownership of the right to use, control or occupy the air space over a designated property.

Alienation: The transfer of real property by one person to another.

Alluvion: Also alluvium. Soil deposited by accretion; increase in land on shore or bank of river due to change in flow of stream.

Amenities: The satisfaction of enjoyable living to be derived from a home; or a beneficial influence arising from the location of the property.

Amortization: The liquidation of a financial obligation on an installment basis.

Annuity: A sum of money or its equivalent that constitutes one of a series of periodic payments.

Appellant: The party who takes an appeal to a higher court.

Appellee: The party against whom the appeal is taken to a higher court.

Appraisal: An estimate of quantity, quality, or value. The process through which conclusions of property value are obtained; also refers to the report setting forth the estimate and conclusion of value.

Appraisal by capitalization: An estimate of value by capitalization of productivity and income.

Appraisal by comparison: Comparability to the sale prices of other similar properties.

Appraisal by summation: Adding together of parts of a property separately appraised to form the whole: for example, value of the land considered as vacant added to the cost of reproduction of the building, less depreciation.

Appurtenance: That which belongs to something else; something which passes as an incident to land, such as a right of way.

Architect: A person whose profession is designing buildings, drawing up plans, and generally supervising construction of the building.

Arpen: French measurement term, being 7/8 of one acre.

Assessed valuation: Assessment of real estate by a unit of government for taxation purposes.

Assessment: A charge against real estate made by a unit of government to cover the proportionate cost of an improvement, such as a street or sewer.

Assignee: The person to whom an agreement or contract is assigned.

Assignment: The method or manner by which a right, a specialty, or contract is transferred from one person to another.

Associate broker: A person who has qualified as a real estate broker, but works for a broker named in the associate broker's license.

Attestation: The witnessing of a signature to an instrument at the request of the person who signed it.

Avulsion: Removal of land from one owner to another when a stream suddenly changes its channel.

Backfill: The replacement of excavated earth into a hole or against a structure.

Balustrade: A small supporting column for a handrail.

Bargain and sale deed: Deed which conveys the property for valuable consideration.

Barge board: A wide trim board placed on the ends of a gable roof.

Base and meridian: Imaginary lines used by surveyors to find and describe the location of lands.

Baseboard: The board skirting the walls of a room at the floor line.

Basement floor: The lowest floor level in a building.

Bench marks: A location indicated on a durable marker by surveyors.

Bilateral contract: Both parties expressly enter into mutual engagements (reciprocal).

Binder: An agreement to cover a down payment for the purchase of real estate as evidence of good faith on the part of the purchaser; in insurance: a temporary agreement given to one having an

Appraisal by summation: Adding together of parts of a property separately appraised to form the whole: for example, value of the land considered as vacant added to the cost of reproduction of the building, less depreciation.

Appurtenance: That which belongs to something else; something which passes as an incident to land, such as a right of way.

Architect: A person whose profession is designing buildings, drawing up plans, and generally supervising construction of the building.

Arpen: French measurement term, being 7/8 of one acre.

Assessed valuation: Assessment of real estate by a unit of government for taxation purposes.

Assessment: A charge against real estate made by a unit of government to cover the proportionate cost of an improvement, such as a street or sewer.

Assignee: The person to whom an agreement or contract is assigned.

Assignment: The method or manner by which a right, a specialty, or contract is transferred from one person to another.

Associate broker: A person who has qualified as a real estate broker, but works for a broker named in the associate broker's license.

Attestation: The witnessing of a signature to an instrument at the request of the person who signed it.

Avulsion: Removal of land from one owner to another when a stream suddenly changes its channel.

Backfill: The replacement of excavated earth into a hole or against a structure.

Balustrade: A small supporting column for a handrail.

Bargain and sale deed: Deed which conveys the property for valuable consideration.

Barge board: A wide trim board placed on the ends of a gable roof.

Base and meridian: Imaginary lines used by surveyors to find and describe the location of lands.

Baseboard: The board skirting the walls of a room at the floor line.

Basement floor: The lowest floor level in a building.

Bench marks: A location indicated on a durable marker by surveyors.

Bilateral contract: Both parties expressly enter into mutual engagements (reciprocal).

Binder: An agreement to cover a down payment for the purchase of real estate as evidence of good faith on the part of the purchaser; in insurance: a temporary agreement given to one having an insurable interest, and who desires insurance subject to the same conditions which will apply if, as, and when a policy is issued.

Blanket mortgage: A single mortgage which covers more than one piece of real estate.

Blight: A reduction in the productivity of real estate due to a variety of causes, which have a harmful effect upon the appearance of the property area affected.

Board foot: Unit of measurement for lumber; one foot long, one foot wide, one inch thick.

Bona fide: In good faith, without fraud.

Bond: Any obligation under seal. A real estate bond is a written obligation, usually issued on security of a mortgage or a trust deed.

Bridging: Small wood or metal pieces used to brace floor joists.

Broker: One employed by another, for a fee, to carry on any of the activities listed in the license law definition of the word.

B.T.U.: British thermal unit. The quantity of heat required to raise the temperature of one pound of water one degree Fahrenheit.

Building code: Regulating the construction of buildings within a municipality by ordinance or law.

Building line: A line fixed at a certain distance from the front and/or sides of a lot, beyond which no building can project.

Bundle of legal rights: Establishes real estate ownership; consists of right to sell, to mortgage, to lease, to will, to regain possession at end of a lease (reversion); to build and remove improvements; to control use within the law. May be compared to a bundle of sticks, each stick representing a separate right or privilege.

Business chance broker: One who negotiates the sale of a mercantile business for another for a fee.

Caveat emptor: "Let the purchaser beware"; the buyer is duty-bound to examine the property he is purchasing and he assumes conditions which are readily ascertainable upon view.

Certificate of no defense: An instrument, executed by the mortgagor, upon the sale of the mortgage, to the assignee, as to the validity of the full mortgage debt.

Certificate of reasonable value: Written statement issued by the V.A. as to the maximum.

Certiorari: A writ obtained from an appellate court, directing a lower court to send up the record for review and determination or for trial by the lower court.

Cestui que trust: The person who has a beneficial interest in an estate, the legal title to which is vested in another person.

Chain: Unit of land measurement—66 feet.

Chain of title: A history of conveyances and incumbrances affecting the title.

Chattel: Personal property, such as household goods or removable fixtures.

Check: See quadrangle.

Chimney cap: The finishing course at the top of the chimney.

Closing statement: An accounting of funds in a real estate sale made by a broker to the seller and buyer, respectively.

Cloud on the title: An outstanding claim or encumbrance which, if valid, would affect or impair the owner's title; a judgment, or dower interest.

Cognovit note: Note authorizing confession of judgment.

Collateral: Security given for the fulfillment of a debt or obligation.

Color of title: That which appears to be good title, but as a matter of fact, is not good title.

Commingle: To mingle or mix a client's funds in the broker's personal account.

Commission: Sum due a real estate broker for services in that capacity; the administrative and enforcement tribunal of real estate license laws.

Common law: Body of law that grew up from custom and decided cases (English law) rather than from codified law (Roman law).

Community property: Property accumulated through joint efforts of husband and wife living together.

Compound interest: Interest paid on original principal and also on the accrued and unpaid interest.

Condemnation: Taking private property for public use, with compensation to the owner, under the right of eminent domain.

Condominium: Individual ownership units in a multi-family structure, combined with joint ownership of common areas of the building and ground.

Conduit: A pipe or channel for conveying fluids or wires.

Confession of judgment: An entry of judgment upon the debtor's voluntary authority to any attorney to do so in his behalf.

Construction loan: Provides for progressive payments of the loan proceeds during erection of the building.

Constructive eviction: Breach of a covenant of warranty or quiet enjoyment; for example, the inability of a purchaser or lessee to obtain possession by reason of a paramount outstanding title.

Constructive notice: Notice given by the public records.

Contract for sale: Also familiarly known as Land Sales Contract,

Contract to Purchase Real Estate, or a Conditional Sales Contract. (See Land Sales Contract).

Conventional mortgage: One which is not insured by the F.H.A. or guaranteed by the V.A.

Conveyance: The means or medium by which title to real estate is transferred.

Cornice: An ornamental projection at the top of a wall.

Covenant: An agreement between two or more persons, by deed, whereby one of the parties promises the performance or nonperformance of certain acts, or that a given state of things does or does not exist.

Coverture: The status of a married woman.

Cubage: Front or width of building multiplied by depth of building and by the height, figured from basement floor to the outer surfaces of walls and roof.

Cul de sac: A passage way with one outlet; a blind alley.

Curtesy: The right which a husband has in his wife's estate at her death.

Curtilage: Area of land occupied by a building and its yard and outbuildings, actually enclosed or considered enclosed.

Damnum absque injuria: A loss which does not give rise to an action for damages against the person causing it.

Dba: Abbreviation for "doing business as."

Declaration of no set-off: *See* Certificate of no defense.

Decree of foreclosure: Decree by a court upon the completion of foreclosure of a mortgage, lien or contract.

Dedication: An appropriation of land by an owner to some public use together with acceptance for such use by or on behalf of the public.

Deed: A writing by which lands, tenements, and hereditaments are transferred, which writing is signed, sealed, and delivered by the grantor.

Default: The nonperformance of a duty, whether arising under a contract, or otherwise; failure to meet an obligation when due.

Defeasance: An instrument which nullifies the effect of some other deed or of an estate.

Deficiency judgment: The difference between the indebtedness sued upon and the sale price or market value of the real estate at the foreclosure sale.

Depreciation: Loss in value, brought about by deterioration through ordinary wear and tear, action of the elements, or functional or economic obsolescence.

Depth table: Tabulation of factors representing the rating of value per front between a selected "standard" depth (usually 100 feet) and other lots of greater or lesser depth.

Devise: A gift of real estate by will or last testament.

Discount: A loan placement charge made by the lending institution to the seller, by increasing the yield on the investment (also known in the trade as Points).

Discrimination: In real estate, prejudice or refusal to rent or sell to a person because of race, color, sex, religion or ethnic origin.

Dispossess: To deprive one of the use of real estate.

Domicile: The place where one has his permanent residence and, usually, is a registered voter.

Dower: The right which a wife has in her husband's estate at his death.

Duplex: A single two-story structure designed for two-family occupancy.

Duress: Unlawful constraint exercised upon a person, whereby he is forced to perform some act, or to sign an instrument, against his will.

Earnest money: Down payment made by a purchaser of real estate as evidence of good faith.

Easement: The right, liberty, advantage or privilege which one individual has in lands of another (a right of way).

Economic life: The period over which a property may be profitably utilized.

Egress: The right to return from a tract of land (used with ingress).

Ejectment: A form of action to regain possession of real property, with damages for the unlawful retention.

Emblements: The right of a tenant to harvest and remove, after his tenancy has ended, such annual products of the land (corn, wheat), as have resulted from his own labor and care; also known as "way-growing crop."

Eminent domain: The right of the people or government to take private property for public use upon payment of compensation.

Encroachment: A building, part of building, or obstruction which intrudes upon or invades a highway or sidewalk or trespasses upon property of another.

Encumbrance: A claim, lien, charge, or liability attached to and binding upon real property, such as a judgment, unpaid taxes, or a right of way; defined in law as any right to, or interest in, land which may subsist in another to the diminution of its value, but consistent with the passing of the fee.

Entity: A thing that has individual notice; a corporation is a legal entity.

Equity: The interest or value which an owner has in real estate over and above the mortgage against it; system of legal rules administered by courts of chancery.

Equity of redemption: Right of original owner to reclaim property sold through foreclosure proceedings on a mortgage, by payment of debt, interest, and costs.

Erosion: The wearing away of land through processes of nature as by streams and winds.

Escheat: Reversion of property to the sovereign state owing to lack of any heirs capable of inheriting.

Escrow: A deed delivered to a third person for the grantee to be held by him until the fulfillment or performance of some act or condition.

Estate: The degree, quantity, nature and extent of interest which a person has in real property.

Estate in reversion: The residue of an estate left in the grantor, to commence in possession after the termination of some particular estate granted by him. In a lease, the lessor has the estate in reversion after the lease is terminated.

Estoppel certificate: *See* Certificate of no defense.

Et al.: An abbreviation for alii, "and others." Also used as an abbreviation for alius, "and another."

Ethics: That branch of moral science, which treats of the duties which a member of a profession or craft owes to the public, to his client, and to the other members of the profession.

Et ux.: Abbreviation for *et uxor*, meaning "and wife."

Eviction: A violation of some covenant in a lease by the landlord, usually the covenant for quiet enjoyment; also refers to process instituted to oust a person from possession of real estate.

Exclusive agency: The appointment of one real estate broker as sole agent for the sale of a property for a designated period of time.

Execution: A writ issued by a court to the sheriff directing him to sell property to satisfy a debt.

Executor: A person named in a will to carry out its provisions.

Ex officio: By virtue of his office. For example, in Iowa and Nebraska, the Secretary of State is ex officio chairman of the Real Estate Commission.

Extender clause: Clause in an exclusive listing contract, which carries the original exclusive period over for an additional period, to protect the broker, if a sale is made to a prospect he obtained during the original listing period.

Extension agreement: Agreement between mortgagee and mortgagor to extend the maturity date of the mortgage after it becomes due.

"Fannie Mae": The secondary mortgage market. It provides a market for mortgages held by primary lenders, such as banks and savings and loan associations and provides the primary market with a ready market for mortgages, so as to permit a greater turnover of money for loans.

Fee-tail estate: An estate of inheritance given to a person and the heirs of his body. If the grantee dies without leaving issue, the estate terminates and would revert to the grantor.

F.H.A.: Federal Housing Authority; an agency of the Federal Government that insures real estate loans.

Fee simple: The largest estate or ownership in real property; free from all manner of conditions or encumbrances.

Finder's fee: A fee or commission paid to a broker for obtaining a mortgage loan for a client or for referring a mortgage loan to a broker. It may also refer to a commission paid to a broker for locating a property.

Fixture: An article that was once personalty, but has become real estate by reason of its permanent attachment in or to the improvement.

Firm commitment: A commitment by the F.H.A. to insure a mortgage on specified property with a specified mortgagor.

Flashing: Metal strips placed around roof openings to provide water tightness.

Forcible entry and detainer: A legal action to recover possession of premises which are unlawfully held.

Foreclosure: A court process instituted by a mortgagee or lien creditor to defeat any interest or redemption which the debtor-owner may have in the property.

Foreshore: Land between high-water mark and low-water mark.

Foundation: The walls of a building below the first or ground floor.

Fraud: The intentional and successful employment of any cunning, deception, collusion, or artifice, used to circumvent, cheat or deceive another person, whereby that person acts upon it, to his detriment, loss, or disadvantage.

Freehold: An estate in fee simple or for life.

Front foot: A standard of measurement, one foot wide, extending from street line for a depth, generally conceded to be 100 feet.

Gable roof: A pitched roof with sloping sides.

G.I.: A member or veteran of the United States military service.

G.I. loan: Loan guaranteed by the Veterans Administration under

Servicemen's Readjustment Act of 1944, as amended; only honorably discharged veterans and their widows are eligible.

General warranty: A covenant in the deed whereby the grantor agrees to protect the grantee against the world.

Gradient: The slope, or rate of increase or decrease in elevation, of a surface, road or pipe, expressed in inches of rise or fall per horizontal linear foot or percent.

Grantee: A person to whom real estate is conveyed; the buyer.

Grantor: A person who conveys real estate by deed; the seller.

G.R.I.: Graduate Realtors Institute; one who successfully completes the three year program given by the state Real Estate Association.

Gross lease: A lease of property whereby lessor is to meet all property charges regularly incurred through ownership.

Ground rent: A rent reserved by a grantor to himself, his heirs and assigns in conveying land in fee.

Habendum clause: The "To Have and To Hold" clause which defines or limits the quantity of the estate granted in the premises of the deed.

Hand money: Same as an earnest money deposit.

Hectare: A metric measure of surface area (2.471 acres).

Hereditaments: The largest classification of property; includes lands, tenements, and incorporeal property, such as rights of way.

Holdover tenant: A tenant who remains in possession of leased property after the expiration of the lease term.

Homestead: Real estate occupied by the owner as a home; the owner enjoys special rights and privileges.

Housing for the elderly: A project designed specially for older persons (62 years or over) which provides living unit accommodations, and common social and activities space, and facilities for health and nursing services for residents.

H.U.D.: Department of Housing & Urban Development.

Hypothecate: To give a stock as security without giving up possession of it.

Inchoate: Not yet vested or completed. Right to dower is inchoate until the husband dies.

Indenture: A formal written instrument made between two or more persons in different interests; name comes from practice of indenting or cutting the deed on the top or side in a waving line.

Ingress: Access to enter a tract of land; used with egress—to go in and out.

Installment contract: Purchase of real estate upon an installment basis; upon default, payments are forfeited.

Ipso facto: By the fact itself.

Irrigation district: Quasi-political districts created under special laws to provide for water services to property owners in the district.

Jalousie: A kind of blind or shutter made with slats fixed at an angle.

Joint and several liability: A debt incurred by two or more persons "jointly and severally" whereby one action may be brought against all of the parties or an action may be brought against one party for the entire debt.

Joint tenancy: Property held by two or more persons together with the distinct character of survivorship.

Judgment: Decree of court declaring that one individual is indebted to another and fixing the amount of such indebtedness.

Judgment d. s. b.: *D. s. b.* is the abbreviation for the Latin *debitum sine brevi*, which means "debt without writ." It is a judgment confessed by authority of the language in the instrument.

Junior mortgage: A mortgage second in lien to a previous mortgage.

Laches: Delay or negligence in asserting one's rights.

Land contract: A contract for the purchase of real estate upon an installment basis; upon payment of last installment, deed is delivered to purchaser.

Land economics: Branch of the science of economics which deals with the classification, ownership, and utilization of land and buildings erected thereon.

Landlord: One who rents property to another.

Lands, tenements and hereditaments: A term used in the early English law to express all types of real estate.

Lease: A contract, written or oral, for the possession of lands and tenements on the one hand and a recompense of rent or other income, on the other hand.

Leasehold: An estate in realty held under a lease.

Legal description: A description recognized by law, which is sufficient to locate and identify the property without oral testimony.

Lessee: A person to whom property is rented under a lease.

Lessor: *See* Landlord.

License: A privilege or right granted by the State to operate as a real estate broker or salesman. An authority to go upon or use another person's land or property, without possessing any estate therein.

License year: Period specified in license law for license; usually different from calendar year.

Lien: A hold or claim which one person has upon property of another as security for a debt or charge; judgments, mortgages, taxes.

Life estate: An estate or interest held during the term of some certain person's life.

Lis pendens: Suit pending; usually recorded so as to give constructive notice of pending litigation.

Listing: Oral or written employment of broker by owner to sell or lease real estate.

Littoral: Belonging to shore as of sea or Great Lakes; corresponds to riparian rights.

Lot line: A legally defined line dividing one tract of land from another.

Louver: A domed turret with lateral openings in a roof.

Mansard roof: A roof with two slopes on each of the four sides, the lower steeper than the upper.

Market value: The highest price which a buyer, willing but not compelled to buy, would pay, and the lowest a seller, willing but not compelled to sell would accept.

Marketable title: Such a title as a court would compel a purchaser to accept; it is free from any encumbrances or clouds.

Marshalling: Where a creditor has two or more funds out of which to satisfy a debt, he cannot so elect as to deprive another individual, who has but one fund, of his security.

Mechanic's lien: A species of lien created by statute which exists in favor of persons who have performed work or furnished materials in the erection or repair of a building.

Meeting of minds: A mutual intention of two persons to enter into a contract affecting their legal status based on agreed-upon terms.

Merchantable title: *See* Marketable title.

Messuage: Dwelling house and adjacent land and outbuildings.

Metes and bounds: A description in a deed of the land location, in which the boundaries are defined by directions and distances.

Mill: One-tenth of one cent; the measure used to state the property tax rate. That is, a tax rate of one mill on the dollar is the same as a rate of one-tenth of one percent of the assessed value of the property.

Monument: An artificial or natural landmark, e.g. the Revolutionary oak tree, a stone peg.

Moratorium: Emergency act by a legislative body to suspend the legal enforcement of contractual obligations.

Mortgage: A conditional transfer of real property as security for the payment of a debt or the fulfillment of some obligation.

Mortgagee: A person to whom property is conveyed as security for a loan made by such person (the creditor).

Mortgagee in possession: A mortgage creditor who takes over the income from the mortgaged property upon a default on the mortgage by the debtor.

Mortgagor: An owner who conveys his property as security for a loan (the debtor).

Multiple listing: The arrangement among real estate board or exchange members whereby each broker brings his listings to the attention of the other members so that if a sale results, the commission is divided between the broker bringing the listing and the broker making the sale, with a small percentage going to the board or exchange.

NAR: National Association of Realtors.

Net lease: A lease, under which lessor receives a fixed rental and lessee pays taxes, utilities and all other operating expenses.

Net listing: A price, which must be expressly agreed upon, below which the owner will not sell the property and at which price the broker will not receive a commission; the broker receives the excess over and above the net listing as his commission.

N.S.F. check: Not sufficient funds check—(not honored by bank).

Nudum pactum: "Naked pact"—no contract.

Nuncupative will: An oral will.

Obsolescence: Impairment of desirability and usefulness brought about by physical, economic, fashion or other changes.

Offset statement: Statement by owner of property or owner of lien against property, setting forth the present status of liens against subject property.

Open listing: An oral or general listing.

Option: The right to purchase or lease a property at a certain price for a certain designated period, for which right a consideration is paid.

Overhang: The part of the roof extending beyond the walls, to shade building and cover walls.

Over-improvement: An improvement which is not the highest and best use for the site on which it is placed by reason of excess in size or cost.

Package mortgage: One which includes personal property within the lien of the mortgage.

Partition: A division made of real property among those who own it in undivided shares.

Party wall: A wall erected on the line between two adjoining properties, belonging to different persons, for use of both properties.

Patent: Conveyance of title to government land.

Percentage lease: A lease of property in which the rental is based upon the volume of sales made upon the leased premises.

Perch: A unit of land measurement; 16½ feet.

Percolation test: A soil test to determine if soil will take sufficient water seepage for use of a septic tank.

Personalty: All articles or property that are not real estate.

Pi: A symbol (π) designating the ratio of the circumference of a circle to its diameter $\pi = 3.1416$.

Plat book: A public record of various recorded plans in the municipality or county.

Plottage: Increment in unity value of a plot of land created by assembling smaller ownerships into one ownership.

Pocket license card: Evidence of licensure, which should be carried by the licensee at all times and presented when requested by any person with whom the licensee is dealing in regard to real estate.

Points: *See* Discount.

Police power: The inherent rights of a government to pass such legislation as may be necessary to protect the public health and safety and/or to promote the general welfare.

Postponement of lien: The subordination of a presently prior lien to a subsequent judgment or mortgage.

Prima facie evidence: Evidence considered in law to be sufficient to establish a fact, if not contradicted.

Principal: The employer of an agent; the person who is ordinarily liable primarily.

Principal meridian: A north-south line projected through a prominent landmark established under the Government Survey system.

Principal note: The promissory note which is secured by the mortgage or trust deed.

Property: The right or interest which an individual has in lands and chattels to the exclusion of all others.

Prospectus: A printed advertisement for a new enterprise, such as rural property or subdivision.

Public policy: That principle of the law, which holds that no person can lawfully do that which has a tendency to be injurious to the public or against the public good.

Public trustee: A person appointed or required by law to execute a trust.

Purchase money mortgage: A mortgage given by a grantee to the grantor in part payment of the purchase price of real estate.

Quadrangle: A tract of the land in the U.S. Governmental Survey System measuring 24 miles on each side of the square, sometimes referred to as a "check."

Quasi contract: An obligation for a party to do something, which is imposed by law.

Quiet enjoyment: The right of an owner to the use of property without interference of possession.

Quiet title: A court action brought to establish title and to remove a cloud on the title.

Quit claim deed: A deed given when the grantee already has, or claims, complete or partial title to the premises and the grantor has a possible interest that otherwise would constitute a cloud upon the title.

Quit notice: A notice to a tenant to vacate rented property.

Quotient: The number obtained when one quantity is divided by another.

Range: A strip of land 6 miles wide determined by government survey, running in a north–south direction.

Ratification: Giving approval by act or conduct of something done by another, without authority.

Realtor: A coined word used to designate an active member of a local real estate board affiliated with the National Association of Realtors.

Redemption: The right of a mortgagor to redeem the property by paying the debt after the expiration date; the right of an owner to reclaim his property after a sale for taxes.

Reduction certificate: A certificate showing the balance due on a mortgage at the time of closing the sale.

Reformation: An action to correct a mistake in a deed or other instrument.

Release: The relinquishment of some right or benefit to a person who already has some interest in the property.

Release of lien: The discharge of certain property from the lien of a judgment, mortgage, or claim.

Remainder estate: An estate in property created at the same time and by the same instrument as another estate and limited to arise immediately upon the termination of the other estate.

Reproduction cost: Normal cost of exact duplication of a property, as of a certain date.

Res gestae: Attendant facts and circumstances to the issue involved.

Res judicata: A matter judicially decided.

Restriction: A device in a deed for controlling the use of land for the benefit of the land.

Restriction covenant: A clause in a deed limiting the use of the property conveyed for a certain period of time.

Reversion: The residue of an estate left to the grantor, to commence after the determination of some particular estate granted out by him.

Right of way: An easement over another's land—also used to describe strip of land used as a roadbed by a railroad or other public utility for a public purpose.

Riparian: Pertaining to the banks of a river, stream, waterway, and so forth.

Riparian owner: One who owns lands bounding upon a river or water course.

Running with the land (easement): An easement which inures to the benefit and advantage of subsequent owners of the land, for which it was originally created.

Satisfaction piece: An instrument for recording and acknowledging payment of an indebtedness secured by a mortgage.

Section: A section of land established by government survey and containing 640 acres.

Seizin: Possession of real estate by one entitled thereto.

Separate property: Property owned by a husband or wife which is not community property; acquired by either spouse prior to marriage or by gift or devise after marriage.

Septic tank system: Private sewage disposal section for an individual home.

Setback: The distance from curb or other established line, within which no building may be erected.

Severalty ownership: Real property owned by one person only; sole ownership.

Siding: Finish covering on exterior walls.

Simple listing: Listing property with a broker for sale or rent other than through exclusive agency or an exclusive right-to-sell contract; an open listing, usually verbal.

Simple proportion: Relationship between four quantities in which the quotient of the first, divided by the second, is equal to that of the third, divided by the fourth; also geometrical proportion—a method for finding the fourth quality in such a relationship when three are given.

Sinking fund: Fund set aside from property which, with accrued interest, will eventually pay for replacement of the improvements.

Sky lease: Lease for a long period of time of space above a piece of real estate; upper stories of a building to be erected by the tenant; upon the termination of lease, the improvement belongs to the lessor.

Special warranty deed: A deed wherein the grantor limits his liability to the grantee to anyone claiming, by, from, through or under him, the grantor.

Specific performance: A remedy in a court of equity compelling the defendant to carry out the terms of the agreement or contract which was executed.

Squatter's rights: Occupancy of land by virtue of long use against the recorded title owner.

Statute of frauds: Requires certain contracts relating to real estate, such as agreements of sale, to be in writing, in order to be enforceable.

Subdivision: A tract of land divided into lots suitable for home-building purposes.

Subletting: A leasing by a tenant to another, who holds under the tenant.

Subordination clause: A clause in a mortgage or lease, stating that rights of the holder shall be secondary or subordinate to a subsequent encumbrance.

Subpoena: A legal order or writ commanding the named individual to appear and testify in a legal proceedings.

Sump pump: An automatic water pump used in basements to raise water to the sewer level.

Surrender: The cancellation of a lease by mutual consent of lessor and lessee.

Survey: The process by which a parcel of land is measured and its area ascertained.

T/A: Abbreviation for "trading as."

Tax: A charge assessed against persons or property for public purposes.

Tax deed: A deed for property sold at public sale by a political subdivision, such as a city, for nonpayment of taxes by the owner.

Tenancy at will: A license to use or occupy lands and tenements at the will of the owner.

Tenancy in common: Form of estate held by two or more persons, each of whom is considered as being possessed of the whole of an undivided part.

Tenant: A person who holds real estate under a lease (lessee).

Tenant at sufferance: One who comes into possession of lands by lawful title and keeps it afterwards without any title at all.

Tenement: Everything of a permanent nature which may be holden.

Termites: Ant like insects which destroy woodwork used in the building.

Terre tenant: One who has the actual possession of land.

Tier: A strip of land 6 miles wide running in an east-west direction, as determined by Government Survey.

Title: Evidence of ownership, which refers to the quality of the estate.

Title by adverse possession: Acquired by occupation and recognized as against the paper title owner.

Title insurance: A policy of insurance which indemnifies the holder for any loss sustained by reason of defects in the title.

Topography: The contour and slope of land, hills, valleys, streams, etc.

Torrens system: A system of title records provided by state law.

Tort: An actionable wrong.

Township: A territorial subdivision, 6 miles long, 6 miles wide, and containing 36 sections, each 1 mile square.

Trust deed: A form of mortgage by which borrower conveys title to a trustee, who holds title for protection of the lender, as security for the loan debt.

Trustee: A person in whom an estate, interest, or power, in or affecting property, is vested or granted for the benefit of another person.

Trustor: One who deeds his property to a trustee.

Ultra vires act: A contract entered in excess of the corporation's express or implied powers of its charter.

Unearned increment: An increase in value of real estate due to no effort on the part of the owner; often due to increase in population.

Unilateral contract: One in which one party makes an express undertaking, without receiving in return any promise of performance from the other.

United States governmental survey system: Also known as the Rectangular Survey System; a method of describing or locating real property by reference to the governmental survey.

Unlawful detainer: The statutory proceedings by which a landlord removes a tenant who holds over after his lease has expired or after his tenancy is terminated by notice or after default in payment of rent or other obligations.

Usury: Charging more than the legal rate of interest for the use of money.

V.A. loan: *See* G.I. loan.

Vara: Spanish term of measurement, being 33⅓ inches.

Vendee: The purchaser of real estate under an agreement.

Vendor: The seller of real estate, usually referred to as the party of the first part in an agreement of sale.

Waiver: The renunciation, abandonment, or surrender of some claim, right, or privilege.

Warranty deed: One that contains a covenant that the grantor will protect the grantee against any claimant.

Waste: Willful destruction of any part of the land or improvements, so as to injure or prejudice the estate of a mortgagee, landlord or remainderman.

Water table: Distance from surface of ground to a depth at which natural ground water is found.

Windowsill: The lower or base framing of a window opening.

Without recourse: Words used in endorsing a negotiable instrument to denote that the endorser will not be liable to a future holder, in event of non-payment.

Writ of execution: A writ which authorizes and directs the proper officer of the court (usually the sheriff) to carry into effect the judgment or decree of the court.

Yield: The annual percentage rate of return on an investment in real estate, stocks or bonds.

Zone: The area set off by a governing body for specific use; such as, residential, commercial, industrial use.

Zoning: An area in a municipality restricted by ordinance for a particular use, such as single family, multiple-family, commercial, or industrial.

"Spot zoning" occurs when tract in question is singled out for treatment, differing unjustifiably from that of similar surrounding land, thereby creating an island having no relevant differences from its neighbors.

Zoning ordinance: Exercise of police power of a municipality in regulating and controlling the character and use of property.

APPENDIX C
COMMON TERMS USED IN THE BUILDING INDUSTRY*

Addenda: Statements or drawings that modify the basic contract documents after the latter have been issued to the bidders, but prior to the taking of bids.

Alternates: Proposals required of bidders reflecting amounts to be added to or subtracted from the basic proposal in the event that specific changes in the work are ordered.

Anchor bolts: Bolts used to anchor structural members to concrete or the foundation.

Approved equal or: The term used to indicate that material or product finally supplied or installed must be equal to that specified and as approved by the architect (or engineer).

As-built drawings: Drawings made during the progress of construction, or subsequent thereto, illustrating how various elements of the project were actually installed.

Astragal: A closure between the two leafs of a double-swing or double-slide door to close the joint. This can also be a piece of molding.

Axial: Anything situated around, in the direction of, or along an axis.

---

*This glossary has been excerpted from *Estimating in Building Construction*, by Frank R. Dagostino, Reston Publishing Company, Inc., Box 547, Reston, Virginia 22090, and is here reproduced with the permission of the copyright holder.

Baseplate: A plate attached to the base of a column which rests on a concrete or masonry footing.

Bay: The space between column center lines or primary supporting members, lengthwise in a building. Usually the crosswise dimension is considered the *span* or *width* module, and the lengthwise dimension is considered the *bay spacing*.

Beam: A structural member that is normally subjected to bending loads and is usually a horizontal member carrying vertical loads. (An exception to this is a purlin.) There are three types or beams:

> **a) continuous beam:** A beam that has more than two points of support.
> **b) cantilevered beam:** A beam that is supported at only one end and is restrained against excessive rotation.
> **c) simple beam:** A beam that is freely supported at both ends, theoretically with no restraint.

Beam and column: A primary structural system consisting of a series of beams and columns; usually arranged as a continuous beam supported on several columns with or without continuity that is subjected to both bending and axial forces.

Beam-bearing plate: Steel plate with attached anchors that is set in top of a masonry wall so that a purlin or a beam can rest on it.

Bearing: The condition that exists whenever one member or component transmits load or stress to another by direct contact in compression.

Bench mark: A fixed point used for construction purposes as a reference point in determining the various levels of floor, grade, etc.

Bill of materials: A list of items or components used for fabrication, shipping, receiving, and accounting purposes.

Bid: Proposal prepared by prospective contractor specifying the charges to be made for doing the work in accordance to the contract documents.

Bid bond: A surety bond guaranteeing that a bidder will sign a contract, if offered, in accordance with his proposal.

Bid security: A bid bond, certified check, or other forfeitable security guaranteeing that a bidder will sign a contract, if offered, in accordance with his proposal.

Bird screen: Wire mesh used to prevent birds from entering the building through ventilators or louvers.

Bond: Masonry units interlocked in the face of a wall by overlapping the units in such a manner as to break the continuity of vertical joints.

Bonded roof: A roof that carries a printed or written warranty, usually with respect to weather-tightness, including repair and/or replacement on a prorated cost basis for a stipulated number of years.

Bonus and penalty clause: A provision in the proposal form for payment of a bonus for each day the project is completed prior to the time stated, and for a charge against the contractor for each day the project remains uncompleted after the time stipulated.

Brace rods: Rods used in roofs and walls to transfer wind loads and/or seismic forces to the foundation (often used to plumb building but not designed to replace erection cables when required).

Bridging: The structural member used to give lateral support to the weak plane of a truss, joist, or purlin; proves sufficient stability to support the design loads, sag channels, or sag rods.

Built-up roofing: Roofing consisting of layers of rag felt or jute saturated with coal tar pitch, with each layer set in a mopping of hot tar or asphalt; ply designation as to the number of layers.

Camber: A permanent curvature designed into a structural member in a direction opposite to the deflection anticipated when loads are applied.

Canopy: Any overhanging or projecting structure with the extreme end unsupported. It may also be supported at the outer end.

Cantilever: A projecting beam supported and restrained only at one end.

Cap plate: A horizontal plate located at the top of a column.

Cash allowances: Sums that the contractor is required to include in his bid and contract sum for specific purposes.

Caulk: To seal and make weathertight the joints, seams, or voids by filling with a waterproofing compound or material.

Certificate of occupancy: Statement issued by the governing authority granting permission to occupy a project for a specific use.

Certificate of payment: Statement by an architect informing the owner of the amount due a contractor on account of work accomplished and/or materials suitably stored.

Change order: A work order, usually prepared by the architect and signed by the owner or his agent, authorizing a change in the scope of the work and a change in the cost of the project.

Channel: A steel member whose formation is similar to that of a "C" section without return lips; may be used singularly or back-to-back.

Clip: A plate or angle used to fasten two or more members together.

Clip angle: An angle used for fastening various members together.

Collateral loads: A load, in addition to normal live, wind or dead loads, intended to cover loads that are either unknown or uncertain (sprinklers, lighting, etc.).

Column: A main structural member used in a vertical position on a bulding to transfer loads from main roof beams, trusses, or rafters to the foundation.

Contract documents: Working Drawings, Specifications, General Conditions, Supplementary General Conditions, the Owner-Contractor Agreement and all Addenda (if issued).

Curb: A raised edge on a concrete floor slab.

Curtain wall: Perimeter walls that carry only their own weight and wind load.

Datum: Any level surface to which elevations are referred (see *Bench mark*).

Dead load: The weight of the structure itself, such as floor, roof, framing and covering members, plus any permanent loads.

Deflection: The displacement of a loaded structural member or system in any direction, measured from its no-load position, after loads have been applied.

Design loads: Those loads specified by building codes, state or city agencies, or owner's or architect's specifications to be used in the design of the structural frame of a building. They are suited to local conditions and building use.

Door guide: An angle or channel guide used to stabilize and keep plumb a sliding or rolling door during its operation.

Downspout: A hollow section such as a pipe used to carry water from the roof or gutter of a building to the ground or sewer connection.

Drain: Any pipe, channel, or trench for which waste water or other liquids are carried off; i.e., to a sewer pipe.

Eave: The line along the sidewall formed by the intersection of the inside faces of the roof and wall panels; the projecting lower edges of a roof, overhanging the walls of a building.

Erection: The assembly of components to form the completed portion of a job.

Equal, or: (see *Approved equal*.)

Expansion joint: A connection used to allow for temperature-induced expansion and contraction of material.

Fabrication: The manufacturing process performed in the plant to convert raw material into finished metal building components. The main operations are cold forming, cutting, punching, welding, cleaning, and painting.

Fascia: A flat, broad trim projecting from the face of a wall, which may be part of the rake or the eave of the building.

COMMON TERMS USED IN THE BUILDING INDUSTRY

Field: The job site or building site.

Field fabrication: Fabrication performed by the erection crew or others in the field.

Field welding: Welding performed at the job site, usually with gasoline-powered machines.

Filler strip: Preformed neoprene material, resilient rubber or plastic used to close the ribs or corrugations of a panel.

Final acceptance: The owner's acceptance of a completed project from a contractor.

Fixed joint: A connection between two members in such a manner as to cause them to act as a single continuous member, provides for transmission of forces from one member to the other without any movement in the connection itself.

Flange: That portion of a structural member normally projecting from the edges of the web of a member.

Flashing: A sheet-metal closure that functions primarily to provide weathertightness in a structure and secondarily to enhance appearance; the metalwork that prevents leakage over windows, door, etc., around chimneys, and at other roof details.

Footing: That bottom portion at the base of a wall or column used to distribute the load into the supporting soil.

Foundation: The substructure that supports a building or other structure.

Framing: The structural steel members (columns, rafters, girts, purlins, brace rods, etc.) that go together to make up the skeleton of a structure ready for covering to be applied.

Furring: Leveling up or building out of a part of a wall or ceiling by wood, metal, or strips.

Glaze (glazing): The process of installing glass in window and door frames.

Grade: The term used when referring to the ground elevation around a building.

Grout: A mixture of cement, sand, and water used to solidly fill cracks and cavities; generally used under setting places to obtain solid, uniform full bearing surface.

Gutter: A channel member installed at the eave of the roof for the purpose of carrying water from the roof to the drains or downspouts.

Head: The top of a door, window, or frame.

Impact load: The assumed load resulting from the motion of machinery, elevators, cranes, vehicles, and other similar moving equipment.

Instructions to bidders: A document stating the procedures to be followed by bidders.

Insulation: Any material used in building construction for the protection from heat and cold.

Invitation to bid: An invitation to a selected list of contractors furnishing information on the submission of bids on a subject.

Jamb: The side of a door, window, or frame.

Joist: Closely spaced beams supporting a floor or ceiling. They may be wood, steel, or concrete.

Kip: A unit of weight, force, or load equal to 1000 pounds.

Lavatory: A bathroom-type sink.

Liens: Legal claims against an owner for amounts due those engaged in or supplying materials for the construction of the building.

Lintel: The horizontal member placed over an opening to support the loads (weight) above it.

Live load: The load exerted on a member or a structure due to all imposed loads except dead, wind, and seismic loads. Examples include snow, people, movable equipment, etc. This type of load is movable and does not necessarily exist on a given member or structure.

Liquidated damages: An agreed-to sum chargeable against the contractor as reimbursement for damages suffered by the owner because of contractor's failure to fulfill his contractual obligations.

Loads: Anything that causes an external force to be exerted on a structural member. Examples of different types are:

   a) dead load: in a building, the weight of all permanent constructions, such as floor, roof, framing, and covering members.
   b) impact load: the assumed load resulting from the motion of machinery, elevators, craneways, vehicles, and other similar kinetic forces.
   c) roof live load: all loads exerted on a roof (except dead, wind, and lateral loads) and applied to the horizontal projection of the building.
   d) seismic load: the assumed lateral load due to the action of earthquakes and acting in any horizontal direction on the structural frame.
   e) wind load: the load caused by wind blowing from any horizontal direction.

Louver: An opening provided with one or more slated, fixed, or movable fins to allow flow of air, but to exclude rain and sun or to provide privacy.

Mullion: The large vertical piece between windows. (It holds the window in place along the edge with which it makes contact.)

Nonbearing partition: A partition which supports no weight except its own.

Parapet: That portion of the vertical wall of a building that extends above the roof line at the intersection of the wall and roof.

Partition: A material or combination of materials used to divide a space into smaller spaces.

Performance bond: A bond that guarantees to the owner, within specified limits, that the contractor will perform the work in accordance with the contract documents.

Pier: A structure of masonry (concrete) used to support the bases of columns and bents. It carries the vertical load to a footing at the desired load-bearing soil.

Pilaster: A flat rectangular column attached to or built into a wall masonry or pier; structurally, a pier, but treated architecturally as a column with a capital, shaft, and base. It is used to provide strength for roof loads or support for the wall against lateral forces.

Precast concrete: Concrete that is poured and cast in some position other than the one it will finally occupy; cast either on the job site and then put into place or away from the site to be transported to the site and erected.

Prestressed concrete: Concrete in which the reinforcing cables, wires, or rods are tensioned before there is load on the member.

Progress payments: Payments made during progress of the work, on account, for work completed and/or suitably stored.

Progress schedule: A diagram showing proposed and actual times of starting and completion of the various operations in the project.

Punch list: A list prepared by the architect or engineer of the contractor's uncompleted or work to be corrected.

Purlin: Secondary horizontal structural members located on the roof extending between rafters, used as (light) beams for supporting the roof covering.

Rafter: A primary roof support beam usually in an inclined position, running from the tops of the structural columns at the eave to the ridge or highest portion of the roof. It is used to support the purlins.

Recess: A notch or cut-out, usually referring to the blockout formed at the outside edge of a foundation, and providing support and serving as a closure at the bottom edge of wall panels.

Reinforcing steel: The steel placed in concrete to carry the tension, compression, and shear stresses.

Retainage: A sum withheld from each payment to the contractor in accordance with the terms of the Owner-Contractor Agreement.

Roof overhang: A roof extension beyond the end or side walls of a building.

Roof pitch: The angle or degree of slope of a roof from the eave to the ridge. The pitch can be found by dividing the height, or rise, by the span; for example, if the height is eight feet and the span is sixteen feet, the pitch is $8/16$ or $½$ and the angle of pitch is $45°$. (See *Roof slope*)

Rolling doors: Doors that are supported on wheels that run on a track.

Roof slope: The angle that a roof surface makes with the horizontal. Usually expressed as a certain rise in 12 inches of run.

Sandwich panel: An integrated structural covering and insulating component consisting of a core material with inner and outer metal or wood skins.

Schedule of values: A statement furnished to the architect by the contractor reflecting the amounts to be allotted for the principal divisions of the work. It is to serve as a guide for reviewing the contractor's periodic application for payment.

Sealant: Any material that is used to close up cracks or joints.

Separate contract: A contract between the owner and a contractor other than the general contractor for the construction of a portion of a project.

Sheathing: Rough boarding (usually plywood) on outside of a wall or roof over which is placed siding or shingles.

Shim: A piece of steel used to level or square beams or column baseplates.

Shipping list: A list that enumerates by part, number, or description each piece of material to be shipped.

Shop drawings: Drawings that illustrate how specific portions of the work shall be fabricated and/or installed.

Sill: The lowest member beneath an opening such as a window or door; also, the horizontal framing members at floor level, such as sill girts or sill angles; the member at the bottom of a door or window opening.

Sill, slip: A sill that is the same width as the opening—it will slip into place.

Sill, lug: A sill that projects into the masonry at each end of the sill. It must be installed as the building is being erected.

Skylight: An opening in a roof or ceiling for admitting daylight; also, the reinforced plastic panel or window fitted into such an opening.

Snow load: In locations subject to snow loads, as indicated by the average snow depth in the reports of the United States Weather Bureau, the design loads shall be modified accordingly.

Soffit: The underside of any subordinate member of a building, such as the undersurface of a roof overhang or canopy.

Soil borings: A boring made on the site in the general location of the proposed building to determine soil type, depth of the various types of soils, and water table level.

Soil pressure: The allowable soil pressure is the load per unit area a structure can safely exert on the substructure (soil) without exceeding reasonable values of footing settlements.

Spall: A chip or fragment of concrete that has chipped, weathered, or otherwise broken from the main mass of concrete.

Span: The clear distance between supports of beams, girders, or trusses.

Spandrel beam: A beam from column to column carrying an exterior wall and/or the outermost edge of an upper floor.

Specifications: A statement of particulars of a given job as to size of building, quality and performance of men and materials to be used, and the terms of the contract. A set of specifications generally indicates the design loads and design criteria.

Stock: A unit that is standard to its manufacturer. It is not custom-made.

Stool: A shelf across the inside bottom of a window.

Stud: A vertical wall member to which exterior or interior covering or collateral material may be attached. Load-bearing studs are those which carry a portion of the loads from the floor, roof, or ceiling above as well as the collateral material on one or both sides. Non–loading-bearing studs are used to support only the attached collateral materials and carry no load from the floor, roof, or ceiling above.

Subcontractor: A separate contractor for a portion of the work (hired by the general contractor).

Substantial completion: For a project or specified area of a project, the date when the construction is sufficiently completed in accordance with the contract documents, as modified by any change orders agreed to by the parties, so that the owner can occupy the project or specified area of the project for the use for which it was intended.

Supplementary general conditions: One of the contract documents, prepared by the architect, that may modify provisions of the General Conditions of the contract.

Square: One hundred square feet.

Temperature reinforcing: Lightweight deformed steel rods or wire mesh placed in concrete to resist possible cracks from expansion or contraction due to temperature changes.

Time of completion: The number of days (calendar or working) or the actual date by which completion of the work is required.

Truss: A structure made up of three or more members, with each member designed to carry basically a tension or a compression force. The entire structure in turn acts as a beam.

Veneer: A thin covering of valuable material over a less expensive body; for example, brick on a wood frame building.

Wainscot: Protective or decorative covering applied or built into the lower portion of a wall.

Wall bearing: In cases where the floor, roof, or ceiling rests on a wall, the wall is designed to carry the load exerted. These types of walls are also referred to as load-bearing walls.

Wallcovering: The exterior wall skin consisting of panels or sheets and including their attachment, trim, facia and weather sealants.

Wall non-bearing: Wall not relied upon to support a structural system.

Water closet: More commonly known as a toilet.

Working drawing: The actual plans (drawings and illustrations) from which the bulding will be built. They show how the building is to be built and are included in the contract documents.

INDEX

A

Apartment leasing, 94-95, 96
Appraisal, in general, 75-83
    appraisers, 75-76
    checklist for homes, 81-83
    for new buildings, 78-81
    land appraisal, 78
    methods, 78
    speculation, 76-77
Arbitration, 34, 161-73
Architect's certificate, 66-67
Articles of partnership, 6-8
    of agreement, 29
Assignment of leases, 93-94
Assignment of property, 38
Attorneys, use of, 5, 8, 29, 35, 41, 87

B

Batter boards, 16
Bidders, 71-73

Bill of sale, 36
Breach of contract, 66
Building terms, 225-34
Bureau of Vital Statistics, 89, 103

C

Call option, 18
Caveat emptor, 33, 39-40
Certificate of indefeasible title, 16
Certificate of partnership, 5
Chain of title, 35
Champerty, 105
Check signing, 6
Claim of lien (*see* Liens)
Cloud on title, 17, 30
Codicils (to wills), 87, 88
Collateral security, 38
Company names, 2, 4, 7
Condominiums, 96-98
    common elements (HOW), 112
Continuing offer, 18
Contracts, in general, 65-73
    defined, 29
    essential parts of, 65-66
    on real estate, 68-71
Cooperatives, 9-10
Corporations, 8-9
Covenants (in leases), 91

D

Death of owners/partners, 2, 4, 29, 87
Dedication of land, 37
Deed, 62
Deed of trust, 34, 39-40
    vs. mortgages, 33, 39-40
Default, 37-38, 76
Depreciation, 3
Directional bearings (*see* Metes and bounds)
Discharge of liens, 34

Discharge of mortgages, 39, 70
Disputes (*see* Arbitration)
Dissolution of partnership, 5
Dower rights, 41

E

Easement by prescription, 37
Eminent domain, 17
Encroachment on land, 37
Encumbrances, 17, 30–34
Entrepreneurship, 1–2
Escheat, 33
Escrow agents, 69
Estoppel certificate, 33
Experience ratings, 152–53

F

Fee simple absolute, 16–17
Fee simple estate, 16–17
Fidelity insurance, 103
Forced sale, 76
Foreclosure, 30, 35, 37, 38, 40, 41, 76
"Free on board" (F.O.B.), 104–05
"Free on rail" (F.O.R.), 105

G–H

Goodwill, 6, 7
Gross lease, 93
Guarantee bonds, 71–73
Homeowner's Warranty (HOW), 109–48
    for condominiums, 112, 115, 121, 152
    homeowner responsibilities, 124
    limited warranty, 148–52
    major structural defects, 118, 145–46
    making a claim, 114–17
Homes, as offices, 3–4

I-J-K

Indefeasible title, certificate of, 16
Individual proprietorship, 1-2
Insurance, in general. 101-05, 152-59
    certificates of, 153-55
    coverage checklist, 155-59
    key man, 4, 7, 8, 97
    mortgage, 103
    personal property, 105-09
Joint tenancy, 37
Judgement, 17, 33, 39
Key man insurance, 4, 7, 8, 97
"Know-How", investment of, 5

L

Land, dedication of, 37
Land appraisal, 78
Land measure, tables of, 13
Land terms, 15
Land title, 30-31, 33, 88
Land use, 54
    See also: Zoning
Latitude, 15
Leases, 91-95
    leaseback, 95-96
    leasehold estate, 92
Legal age, 23
Legal description, 15
Legal forms, sample list, 43-52
Legal terms, 175-203
Letters patent, 9
Liens (claims), 30-34
Life estate, 36
Limited partnership, 8
Liquidated damages, 66-67
Listings, all types, 70-71
Longitude, 14

INDEX

M

Mandatory insurance, 101-02
Material supplier's lien, 31
Mechanic's liens, 17, 31-34
Memorandum of association, 9
Metes & bounds, 14-15
Mortgages, 33, 34-35, 39
    vs. deed of trust, 33, 39-40
Mortgage insurance, 103

N-O-P

Net lease, 93
Notaries public, 40, 61-63
Offices, in homes, 3-4
Operating expenses, 3
Options (to purchase), 18, 36
Oral agreements, 68, 71
Partnership agreements, 4-8, 63
    articles of, 6-8
Percentage lease, 93
Personal property inventory, 105-09
Points of law, in general, 40-41
Power of attorney, 38, 63
Priority of mortgage, 35
Put option, 18

R

Range, defined, 14
Real estate contracts, 68-71
Real estate listings, all types, 70-71
Real estate terms, 205-23
Registration of liens, 33
Rescission, 66
Retainage funds, 67
Riparian owner, 36

S

Sandwich Leases, 92
Satisfaction piece, 40, 70
Setback ordinance, 41
Severalty, 37
Severalty ownership, 33
Sewer lines, 16, 76
Sole proprietorship, 1-2
Specifications, 67, 68, 71
Specific performance, 66
Speculation building, considerations, 76-77
Statute of frauds, 41
Statute of limitations, 41
Straddle option, 18
"Subject to" clauses, 69-70
Subpoena, 36
Subrogation, 103
Surety bonds, 73
Surrogage, 89
Surveys, use of, 15

T

Tables of land measure, 13
Tax liens, 31
Tenants in common, 37
Tenders (*see* Bidders)
Timesharing, 97-98
Title (*see* Land title)
Torts, 23-24, 28, 36, 38

W-Z

Water drainage, 76
Water supply, 77
Wills, 85-89
Worker's compensation, 102, 153, 155, 157-58
Writ of judgment (*see* Judgment)
Zoning, 18-21, 53-59, 76